Charles Johnson

D0982797

THE ANALYSIS
OF
CROSS-CLASSIFICATIONS

H. T. Reynolds, Associate Professor at the University of Delaware, received his Ph.D. in political science from the University of North Carolina. He has written several books and articles on political behavior and research methods.

THE ANALYSIS
OF
CROSS-CLASSIFICATIONS

H. T. Reynolds

THE FREE PRESS
A Division of Macmillan Publishing Co., Inc.
New York

Collier Macmillan Publishers
London

Copyright © 1977 by The Free Press
A Division of Macmillan Publishing Co., Inc.

All rights reserved. No part of this book may be reproduced
or transmitted in any form or by any means, electronic or
mechanical, including photocopying, recording, or by any
information storage and retrieval system, without permission
in writing from the Publisher.

The Free Press
A Division of Macmillan Publishing Co., Inc.
866 Third Avenue, New York, N.Y. 10022

Collier Macmillan Canada, Ltd.

Library of Congress Catalog Card Number: 76-51589

Printed in the United States of America

printing number

  2 3 4 5 6 7 8 9 10

Library of Congress Cataloging in Publication Data

Reynolds, Henry T
      The analysis of cross-classifications.

      Includes bibliographical references and index.
      1. Discriminant analysis. 2. Social sciences
—Statistical methods. I. Title.
QA278.65.R48   519.5′3   76-51589
ISBN 0-02-926390-5

For Lisa

CONTENTS

PREFACE

Although social scientists strive for the same precision as their colleagues in the natural sciences, they confront a hard reality: social and political behavior and motivations are exceedingly difficult to quantify. Frequently an investigator's only recourse is classification. Classifications in the form of nominal and ordinal variables are so common that hardly any social scientist, whether student or practitioner, ever completely avoids them.

Yet when confronted with categorized data, researchers typically respond either by doing very little—perhaps they compute a chi square or a single measure of association—or by treating the variables as if they were internal scales and undertaking complex multivariate analyses. Both responses seem unsatisfactory and unnecessary, unsatisfactory because they possibly overlook subtleties of the data or produce misleading, even erroneous conclusions, and unnecessary in view of the plethora of techniques developed explicitly for categorical variables.

This book describes methods for analyzing cross-classifications, the most common way of displaying and studying nominal and ordinal variables. Many of these procedures have been available for years but have been little used in the social sciences, probably because they originally emerged in other disciplines such as the health sciences. Others have only recently been developed. Whatever the case, they permit one to investigate cross-classified data more systematically and extensively than is commonly done.

The purpose is to provide an intuitive, nonrigorous description of the techniques. Instead of giving a formal presentation of the methods I have tried to explain and illustrate their computation, their interpretation, and especially their practical strengths and weaknesses. Consequently, the material should be understandable to anyone with training in applied statistics through the rudiments of regression and analysis of variance.

Of course, an intuitive approach to these topics requires some sacrifice in mathematical and statistical exactitude. Furthermore, a book of this sort must be selective. Instead of attempting to write an encyclopedia of categorical data analysis, an undertaking doomed to fail, I have written a book presenting the basic ideas of the most common and most useful approaches. For a thorough and rigorous understanding of the techniques, the sources, cited throughout the text, are indispensable.[1]

The book follows a simple outline. The first three chapters cover bivariate tables while the last four deal with multivariate analysis. With the exception of Chapters 5 and 6, which form a unit, each chapter is self-contained. Although matrix notation is used heavily in Chapter 7, Appendix A should provide enough background for those who are unfamiliar with the terminology.

Several people have read and commented on various portions of the manuscript. I am especially grateful to Herbert Kritzer, Shelby Haberman, Hubert Blalock, and William Reynolds for their helpful corrections and suggestions. Of course, none of them is responsible for any remaining errors. I also wish to thank Claude Conyers of The Free Press and copy editor Lynne Lackenbach for their excellent assistance in preparing the manuscript for publication.

My work on this book has been greatly facilitated by generous support from the Graduate College of the University of Delaware. In addition, part of the manuscript was written with assistance from the National Science Foundation (grant GS-38156). The support of these institutions is gratefully acknowledged.

I am also grateful to the Literary Executor of the late Sir Ronald A. Fisher, F.R.S., and to Longman Group Ltd., London, for permission to reprint Table IV from their book *Statistical Tables for Biological, Agricultural and Medical Research*, 6th ed. (1974).

Finally, I owe a special debt of gratitude to my wife, Lisa, without whose love and encouragement I could not have finished.

---

1. I have relied heavily on Bishop, Fienberg, and Holland (1975) and Quade (1974), as well as on Leo A. Goodman's many works.

THE ANALYSIS
OF
CROSS-CLASSIFICATIONS

1 ANALYSIS OF TWO-WAY TABLES

1.1 INTRODUCTION

That social scientists attempt to explain human behavior scientifically is widely known and accepted. In this respect they resemble their colleagues in the natural sciences, who must choose significant problems to study, identify and measure appropriate variables, test hypotheses, and relate their findings to theory. Social scientists have the added problem, however, of conceptualizing and measuring the innumerable complexities and nuances of human affairs.

There is, of course, no lack of theorizing. The problem lies in testing these theories. Faced with subtle and abstract concepts, an investigator's only recourse is often classification, the assignment of subjects to categories. The resulting measures, ubiquitous in nearly every field in the social sciences, present formidable difficulties. Nowhere is this situation more apparent than in the study of voting behavior.

Perhaps no single topic in political science has been studied more prodigiously. Data from every conceivable type of research design, not to mention countless pearls of conventional wisdom, have been advanced to explain why people vote as they do. In spite of these efforts, however, political scientists have still not constructed a generally accepted theory of voting.

Clearly, part of the problem lies in the nature of the subject matter. Electoral choice, involving a myriad of variables, cannot be examined separately from its political and social context. Consequently, it is an exceedingly complex topic. But equally troublesome is the existing level of measurement.

In the absence of quantitative measures of the most important concepts, political scientists rely on classification. Instead of measuring a voter's exact level of partisanship, he is classified as simply pro-Democratic, neutral, or pro-Republican. In a large survey, all kinds of people with disparate needs, interests, and motives are lumped together under common labels. Apart from any substantive considerations, such variables are not so easy to analyze statistically as one might suppose.

Table 1.1 shows the relationship between party identification and vote for U.S. senator.[1] Superficially, the table seems to reveal all there is to know about the relationship. Democrats prefer Democratic senatorial candidates (after all, 84 percent of them chose the Democrat), whereas Republicans just as strongly prefer Republican candidates. The Independents, as expected, divide their vote almost evenly. In short, the variables seem to be moderately associated. Yet important questions remain.

TABLE 1.1.   **Vote for U.S. Senator by Party Identification**

		B: Party			
		Democrat	Independent	Republican	Total
A: Vote	Democrat	84% (1103)	47% (309)	13% (115)	1527
	Republican	16% (207)	53% (343)	87% (766)	1316
	Total	100% (1310)	100% (652)	100% (881)	2843

Note: Numbers in parentheses are number of cases.
Source: Cowart (1973, p. 841, table 2).

Terms such as "moderately associated" are rather vague. Is it possible to describe the form and strength of the relationship more precisely? Does the relationship hold for all types of people? Is it stronger in some parts of the table than others? Suppose that additional variables are included in the analysis. How is the original association affected? Do the added variables substantially increase knowledge of voting behavior? Which variable is the most important explanation? Can the interrelationships be explained by a general model? Finally, since the data come from a sample survey, how representative are they of the population as a whole?

Even with quantitative measures, these questions are hard to answer. With completely categorized variables, the obstacles are formidable indeed. But answering them is essential for a thorough understanding of the

---

1. These data are derived from Cowart (1973, p. 841, table 2). The data, originally collected by the Survey Research Center, University of Michigan, are a combination of samples taken in 1956, 1960, 1964, and 1968. Hence, "vote for senator" does not refer to a particular year.

data. Dismissing a cross-tabulation with the statement that the variables are or are not related—certainly a widespread practice—risks throwing away a great deal of information.

Fortunately, one can do better. The analysis of cross-classifications has been the object of a vast amount of research. Although problems persist, significant progress has been made in the last few years, particularly in multivariate analysis. In fact, advances in this methodology have outstripped their application in substantive fields. Thus, researchers can now turn to a wide variety of tools for the close and careful examination of cross-tabulation of categorical variables.

In this sense the present chapter is more suggestive than exhaustive: it describes methods for the detailed analysis of two-way tables. Not every technique is covered—that is precluded in a short work like this—but enough material is presented to encourage more thorough analyses than are usually performed.

Before describing these approaches, however, it is first necessary to present preliminary information pertaining to categorical data, sampling, and notation.

1.1.1 The Nature of Categorical Variables.   Classification, the simplest form of measurement, means assigning individuals to classes on the basis of a specific trait or attribute such as candidate preference or party identification. Ideally, the classes are homogeneous with regard to the underlying property and, of course, should be mutually exclusive and exhaustive. They may or may not have an implicit numerical ordering.

In a nominal scale, the members of one category differ from individuals in other categories, but by itself the scale does not reveal the magnitude of the differences. Nor do the classes stand in any particular order with respect to one another; the first is not necessarily less than or greater than the last.

Ordinal scales, by contrast, do involve implied measurement. "Discrete numerical" variables (e.g., the number of organizations to which a person belongs) are simply enumerations of objects or events. More commonly, the classes of an ordinal variable are ordered along a dimension without indicating precise magnitudes. By virtue of the ordering among the categories, ordinal scales contain information permitting one to specify relationships more precisely. Therefore, they are usually analyzed differently than nominal variables.

In either event, however, this book and the techniques it describes are neutral regarding the processes generating the data. Categorical variables may measure truly discrete phenomena such as race, sex, or number of siblings. In most instances, however, they probably represent measurement error, because the underlying traits are not measured quantitatively. Attitudes, for instance, probably do not exist in a single pro-con dichotomy but rather in gradations from, say, strongly favorable through strongly unfavorable. For one reason or another, an investigator's operational techniques prevent him from capturing the full richness of people's opinions, and he merely pigeonholes them into two or three groups.

Whatever the case, statistical procedures assume the meaningfulness of the categories. They will "work" with any data set. A social scientist, on the other hand, always has to think carefully about the measurements in order to interpret the results. There is a widespread tendency in many fields to compress variables into a small, manageable number of categories. As compelling as the need seems however, collapsed variables lead to trouble. Dichotomizing what is really a continuous variable may produce misleading, even erroneous conclusions, no matter what technique is used. (See Sections 2.6.6 and 5.6 for examples.)

The point is, then, that statistics—however mathematically sophisticated and elegant—cannot make poorly measured variables into good ones; statistical techniques are valid only to the extent that the data are meaningful for the problem at hand. As a general rule, an investigator should not combine categories but should strive for as much precision in measurement as possible.

1.1.2 Sampling Models.   Cross-tabulations are produced by several means. In the most common, a simple random sample, only the sample size, n, is fixed in advance. In other words, one randomly selects n subjects from the population without specifying the marginal totals ahead of time. Referring to Table 1.1, for example, 1310 Democrats appeared in the sample by chance; that total was not determined by the research design. Variables sampled in this manner are sometimes called responses (Bhapkar and Koch, 1968a).

When analyzing data based on this sampling scheme, one usually assumes that the observations are drawn from a population table that follows a *multinomial* distribution. The multinomial distribution, described in most elementary statistics books, underlies many statistical methods for categorical data. Assuming a multinomial distribution is somewhat analogous to assuming normality in tests of means. In a way it is a rather weak assumption, because it asserts only that the data follow a probability structure.

Other kinds of sample design and distribution are valid. Frequently one set of marginals is fixed before the study begins. For example, an investigator may decide to interview equal numbers of Democrats, Republicans, and Independents. Or he may include twice as many partisans as Independents. In either case, the marginal totals associated with party identification do not arise by chance but are predetermined by the analyst. Statisticians call these variables "factors."

If each category of the factor has been sampled separately from the others, one usually considers the data as having come from a series of independent multinomial distributions. Each level of the factor thus represents a population for which the multinomial is applicable. The probability structure of a cross-classification with one set of marginals fixed is called a *product-multinomial.* Again, this assumption does not appear overly restrictive if the samples are in fact independent.

Other types of sample are commonplace. In a two-way table both sets of marginal totals may be fixed as in certain experiments; in other situations, nothing—neither the marginals nor the sample size—is predetermined. Furthermore, most large sample surveys involve complex designs including clustering and stratification.

For the most part, the techniques described below can be applied to such data, although modifications are often necessary. To keep the presentation simple, let us generally assume that the variables have a multinomial or product-multinomial distribution. This assumption need not be too confining, however, since it will often be met in an approximate sense.

Sample size is important. Without exception the statistical tests rest on *asymptotic* methods. Roughly speaking, asymptotic results hold only for large samples. Suppose that one wanted to know the probability that a particular pattern of observed frequencies came from a population having certain characteristics. Ideally, one would compute the exact probability of its occurrence. The problem is that such calculations are usually prohibitively time-consuming and difficult. Fortunately, simplifying approximations are available, but they generally assume large samples.

The commonplace chi square statistic, for example, has an approximately chi square distribution under the hypothesis of independence. Its utility lies in the adequacy of the approximation. Yet unless the expected frequencies (see Section 1.2) are reasonably large, it might produce misleading inferences. Hence, along with the other techniques explained throughout this book, it requires relatively sizable n's. (A shorthand way of expressing this provision is to use the word "asymptotic.")

It is difficult to define "large" because, among other things, each statistic or technique has to be considered in a specific context. Furthermore, statisticians do not agree among themselves. Surveys containing at least 75 to 100 cases are probably satisfactory for most purposes, unless the observations are distributed in peculiar ways. (More precise rules of thumb are given later.) With smaller samples, the investigator should turn to exact methods.

1.1.3 Notation. In order to put the various methods in a common framework and simplify their presentation, it is convenient at this point to introduce some simple notation.

We denote tables with sets of letters, enclosed by braces, that represent the appropriate variables. The notation $\{AB\}$, as an example, means a two-way table between variables labeled for convenience A and B.

Observed cell frequencies are denoted with small f's, with subscripts standing for the specific level of the variables. Thus, in a two-way or two-dimensional table where A, the row variable, has I categories and B, the column variable, has J categories, f_{ij} represents the frequency in the ijth cell (for $i = 1, \ldots, I$; $j = 1, \ldots, J$). (In Table 1.1, for example, f_{11} corresponds to the 1103 cases in the first row and first column.) Similarly, in a three-dimensional table such as Table 4.1 showing the relationship between voting and party identification within levels of partisan attitude, f_{ijk} stands for the number of observations in the ijth cell in the kth layer of C, the third variable. (For instance, f_{111}, the number of Democrats with pro-Democratic attitudes who voted for a Democratic candidate, is 620.) Frequencies in higher-dimensional tables are denoted in a similar fashion.

1.1.4 Marginal Tables. Marginal totals and tables play a particularly important role in the analysis of cross-classifications. A marginal total is formed by adding frequencies over one or more subscripts. In an $I \times J$ table, for example, the first row's marginal total is

$$f_{1+} = f_{11} + f_{12} + \cdots + f_{1J} = \sum_j f_{1j}.$$

Note that plus signs in subscripts indicate summation over the particular subscript. Moreover, the symbol $\sum_j$ means summation over all values of j; it is a simpler way of writing $\sum_{j=1}^{J}$. In Table 1.1, the marginal total in the first row is

$$f_{1+} = 1103 + 309 + 115 = 1527.$$

Marginal tables are derived from higher-dimensional tables by summing frequencies over one or more subscripts. Table 1.1, viewed as a marginal table formed from Table 4.1, contains entries f_{ij+}. For example, the first frequency in Table 1.1 is found from Table 4.1 as follows:

$$f_{11+} = f_{111} + f_{112} + f_{113} = 620 + 367 + 116 = 1103.$$

It would, of course, be possible to derive the vote by attitude marginal table with frequencies f_{i+k} by adding over the categories of party identification. The entry in the first cell would be

$$f_{1+1} = f_{111} + f_{121} + f_{131} = 620 + 89 + 13 = 722.$$

With higher-dimensional tables, one can compute even more marginal tables. Suppose that one has four variables, A, B, C, and D, with I, J, K, and L categories, respectively. The frequency in the $ijkl$th cell is f_{ijkl}. Three- and two dimensional tables are found from the original table by summing the appropriate cell frequencies. The three-dimensional $\{ABC\}$ marginal table has entries

$$f_{ijk+} = f_{ijk1} + f_{ijk2} + \cdots + f_{ijkL} = \sum_l f_{ijkl}.$$

By the same token, entries in the $\{AB\}$ marginal table are

$$f_{ij++} = f_{ij11} + f_{ij12} + \cdots + f_{ij1L} + f_{ij21} + \cdots + f_{ijKL}$$

$$= \sum_k \sum_l f_{ijkl}.$$

From these considerations, it is apparent that marginal tables can be denoted either by sets of letters corresponding to the variables (for example, $\{BC\}$) or by frequencies with appropriate subscripts and plus signs (for example, f_{+jk} for a two-way table between B and C).

Besides tables of observed frequencies, one often works with population probabilities and expected frequencies. For two variables, let $P(A_iB_j)$ denote the probability that an individual is in the ith class of A and the jth class of B in an $I \times J$ population cross-classification. To simplify the notation, P_{ij} often replaces $P(A_iB_j)$. Expected frequencies are denoted by F_{ij}. Observed proportions are denoted with lowercase p's.

The layout of tables containing these values follows exactly the same guidelines as observed contingency tables. In a two-way table, P_{i+}, for instance, means the marginal probability of being in the ith category of A and is obtained by adding the probabilities in the ith row:

$$P_{i+} = P_{i1} + P_{i2} + \cdots + P_{iJ},$$

assuming that the table has J columns.

1.2 A SHORT REVIEW OF THE CHI SQUARE TEST FOR INDEPENDENCE

The familiar chi square statistic tests for independence between the row and column variables in an $I \times J$ cross-classification. In general terms, independence means that the probability of one event (e.g., voting Democratic) is not affected by the occurrence or nonoccurrence of another event (e.g., being a Democrat). Let P_{ij} be the probability of the joint occurrence of particular values (the ith and jth) of the variables A and B, respectively, and let P_{i+} and P_{+j} be the probabilities of their separate occurrences. (That is, P_{i+}, for instance, is the probability that that member of a population belongs in the ith category of A regardless of his classification on *B*.) Statistical independence holds if

$$P_{ij} = P_{i+}P_{+j} \quad \text{for } i = 1, \ldots, I; j = 1, \ldots, J.$$

This formula simply expresses the idea that the probability of, say, a Republican's voting for a Democratic candidate is the product of the probability that he is a Republican times the probability that he votes Democratic. If the proposition holds for all combinations of *i* and *j*, the two variables are statistically independent.[2] Independence, then, implies that knowing the value of one variable says nothing about the values of the other. Conversely, the absence of independence suggests that at least some categories are associated; knowing a person's party affiliation gives clues about how he votes.

To test the hypothesis that an observed cross-classification fits the model of independence, one estimates P_{i+} and P_{+j} with the marginal proportions f_{i+}/n and f_{+j}/n, respectively, where *n* is the sample size. Estimated expected frequencies under the model are

$$\hat{F}_{ij} = n\left(\frac{f_{i+}}{n}\right)\left(\frac{f_{+j}}{n}\right) = \frac{f_{i+}f_{+j}}{n}. \tag{1.1}$$

The expected values are compared with the observed values, using the familiar goodness-of-fit chi square statistic

$$GFX^2 = \sum_{ij} \frac{(f_{ij} - \hat{F}_{ij})^2}{\hat{F}_{ij}} = \sum_{ij} \frac{f_{ij}^2}{\hat{F}_{ij}} - n, \tag{1.2}$$

where $\sum_{ij}$ means summation over all cells in the table.[3] Most readers are doubtlessly well acquainted with GFX^2. An alternative but essentially equivalent statistic is the likelihood-ratio chi square:

$$LRX^2 = 2 \sum_{ij} f_{ij}\left[\log\left(\frac{f_{ij}}{\hat{F}_{ij}}\right)\right]$$

$$= -2 \sum_{ij} f_{ij}\left[\log\left(\frac{\hat{F}_{ij}}{f_{ij}}\right)\right], \tag{1.3}$$

where log refers to the natural (base *e*) logarithm. Although less widely known than GFX^2, the likelihood-ratio chi square has the advantage of

---

2. Statistical independence is occasionally expressed in another manner: $P_{ij} = \alpha_i\beta_j$, for $i = 1, \ldots, I, j = 1, \ldots, J$ where α_i and β_j are positive constants. In the present context, the two formulations are equivalent, since α_i and β_j can be interpreted as marginal proportions.

3. Most statistics books use X^2 to denote the goodness-of-fit chi square. GFX^2 is used here to distinguish it from the likelihood-ratio statistic given next.

being divisible into additive portions, much as the total sum of squares in analysis of variance is partitioned. Log-linear models (Chapter 5), as well as some methods presented later in this chapter, take advantage of this feature.

Under the null hypothesis of independence, both GFX^2 and LRX^2 have approximately chi square distributions with $v = (I-1)(J-1)$ degrees of freedom, provided that the sample size is sufficiently large (see below). They are asymptotically equivalent in the sense that one will reach the same decision no matter which statistic he uses.

It is easy to verify that in Table 1.1, $GFX^2 = 1085.97$ and $LRX^2 = 1197.59$. These values can be compared to the tabulated chi square distribution (see Appendix B). With 2 degrees of freedom, their statistical significance is quite evident; the hypothesis of independence is rejected.

1.2.1 Chi Square Tests Are Approximations. Probabilities found in the chi square table are approximations. The adequacy of these approximations and hence the tenability of one's decisions assume that several conditions have been met. Presumably, the underlying distribution is a multinomial (if only n is fixed by the sample design) or a product multinomial (if one set of margins is fixed). Random sampling ensures that the observations are independent. Finally, the categories must be mutually exclusive and exhaustive.

Social scientists are normally willing to make these assumptions. The main stumbling block lies in the sample size. Because the distribution of GFX^2 and LRX^2 only approximates the theoretical distribution, one has to be certain that the approximation is reasonable. In general, the larger the sample size, the better the fit is. Yet other factors, including the true marginal distributions, the number of cells in the table, and the significance level, also affect the approximation's adequacy. Although there is no consensus among statisticians—in fact, they continue to debate the topic with considerable vigor—a safe rule of thumb is that the sample size should be large enough and distributed in such a way that each expected frequency is greater than 5. In larger tables the rule may be relaxed slightly: as long as most cells, say 90 percent, have expected frequencies greater than 5, the remaining cells can have expectations as small as 1 or 2 (see Cochran, 1954, for example).

The problem frequently appears in the analysis of 2×2 tables.[4] Here there is little agreement at all. Many statisticians suggest adding or

---

4. The goodness-of-fit chi square in a 2×2 table is readily computed by

$$GFX^2 = \frac{n(f_{11}f_{22} - f_{12}f_{21})^2}{f_{1+}f_{2+}f_{+1}f_{+2}}.$$

subtracting $\frac{1}{2}$ from each frequency, making sure the marginal totals remain the same (see Blalock, 1972). Others argue that this procedure sometimes "overcorrects" the data and suggest using $\frac{1}{2}n$ instead (Smith, 1976; Pirie and Hamdan, 1972).[5]

If in doubt about the sufficiency of a sample size in a 2×2 table, one's safest alternative is to compute Fisher's exact test. This test, found in most introductory texts, gives exact rather than approximate probabilities. It is appropriate when both marginals are fixed or when one is willing to have a test conditional on a given set of marginals. In this respect its interpretation is limited, but some statisticians feel that its use is preferable to corrections for continuity. This is especially true since widely available computer programs have eliminated the tedium of its computation.

It is difficult to correct for continuity in larger tables. The only practical solution may be to combine certain categories or eliminate them altogether in order to keep the expected values above 5. As a last resort, such manipulations should be kept to a minimum. If only two or three cells in a large table have small expected values, they can probably be ignored.

Although the calculation of the expected values, $\hat{F}_{ij}$, should be familiar to the reader, one point is worth mentioning here because it recurs up again in later chapters. The expected frequencies under the hypothesis of independence sum to the marginal totals. In other words,

$$\hat{F}_{i+} = f_{i+} \qquad \text{and} \qquad \hat{F}_{+j} = f_{+j}, \tag{1.4}$$

for all i and j. This property can be seen in Table 1.1. The expected frequencies in the first column are $\hat{F}_{11} = 703.61$ and $\hat{F}_{21} = 606.39$. Their sum, 1310, is simply the marginal total in the first column.

Estimates that have this property are said to *fit* the marginal totals. Alternatively, one describes the marginals as *fitted* under a model. This fact has no practical application now, but is quite important is analyzing multivariate models (Chapter 6).

1.2.2 Limitations of the Chi Square Test. Mosteller (1968, p. 1) writes:

> I fear that the first act of most social scientists upon seeing a contingency table is to compute a chi-square for it. Sometimes the process is enlightening, sometimes wasteful, but sometimes it does not go far enough.

The chi square technique as normally applied has two potential drawbacks. As with any test statistic, the sample size affects its magnitude. For a given departure from independence, its magnitude is

---

5. For a discussion of these problems, see Conover (1974).

proportional to the sample size. Multiplying each observed frequency by, say 10, will increase GFX^2 tenfold, other things being equal. In practical terms, this means that one can always find a significant relationship by making the sample large enough. In public opinion surveys, where n often exceeds 1500, the difficulty of separating substantive from statistical significance is particularly acute. The obvious answer is to compute measures of association in conjunction with chi square, a procedure taken up in Chapter 2.

The conventional chi square test presents another problem of interpretation since it is not directed at any particular alternative hypotheses. It only measures departures of expected from observed values and does not point to any "pattern of deviations . . . that may hold if the null hypothesis of independence is false" (Cochran, 1954, p. 417). When the chi square is significant, in other words, it does not show the way in which the variables are related. Hence, by itself it perhaps hides as much as it reveals.

For these reasons it is desirable to modify and extend the usual test. Detailed analyses permit the investigator to locate more precisely the source of a significant relationship and to explore various subhypotheses. A thorough ransacking of the two-way table is desirable because social scientists frequently know ahead of time that a result will be significant. By relying solely on chi square tests, they gain little new information. At the same time, they might be missing important insights by not subjecting the data to closer scrutiny.

1.3 EXAMINING RESIDUALS

Perhaps the simplest first step after finding a significant chi square is to examine the pattern of residuals. Studying the residuals may show more clearly where the independence model breaks down. This approach amounts to comparing each observed frequency with its expected value to see which terms contribute most to the chi square.

Instead of looking at the differences $(f_{ij} - \hat{F}_{ij})$, many of which are affected by marginal totals, Haberman (1973) recommends computing *standardized residuals:*

$$e_{ij} = \frac{f_{ij} - \hat{F}_{ij}}{\sqrt{\hat{F}_{ij}}}, \tag{1.5}$$

where f_{ij} and $\hat{F}_{ij}$ are observed and expected frequencies, respectively.[6]

---

6. Note, incidentally, that $GFX^2 = \sum_{ij} e_{ij}^2$.

Better still, he suggests, is calculating *adjusted residuals:*

$$d_{ij} = \frac{e_{ij}}{\hat{v}_{ij}} \qquad (1.6)$$

where $\hat{v}_{ij}^2$ is an estimate of the variance of the e_{ij}:

$$\hat{v}_{ij}^2 = \left(1 - \frac{f_{i+}}{n}\right)\left(1 - \frac{f_{+j}}{n}\right).$$

Assuming a multinomial distribution and sufficiently large n, each d_{ij} is approximately distributed as a standard normal variable (i.e., a normally distributed variable with mean zero and variance equal to 1.0).

Consequently, their values can be compared with percentiles of the normal distribution. Values greater than 1.64 (the 95th percentile of the standard normal distribution) suggest a significant discrepancy between the observed and expected frequencies. One should be cautious in making probability statements about the d's, since he will usually be analyzing a set of them. But practically speaking, those that are quite large (greater than, say, 1.64) suggest where the independence model breaks down. Adjusted residuals then would be helpful in detecting "outliers," that is, frequencies that are far greater or smaller than they should be under the model of independence.

An example further illustrates the point. The data in Table 1.2, taken from the 1974 American National Election Study conducted by the Survey Research Center at the University of Michigan, show the relationship between vote for Senate and region. Although the $GFX^2 = 23.156$ with 4 degrees of freedom suggests a weak association, the form of the relationship is not completely clear. The percentages, one might surmise,

TABLE 1.2. **Vote for Senate in 1974 by Region**

		East	Midwest	Border	South	West	Total
		B: Region					
	Republican	55%	42%	29%	51%	41%	42%
		[2.40]	[−.09]	[−2.57]	[1.02]	[−.23]	
A: Vote		{3.48}	{−.03}	{−3.77}	{1.38}	{−.36}	
	Democratic	45%	58%	71%	49%	59%	58%
		[−2.04]	[.02]	[2.18]	[−.87]	[.20]	
		{−3.48}	{.03}	{3.77}	{−1.38}	{.36}	
	Total	100%	100%	100%	100%	100%	100%
		(152)	(229)	(168)	(55)	(234)	(838)

Note: Numbers in brackets are standardized residuals; numbers in braces are adjusted residuals; numbers in parentheses are number of cases.

Source: 1974 American National Election Study (see Appendix C).

indicate that the independence model breaks down in the first, third, and fourth columns, since the percent voting Democratic in those columns differs from the marginal proportion.

Yet the adjusted residuals show that the fit is poor only in the first and third columns. It is interesting to note that there is an "excess" of Democratic voters in the border states and an excess of Republican voters in the East, a surprising result in view of recent trends in American politics. In any event, the other cells contribute relatively little to the total chi square.

Besides analyzing the residuals in this fashion, one can plot them to detect deviations from independence. Methods similar to those illustrated by Draper and Smith (1966) for plotting residuals obtained from regression analysis can also be employed in contingency tables. For example, one might construct graphs of the adjusted residuals plotted against individual cell values or against values of the standard normal distribution (see Draper and Smith, 1966, p. 87).

Still other types of residuals can be defined (see Bishop, Fienberg, and Holland, 1975, pp. 136–41). The benefit of these techniques is that by examining a model's fit cell by cell, one is better able to interpret chi squares. In two-way tables, the methods supplement the practice of looking at percents; in multidimensional tables the systematic examination of residuals is indispensible in model fitting.

1.4 PARTITIONING CHI SQUARE

When analyzing a large cross-classification, it is frequently worthwhile to supplement the overall chi square analysis with tests for specific subhypotheses. Dividing the original array into subtables, one computes a chi square for each. The component chi squares, which are independent, sum to the total chi square. (The sum will be exact if the LRX^2 is used; approximate if GFX^2 is used.) In addition to testing certain subhypotheses, this method allows one to see which portions of the table contribute most to the overall chi square.

1.4.1 A General Method of Partitioning. Goodman (1968), following earlier statisticians, proposes partitioning the test for independence in an $I \times J$ table into two (asymptotically) independent parts. (1) The first is a test in a subtable formed from the first J' columns ($J' < J$) and the I rows. This table, an $I \times J'$ array, has $(I-1)(J'-1)$ degrees of freedom. Alternatively, one could construct the table from the first I' rows ($I' < I$) and J columns, producing an $I' \times J$ table with $(I'-1)(J-1)$ degrees of freedom, or from the first I' and J' rows and columns, leaving an $I' \times J'$ table with $(I'-1)(J'-1)$ degrees of freedom. (2) The second test involves a subtable composed of the remaining columns, $J'+1$, $J'+2, \ldots, J$, and a column obtained by adding the entries in the first J' columns. The second table is $I(J-J'+1)$ and has $(I-1)(J-J')$ degrees of freedom. As before, one could construct the second table from partitions of rows instead of columns or from partitions of both rows and columns.

Furthermore, the partitioning can be applied successively to each subtable to obtain finer subdivisions of the original table. Under the null hypothesis of independence in the original table, the tests are asymptotically independent; and if LRX^2 is computed, the sum of the components will equal the overall chi square.

Two examples illustrate the method. (For still another example, see Section 1.5.) First, consider a rearrangement of Table 1.1 in which the second and third columns are interchanged. Switching the columns does not, of course, change the value of either chi square, but it facilitates the interpretation of the partitioning. (One should always specify the table's layout before examining the data.)

In the 2×3 table the overall chi squares are $GFX^2 = 1085.97$ and $LRX^2 = 1197.59$, as noted previously. Now consider a 2×2 table formed from the first two columns of the rearranged table:

	Democrats	Republicans
Democrat	1103	115
Republican	207	766
Total	1310	881

In this table, which compares the voting behavior of Democrats and Republicans, the $GFX^2 = 1079.99$ and $LRX^2 = 1184.04$, both with 1 degree of freedom.

Next look at the table formed from the remaining column and a column obtained by adding the frequencies in the first two:

	Partisans (Dems. & Reps.)	Independents
Democrat	1218	309
Republican	973	343
Total	2191	652

Here, $GFX^2 = 13.58$ and $LRX^2 = 13.55$. The chi squares in both substables can be compared to the tabulated chi square distribution with 1 degree of freedom. The results are perhaps best summarized in an analysis-of-variance-type table:

Component Due to:	GFX^2	LRX^2	df
Democrats vs. Republicans	1079.99	1184.04	1
Partisans vs. Independents	13.58	13.55	1
Total (overall)	1093.57	1197.59	2

The total for LRX^2 agrees with the overall LRX^2 computed in the original 2×3 table. Although the total GFX^2 does not equal the overall GFX^2, they are close enough for practical purposes. (Under the null hypothesis they are asymptotically equivalent.)

Clearly, the main source of the overall chi square lies in the differences in the candidate preferences between Democrats and Republicans. Partisans (i.e., Democrats and Republicans) as a whole do not differ much from Independents, since the proportions voting Democratic are not too dissimilar.

None of these findings is surprising, especially in view of previous research on voting behavior. But the example is intended only to supply a simple illustration of the technique. In larger tables with many more cells, detailed partitioning is frequently enlightening. It also provides a way to test systematically and objectively certain subhypotheses within the context of a large table.

1.4.2 Partitioning into 2×2 Tables.   It might be instructive to see how an $I \times J$ cross-classification is partitioned into $T = (I-1)(J-1)$ tables, each with 1 degree of freedom.

The partitioning can be achieved by repeatedly applying Goodman's algorithm described above. An equivalent method is to let f_{ij} (for $i = 2, 3, \ldots, I; j = 2, 3, \ldots, J$) be the bottom right-hand entry in each 2×2 table. The other cells are obtained by adding frequencies in the cells above and to the left of the IJth cell. The tth partition of the original table thus has the form

$$
\begin{array}{ccc|c}
f_{11} & + \cdots + f_{1(j-1)} & & f_{1j} \\
& & & + \\
+ f_{21} & + \cdots + f_{2(j-1)} & & f_{2j} \\
\cdot & \cdot \quad \cdot & & \cdot \\
\cdot & \cdot \quad \cdot & & \cdot \\
\cdot & \cdot \quad \cdot & & \cdot \\
& & & + \\
+ f_{(i-1)1} & + \cdots + f_{(i-1)(j-1)} & & f_{(i-1)j} \\
\hline
f_{i1} & + \cdots + f_{i(j-1)} & & f_{ij}
\end{array}
$$

TABLE 1.3. **Voting in 1956 State and Local Elections by Attitudes on Government-Guaranteed Jobs**

		B: Attitude*			
		Liberal	Moderate	Conservative	Total
	Mostly Democratic	46% (312)	38% (34)	32% (115)	461
A: Vote	Even	23% (159)	27% (24)	30% (110)	293
	Mostly Republican	31% (210)	36% (32)	38% (137)	379
	Total	100% (681)	101% (90)	100% (362)	1133

* "The government in Washington ought to see to it that everybody who wants to work can find a job." For convenience, respondents who agree are called liberal; those who disagree are called conservative; and those in between are called moderate.

Note: Numbers in parentheses are number of cases.

Source: The 1956 Election Study (see Appendix C).

Note that in each 2×2 table the bottom right-hand cell contains a single frequency, whereas the other cells contain combinations of frequencies (except when $t = 1$). One computes a chi square statistic with 1 degree of freedom for each subtable, with their sum being asymptotically equivalent to the overall chi square under the null hypothesis.[7] (We assume that each subtable contains enough frequencies to make each approximation reasonable.)

As an example, the data in Table 1.3 show the relationship between people's attitudes on the government's role in guaranteeing jobs and their votes in state and local elections. The significant (at the .001 level) chi squares, $GFX^2 = 19.81$ and $LRX^2 = 20.09$ with 4 degrees of freedom, suggest a closer look at the relationship. In particular, one wonders if moderates behave more like liberals or conservatives, or if they are somewhere in between. Percents are helpful in answering this question, but nevertheless a more systematic and detailed analysis might be revealing.

The first subtable consists of the four cells in the upper left corner of Table 1.3 (that is, $f_{ij} = f_{22}$). It compares liberals and moderates on their

---

7. Castellan (1965) gives a formula for the calculation of the goodness-of-fit chi square in the tth table. Although it would be ideal for a computer algorithm, it is probably easier when working manually to form the 2×2 tables and compute the chi square directly.

propensity to vote mostly Democratic:

	a	
	Liberals	Moderates
Dem.	312	34
Even	159	24
Total	471	58

The remaining subtables are formed by applying Goodman's algorithm or by the method just suggested:

	b	
	Lib–Mod.	Cons.
Dem.	346	115
Even	183	110
Total	529	225

	c				d	
	Lib.	Mod.			Lib.–Mod.	Cons.
Dem.–Even	471	58		Dem.–Even	529	225
Mostly Rep.	210	32		Mostly Rep.	242	137
Total	681	90		Total	771	362

As in the previous analysis, the results are best summarized in a form similar to an analysis-of-variance table:

Subtable	Component Due to:	GFX^2	LRX^2	df
a	Liberals vs. moderates on voting Dem. or Even	1.34	1.30	1
b	Lib. and Mod. vs. Cons. on voting Dem. vs. Even	13.57	13.41	1
c	Lib. vs. Mod. on voting Dem.–Even vs. Rep.	.82	.81	1
d	Lib. and Mod. vs. Cons. on voting Dem.–Even vs. Rep.	4.61	4.57	1
	Total (overall)	20.34	20.09	4

Partitioning indicates that the bulk of the association lies in subtables b and d, which contrast liberals and moderates with conservatives. Actually, if one partitions the table in a different manner, it turns out that most of the chi square is attributable to differences between liberals and conservatives. In this sense, the presence of the moderates seems to dampen the relationship. Stated in other words, there is more ideological polarization than a cursory glance at the overall chi squares or percents indicates.

There are numerous other ways that an overall chi square can be partitioned into additive components (see Lancaster, 1949; Kimball, 1954; Kastenbaum, 1960; Maxwell, 1961; Bresnahan and Shapiro, 1966; Goodman, 1969a). The present treatment, moreover, emphasizes tests for relationships rather than estimates of their magnitude. The next chapter describes a method of partitioning based on a measure of association. All of these approaches, however, involve the same basic concepts and usually lead to the same substantive conclusions.

1.5 QUASI-INDEPENDENCE

Just as an investigator is interested in independence in an $I \times J$ table, he may also wish to know if independence exists within a subset of the cells of a table. Denote this subset by S. It might consist of all the off-diagonal cells in a square table or a group of cells in, say, the upper right corner of a rectangular table. Whatever the case, the cells in S are *quasi-independent* if

$$P_{ij} = \alpha_i \beta_j \qquad \text{for all cells } (i, j) \text{ in } S, \qquad (1.7)$$

where α_i and β_j are positive constants (see note 2; Goodman, 1968). This is simply the usual definition of independence applied to a subset of the cells in an $I \times J$ table. In this sense, quasi-independence means conditional independence, the condition being that only a subset of cells are considered. The idea is that although two variables as a whole may be associate, there might be independence within certain combinations of their categories.

Hypotheses of quasi-independence occur in two contexts. Some tables are naturally incomplete or truncated because they contain "structural" zeros. Consider, for example, the relationship between birth order and the number of siblings. The observed table relating these variables must be triangular, since an individual's birth order cannot exceed the number of siblings in his family. Certain cells in the table contain only zeroes. (These zero entries must be distinguished from sampling zeros that occur by chance.) Since one portion of the table has only zeroes—more exactly, does not contain any entries because none are possible—one may wish to test the hypothesis that the remaining classifications are quasi-independent.

Even in complete tables, one may wish to delete certain cells in order to test for quasi-independence in the remaining ones. Since complete tables are more common in the social sciences than truncated cross-classifications, we give an example of this kind of analysis.

Table 1.4 shows the relationship between the party identification of 1852 parents and their high-school-aged children. The highly significant overall chi square, $LRX^2 = 823.90$ with 36 degrees of freedom, implies a strong association. But a researcher might feel that a more detailed investigation is needed. His reasoning is this: parents and children tend to agree on party identification. Yet most of the relationship is perhaps due to agreement among Democrats. As a consequence of the prevailing liberalism of high schools and the youth culture, sons and daughters of Independents and Republicans, he believes, are more apt to defect from their parents' politics. Therefore, when Democrats are excluded, the relationship in the remaining cells may be nil.

The test for quasi-independence requires deleting the appropriate cells and testing for independence in the remainder. The degrees of freedom equals the usual degrees of freedom minus the number of deleted cells. Assuming that d cells have been deleted from an $I \times J$ table, the degrees of freedom are $v = (I-1)(J-1) - d$. Any number of cells might be removed. The only restriction is that the removal of cells does not leave two (or more) separate tables. Separate tables occur when the cells in S can be divided into two mutually exclusive sets, S_1 and S_2, where S_1 and S_2 have no rows or columns in common. Separate tables should be analyzed in the usual way, as if they were two distinct tables. Expected values under the hypotheses of quasi-independence cannot,

TABLE 1.4. **High School Students and Their Parents' Party Identification**

		B: Parents' Party							
		SD	D	ID	I	IR	R	SR	Total
	·SD	180	108	30	20	2	5	3	348
	D	147	167	39	30	10	38	17	448
	ID	63	78	38	30	14	30	14	267
A: Student's	I	33	49	32	50	17	42	14	237
Party	IR	9	13	14	23	17	35	45	156
	R	16	29	14	17	23	92	61	252
	SR	9	13	4	10	9	35	64	144
	Total	457	457	171	180	92	277	218	1852

Key: SD = Strong Democrat, D = Democrat, ID = Independent-Democrat, I = Independent, SR = Strong Republican, R = Republican, IR = Independent-Republican.

Source: Jennings, The Student-Parent Socialization Study (see Appendix C).

unfortunately, be calculated from formula (1.1). Instead, other methods are necessary.

For some hypotheses the original table may be partitioned by the methods outlined in Section 1.4.1. Suppose that we want to remove the four cells in the upper left-hand corner of Table 1.4. (These cells pertain to strong and moderate Democrats.) The table with a "chunk" of cells removed can be represented as

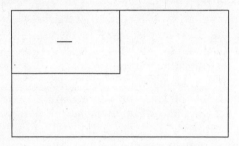

where the dash indicates the eliminated cells. This truncated table is now the object of interest, because one wants to know if its cells are quasi-independent.

Using the methods described in Section 1.4.1, one partitions the truncated table into a 5×5 subtable, a 3×5 subtable, and a 5×3 subtable, as shown in Table 1.5. Starting in the lower right corner, let $I' = J' = 5$. This leads to Table 1.5a. Next, consider the subtable consisting of the remaining two rows and a row obtained by adding the corresponding entries in the first I' rows (Table 1.5b). The last subtable (Table 1.5c) is found in the same way except that it consists of the remaining two columns plus a column obtained by adding the entries in the first J' columns.

One then computes a likelihood-ratio chi square for each subtable.[8] Under the null hypothesis of quasi-independence in the population table corresponding to Table 1.4, each of these statistics has an approximate chi square distribution with appropriate degrees of freedom (Goodman, 1968). Their sum, denoted LRX_+^2, constitutes the test for quasi-independence. It has a chi square distribution under the hypothesis with degrees of freedom obtained either by summing the degrees of freedom in the three subtables or by subtracting the number of missing cells from the degrees of freedom in the original table. Since $LRX_a^2 = 167.95$ (with 16 df), $LRX_b^2 = 88.40$ (with 8 df), and $LRX_c^2 = 121.68$ (with 8 df), the chi square for quasi-independence is $LRX_+^2 = 378.03$ with 32 degrees of

---

8. The goodness-of-fit chi square could also be calculated, but its partition in these tables would not be exact.

TABLE 1.5.   **Subtables Formed by Partitioning Table 1.4**

a

		B: Parents					
		ID	I	IR	R	SR	Total
	ID	38	30	14	30	14	126
	I	32	50	17	42	14	155
A: Students	IR	14	23	17	35	45	134
	R	14	17	23	92	61	207
	SR	4	10	9	35	64	122
	Total	102	130	80	234	198	744

$$LRX_a^2 = 167.95$$

b

		B: Parents					
		ID	I	IR	R	SR	Totals
	SD	30	20	2	5	3	60
A: Students	D	39	30	10	38	17	134
	*	102	130	80	234	198	744
	Total	171	180	92	277	218	938

$$LRX_b^2 = 88.40$$

c

		B: Parents			
		SD	D	*	Total
	ID	63	78	126	267
	I	33	49	155	237
A: Students	IR	9	13	134	156
	R	16	29	207	252
	SR	9	13	122	144
	Total	130	182	744	1056

$$LRX_c^2 = 121.68$$

* Row (or column) formed by combining entries in first five rows (or columns).

freedom. This is the chi square, in other words, for the table with the block denoted by the dash removed. There is still a strong association in this truncated table.

One table remains. It is constructed from the last $I - I'$ rows (plus a row consisting of the entries in the first I' rows) and the last $J - J'$ columns (plus a column consisting of the entries in the first J' columns). (Remember that we are counting from the bottom right-hand corner instead of the upper left-hand cell.) This table is

	d			
	SD	D	Remaining Columns	Total
SD	180	108	60	348
D	147	167	134	448
Remaining Rows	130	182	744	1056
Total	457	457	938	1852

Here the likelihood-ratio chi square is 445.87 with 4 degrees of freedom. In a sense, it gives the contribution of the deleted cells to the overall chi square.

All these results can be summarized in an analysis-of-variance-type table:

Component Due to:	LRX^2		df	
Quasi-independence	378.03		32	
Subtable a		167.95		16
Subtable b		88.40		8
Subtable c		121.68		8
Entries in deleted cells (i.e., association among Democrats)	445.87		4	
Total (overall)	823.90		36	

Even though the cells are not quasi-independent, it nevertheless appears that a great deal of the relationship in the original array is due to the Democrats. Thus, the investigator's supposition seems well founded.

Notice that the hypothesis of quasi-independence is itself partitioned into three components. Actually, it could be further partitioned by treating each subtable in the same fashion as the original tables. Such analysis might yield interesting insights, but should be guided by theoretical considerations in order to avoid meaningless data dredging.

The preceding methods work when a single cell or a block of adjoining cells is removed. One first forms the truncated table and partitions it with the procedures outlined in Section 1.4. Each subtable has a LRX^2 that under the null hypothesis will have an asymptotic chi square distribution with given degrees of freedom. The sum of the separate chi squares provides the test for quasi-independence. The chi square pertaining to the missing cell (s) can be found either by completing the partitioning (as above) or by subtracting LRX^2_+ from LRX^2.

This method, however, requires partitioning. Goodman (1968), on the other hand, gives explicit formulas for computing estimated expected values under the hypothesis of quasi-independence. These formulas save one the trouble of partitioning the table. They are not presented here because different formulas are needed for different types of table and because the partitions themselves supply interesting information.

For some models neither the partitioning scheme nor the formulas will work. Suppose, for example, that an investigator wanted to delete all the cells on the main diagonal of Table 1.4, feeling that the relationship is due solely to students inheriting their parents' preferences exactly. The test for quasi-independence when the cells in the main have been removed requires a different approach.[9]

The estimated expected frequencies have to be computed by an algorithm called *iterative proportional fitting*. In this algorithm, described in Chapter 6, one makes preliminary estimates of the expected values, then successively adjusts them until they satisfy the criterion that the marginal totals of the estimates equal the marginal totals of the observed frequencies. That is,

$$\hat{F}_{i+} = f_{i+} \qquad \text{and} \qquad \hat{F}_{+j} = f_{+j}$$

for all i and j in S. Iterative proportional fitting is not difficult to grasp but is computationally tedious and not especially instructive.[10]

The algorithm's major advantage is its applicability to all tests of quasi-independence. After obtaining the estimated values, one calculates the chi square statistic and its degrees of freedom in the usual manner. The only difference is that the summations in (1.2) and (1.3) are only over the cells in the incomplete table. (The degrees of freedom, remember, equal the degrees of freedom in the original table minus the number of deleted cells.) In the present example, where the seven cells in the main diagonal have been removed, the results are

Component Due to:	LRX^2	df
Quasi-independence (i.e., nondiagonal cells)	452.66	29
Main diagonal cells	371.24	7
Total (overall)	823.90	36

9. See Bishop, Fienberg, and Holland (1975, pp. 192–202), for a general way of determining which truncated tables require the alternative approach.

10. Goodman (1968) gives an algorithm slightly different from the one presented in Chapter 6. Although his has a few advantages, it seems simpler to present only one, especially since they lead to equivalent results.

Quasi-independence does not hold, but the diagonal cells contribute substantially to the over chi square.

Partitioning and testing for quasi-independence are performed in a variety of ways. In fact, this description has only skimmed the surface. It is a prodigiously studied topic involving many mathematical nuances.[11]

Yet the motivation and basic ideas are straightforward. So far it has been applied mainly to social mobility tables (Goodman, 1965b, 1969a; Pullum, 1970; Boudon, 1973), but the technique has great potential in a number of areas, especially when an investigator wants more than a cursory analysis of the data (see, for example, Hallinan and Moore, 1975).

1.6 THE ANALYSIS OF SQUARE TABLES

Square tables (i.e., cross-classifications for which $I = J$) are commonplace in the social sciences. They occur, for example, in socialization studies were parents and children are cross-classified on the same variable (see Tables 1.4 and 1.6); in panel studies where respondents are measured on the same variables at two different times; and in cross-section surveys where individuals are classified on variables having the same number of categories. They arise in other contexts as well, such as in experiments involving matching.

A test of independence would of course be appropriate, since the strength of the relationship is of interest. But the usual chi square test may not add much to one's understanding of the association. After all, in a cross-tabulation of parents and children, one is not surprised to find an association. There are, however, at least two other hypotheses worthy of exploration.

1.6.1 Symmetry.   It may be interesting to know if there is symmetry in the proportions in off-diagonal cells. More formally, the hypothesis of symmetry is

$$P_{ij} = P_{ji} \qquad \text{for all } i \neq j. \tag{1.8}$$

The hypothesis asserts, for example, that the proportion in cell $(2, 1)$ is the same as the proportion in cell $(1, 2)$.

According to Bishop, Fienberg, and Holland (1975, p. 283), the estimated expected values under the hypothesis of symmetry are

$$\hat{F}_{ij} = \begin{cases} \dfrac{f_{ij} + f_{ji}}{2} & \text{for } i \neq j \\ f_{ij} & \text{for } i = j. \end{cases} \tag{1.9}$$

---

11. For more thorough discussions, see Bishop and Fienberg (1969), Bishop, Fienberg, and Holland (1975), Fienberg (1970b, 1972) Mantel (1970), and Goodman (1968, 1972c).

TABLE 1.6. **Relationship between Respondents' Votes and Spouses' Votes in 1968 Presidential Election**

		B: *Respondent's Spouse Vote*		
		Nixon	Humphrey	Wallace
	Nixon	1586 [1586] {1}	117 [110] {.5}	49 [41.5] {.5}
A: *Respondent Vote*	Humphrey	103 [110] {0}	1540 [1540] {1}	40 [28.5] {0}
	Wallace	34 [41.5] {.5}	17 [28.5] {.5}	359 [359] {1}
	Total	1723	1674	448

Note: Numbers in brackets are expected frequencies under hypothesis of symmetry; numbers in braces are weights used in calculating weighted κ (see Section 2.7).

Source: Kovenock et al., Comparative State Electron Project (see Appendix C).

These values can be used in the expressions for the goodness-of-fit chi square (1.2) and the likelihood-ratio chi squares (1.3). Assuming sufficiently large samples, they have approximately chi square distributions with $I(I-1)/2$ degrees of freedom.

The data in Table 1.6 illustrate the test for symmetry. Since $GFX^2 = 12.883$ and $LRX^2 = 13.168$ with 3 degrees of freedom, the hypothesis of symmetry does not hold. Yet note that the huge sample size contributes heavily to the chi squares. As a practical matter, the cell proportions seem relatively symmetrical.

This procedure provides a test of the hypothesis of symmetry; the next chapter introduces statistics for measuring the amount of agreement in square tables.

1.6.2 Marginal Symmetry.   Perhaps of more interest than symmetry is the hypothesis that the marginal proportions or totals are symmetrical. In an $I \times I$ table the hypothesis of *marginal symmetry* (often called marginal homogeneity) asserts that

$$P_{i+} = P_{+i} \qquad \text{for all } i. \tag{1.10}$$

This is an interesting hypothesis because one frequently wants to know if the marginal distributions for two groups are the same. In the study of political socialization, for example, a test for independence shows to what extent students share their parents' opinions; a test for marginal symmetry, by contrast, shows to what extent students as a group have the same opinions as their parents.

Symmetry implies marginal symmetry. Consequently, if the test for symmetry is nonsignificant, marginal symmetry also holds. On the other hand, if the data do not fit the hypothesis of symmetry, it is still possible that marginal symmetry exists. Unfortunately, the test for marginal homogeneity involves rather complex calculations. Chapter 7, however, shows how the test can be computed within a general weighted regression framework. The interested reader is also referred to Bishop, Fienberg, and Holland (1975, chap. 8) for alternative techniques.

1.7 SUMMARY

This chapter has been more suggestive than exhaustive. The underlying theme is that an investigator does not have to rest with the usual chi square test for independence but can instead explore the data in a number of ways. Ideally, his theory and substantive knowledge will suggest specific hypotheses, for it makes little sense to ransack a cross-classification in hopes of finding something significant. But a problem is usually formulated well enough for the analyst to make meaningful tests.

There are innumerable other ways of extending the chi square test, particularly when the dependent variable is a dichotomy.[12] Most of these techniques, fortunately, involve a logic similar to the methods described above, and the interested reader should have little trouble finding a procedure suited to his particular needs.

---

12. The reader ought to consult, among others, Cochran (1954), Armitage (1955), Daly (1962), Maxwell (1961), Mantel and Haenszel (1959), Mantel (1963), and Simon (1974).

2 MEASURES OF ASSOCIATION FOR NOMINAL DATA

2.1 INTRODUCTION

Finding a significant chi square is somewhat like hearing that one basketball team defeated another. Knowing who won the game does not tell the score and therefore does not reveal if the teams were evenly matched or if one was vastly superior to the other. A chi square test indicates only that two variables may or may not be statistically independent. By itself it does not give the strength or form of the relationship. For these purposes a measure of association is used.

A measure of association, a numerical index, describes the strength or magnitude of a relationship. Although literally dozens of measures exist, they can be classified into two broad groups: nominal and ordinal. We deal here only with nominal measures; ordinal indices are covered in the next chapter. But within this group of nominal measures there are numerous alternatives, each having different characteristics. Finding the most appropriate coefficient for a particular problem involves at least two interrelated considerations: the measure's interpretation and its sensitivity to confounding influences.

2.1.1 The Interpretation of Measures of Association. Since a measure of association, a single number, supposedly summarizes the information in a table, it should have a clear interpretation. The numerical value of most measures lies between 0 and 1.0, zero if the variables are completely unrelated according to some definition of a nil relationship, and 1.0 if the variables are perfectly associated, again according to some criterion of "perfect." The meaning of intermediate values depends on how the measure is operationally defined.

Nil Associations. To say that the association between two variables is

"nil" usually—but not always—implies that they are statistically independent. If independence holds for a population table, most measures of
association are defined so that they are zero. For samples drawn from that
population, the measures will equal zero subject to sampling error. Thus,
values close to zero typically indicate a weak relationship.

A few measures of association are zero even in the absence of
statistical independence. Lambda, an index described below, frequently
equals zero when the marginal totals are highly skewed—that is, most
cases fall in one category—but the variables are not independent. Many
social scientists view this property as an inherent weakness in the measure. On the other hand, one can define "nil" to mean something besides
independence (Weisberg, 1974). Such definitions are rare, however, and
throughout this book we use statistical independence as the definition of
nil association.

Perfect Association. Having only rough classifications, an investigator
may not worry about defining or measuring perfect association. After all,
classified variables often represent measurement error where individuals
are lumped together into categories out of convenience or necessity.
Were more refined divisions available, the observed pattern of relationship might be different. Hence, defining perfect association for nominal
data might be premature; if nothing else, it assumes the meaningfulness
of the observed classifications.

Nevertheless, it is common to conceptualize perfect association even
for categorical variables. There are at least three different ways of doing
so.

Strict perfect association implies that each value of one variable is
uniquely associated with a value of the other. Table 2.1a presents an
example. Note that for this condition to hold, the numbers of categories
of A and B must be equal. Here knowledge of a person's B category
implies perfect prediction of his score on A. Under this relationship,
"normed" measures of association equal 1.0, except for sampling error in
the case of samples.

If one variable has more classes than another (that is, the rows and
columns do not equal), the definition of perfect association has to be
modified. In Table 2.1b, for instance, a column category completely
specifies a row category. In other words, the members of a column
classification are as homogeneous as possible with respect to A in the
sense that there is only one nonzero row entry per column. Different B
categories are generally associated with different A categories, but since
the classes on B outnumber those on A, the association is not unique.

Not every measure of association achieves its maximum value in this
case. Hence, if one feels that this type of table represents perfect
association, he should choose a measure that does attain its maximum
value.

TABLE 2.1.   **Hypothetical Data Illustrating Definitions of Perfect Association**

a. "Strict" Perfect Association				b. "Implicit" Perfect Association				

		B					B		
	100	0	0			0	100	0	100
A	0	0	100	A		100	0	0	0
	0	100	0			0	0	100	0
Total	100	100	100	Total		100	100	100	100

c. "Weak" Perfect Association

		B		
	100	0	0	
A	100	0	0	
	100	100	100	
Total	300	100	100	

Table 2.1c illustrates a relationship that a few social scientists consider perfect. Here, the categories of, say, *B* are as homogeneous as possible with respect to *A*, given the marginal totals.

Most measures do not attain their maximums for relationships of this sort. In Table 2.1c, the problem lies in the first column and last row, which contain the preponderance of cases. Knowing an individual's score on one of these classes does not help predict his classification on the other variable. Furthermore, if more refined classifications could be obtained, one still has no assurance that the association would be perfect in any of the above senses.

Nonetheless, one could argue that these data exhibit perfect association, in which case he should choose an appropriate measure.

Intermediate Values. Since most indices are normed so that they have intelligible lower and upper bounds, one has some basis for choosing among them. He simply selects the one based on the definitions of nil and perfect relationship most in agreement with his research needs.

The rub lies in interpreting intermediate values. Suppose that an investigator wants statistical independence and strict association to define nil and perfect association. His choice of measures is narrowed somewhat, but he still has to make sense of values lying between 0 and 1.0.

The decision turns on the measure's operational definition. Some, like measures based on chi square, do not have intuitively appealing interpretations. Others, proportional-reduction-in-error indices, for example, are more easily understood but depend on looking at a cross-classification in a particular way. Thus, each measure has to be examined separately in order to grasp its underlying logic and meaning.

The choice can be narrowed slightly by deciding whether a symmetric or asymmetric measure is appropriate. If one's theory or common sense suggests that A causes B, then he would perhaps want an asymmetric measure since he is trying to predict the classes of a clearly defined dependent variable. In many instances, however, neither variable is considered dependent; here the best selection may be a symmetric index, one that gives the same value whatever variable is considered dependent.

2.1.2 Confounding Factors.   A problem common to all indices is their sensitivity to factors that have little to do with inherent relationships but that affect the measure's numerical values. For example, the number of cases affects the magnitude of the chi square statistic: the greater the sample size, the larger the value of chi square, other things being equal. Measures of association eliminate the effects of sample sizes—this is one reason for calculating them in the first place—but similar types of factors influence their interpretation. Two of the most common problems are skewed marginal distributions and unequal numbers of rows and columns.

   Marginal Distributions. Variation in nominal data is indicated by marginal distributions.[1] In some variables the observations are more or less evenly distributed, whereas in others they are concentrated in one or two categories. Whatever the situation, one may reasonably view variation as extraneous to the inherent relationship between two variables. After all, observed variation results from the underlying population distribution as well as from sampling effects and the frequently arbitrary choice of cutpoints.

---

   1. There are a variety of indices of variation in nominal data. Among the best known are the following:

$$\text{Index of qualitative variation:}\quad IQV = \frac{1 - \sum_i (f_{i+}/n)^2}{(I-1)/I}$$

$$\text{Deviation from the mode:}\quad DM = 1 - \frac{\sum_i (f_{m+} - f_{i+})}{n(I-1)}$$

$$\text{Index of relative uncertainty:}\quad H = \frac{-\sum_i f_{i+}/n \, \log\,(f_{i+}/n)}{\log I}$$

where the summation is over all I categories of the variable, f_{m+} is the frequency in the modal category, and log is the natural logarithm. These indices vary between 0 and 1.0. The value 0 implies no variation (i.e., all cases in a single category), whereas 1.0 implies maximum variation (i.e., the same number of cases in each cell). The reader may find them useful in comparing marginal distributions and for other purposes. They are less useful for ordinal variables, however, because they do not take account of the ordering among the categories. It is also hard to give intermediate values an intuitive or operational meaning.

Many indices of association, however, are sensitive to marginal distributions in the sense that skewness in one or both variables tends to decrease a measure's magnitude. This in turn leads to confusion.

Suppose that two investigators studying the same phenomenon use identical methods in categorizing A and B. One researcher, however, samples a population with relatively little variation in B; the other samples a population with more variation. Now, the inherent relationship between A and B (as measured by, say, percents) may be the same in both populations, but they could report opposite conclusions even though they calculate the same statistics, because the observed marginal distributions differ.

Since only a few indices, whether nominal, ordinal, or interval, are impervious to marginal distributions, an investigator has to pay particular attention to marginal totals. When one or both variables are highly skewed, he should decide whether or not the relative absence of variation is substantively meaningful. If he wants to know what more even distributions would produce, he can adjust the observed data (see next section) or select a less sensitive measure. On the other hand, the lack of variation may itself be theoretically important, and in that case he would want to preserve the original marginal distributions. The point is simply that one must be aware of the possible confounding effects of marginal distributions.

Nonsquare Tables. The number of rows and columns frequently do not equal. Tabular asymmetry usually occurs by happenstance and ought not to change the inherent relationship between two variables. Yet a surprisingly large number of measures are affected by it.

The difficulty arises because some measures cannot attain their maximums if the rows do not equal the columns. Suppose that interest lies in the hypothesis that two variables are "implicitly" perfectly correlated. In order to test this proposition, one requires an appropriate measure that can attain its maximum in nonsquare tables.

2.1.3 Standardizing Tables.   There are two general ways to solve problems of this sort, particularly those involving skewed marginal totals. A common approach is to compute a "maximum" version of a measure—maximum *given* the table size or marginal distribution—and then divide this version into the observed value.

A more sophisticated method is to *standardize* or *smooth* a table of observed frequencies to conform to any set of desired marginal totals. The easiest method is to compute percents and then treat the percents as though they were raw frequencies. Percentaging effectively standardizes a variable because it assumes that each category of the independent variable has exactly 100 cases, thereby removing the effects of the unequal marginals.

Obviously, percentaging affects only one variable. It is possible, though, to standardize both variables to make them conform to any desired marginals. Moreover, standardization does not change inherent relationships, at least according to one criterion of association (Mosteller, 1968; K. W. Smith, 1976).

Two-variable standardization, an interative procedure, begins with the investigator selecting the desired marginal totals, denoted f_{i+}^* and f_{+j}^* $(i = 1, \ldots, I; j = 1, \ldots, J)$. For example, he might want to transform a table so that there are equal numbers of cases in each category, thereby removing the effects of the uneven marginal distributions.

At the first step he adjusts the data to conform with one set of desired marginals. But at this point they do not agree with the second set, so in the next step he further adjusts the frequencies. In so doing, the fit with the first set of marginals is lost. Hence a new cycle begins. Fortunately, the data quickly converge to the desired marginals, usually in less than 10 cycles. The work is done when the values obtained at the end of one cycle do not differ from those obtained at the previous cycle by more than, say, .01.

More formally, let f_{ij}^s denote a standardized frequency at step s. At the outset (that is, at step $s = 0$), let $f_{ij}^0 = f_{ij}$, the observed frequency. Then at the sth step,

$$f_{ij}^s = \left(\frac{f_{ij}^{s-1}}{f_{i+}^{s-1}} \right) f_{i+}^* \qquad (2.1a)$$

where f_{i+}^{s-1} is the marginal total in the ith row obtained from the adjusted frequencies in the previous step and f_{i+}^* is the desired row marginal total. At the next step,

$$f_{ij}^{s+1} = \left(\frac{f_{ij}^s}{f_{+j}^s} \right) f_{+j}^* \qquad (2.1b)$$

where f_{+j}^* is the desired marginal total for the column variable. The calculation of f_{ij}^{s+1} ends the cycle. The procedure continues until all values obtained at the end of one cycle do not differ by more than δ (a small number, usually .01) from the estimates found in the previous cycle.

Table 2.2a shows the association between attitudes toward capital punishment and beliefs about the court's treatment of criminals. Both variables, but especially A, are skewed, and one wonders what the relationship would be if they were more evenly distributed.

Table 2.3 illustrates the iterative procedure for adjusting the data to fit equal marginal totals. (Table 2.2b presents the standardized frequencies.) Note that most measures of association, described later, increase in magnitude.

Standardization, which generalizes to multidimensional cross-classifications, facilitates the comparison of tables. Data collected from different populations or at different times often exhibit different amounts of variation. If marginal variation affects a measure of association, using that measure for comparison may raise as many questions as it answers. Standardization provides one solution.

TABLE 2.2. **Example of Unstandardized and Standardized Tables**

a. Original Table

		B: Attitude toward Capital Punishment		
		Favors	Opposes	Total
A: Belief about	Too Harsh	17	51	68
Courts' Treatment	About Right	126	206	332
of Criminals	Too Easy	751	332	1083
	Total	894	589	1483

$$\hat{\alpha}_{11} = .147 \qquad \hat{\alpha}_{21} = .270 \qquad \hat{\tau}_A = .072 \qquad \hat{T} = .218$$
$$\hat{\lambda}_A = .0 \qquad \hat{\Phi}^2 = .096 \qquad \hat{C} = .295 \qquad \hat{V} = .096$$

b. Standardized Table

		B: Attitude toward Capital Punishment		
		Favors	Opposes	Total
A: Belief about	Too Harsh	150.8	343.5	494.3
Courts' Treatment	About Right	220.6	273.8	494.4
of Criminals	Too Easy	370.1	124.2	494.3
	Total	741.5	741.5	1483.0

$$\hat{\alpha}_{11} = .147 \qquad \hat{\alpha}_{21} = .270 \qquad \hat{\tau}_A = .069 \qquad \hat{T} = .261$$
$$\hat{\lambda}_A = .222 \qquad \hat{\Phi}^2 = .137 \qquad \hat{C} = .347 \qquad \hat{V} = .137$$

Source: J. Davis, General Social Survey (see Appendix C).

TABLE 2.3. **Example of Iterative Calculations to Standardize Table 2.2a**

Cell			Cycle 1		Cycle 2		$\cdots$	Cycle 6	
i	j	f^0	f^1	f^2	f^3	f^4	$\cdots$	f^{11}	f^{12}
1	1	17	123.58	140.12	146.83	149.30	$\cdots$	150.82	150.82
1	2	51	370.75	331.61	347.50	341.85	$\cdots$	343.51	343.51
2	1	126	187.61	212.71	215.89	219.52	$\cdots$	220.56	220.56
2	2	206	306.72	274.35	278.44	273.91	$\cdots$	273.77	273.77
3	1	751	342.79	388.66	366.51	372.68	$\cdots$	370.11	370.11
3	2	332	151.54	135.54	127.82	125.74	$\cdots$	124.22	124.22

Note: Computations were actually carried out to more significant digits than reported.

2.2 NOMINAL MEASURES OF ASSOCIATION FOR 2×2 TABLES

One of the most familiar and most extensively studied types of cross-classification in the social sciences is 2×2 tables. Formulas and calculations are usually much simpler in the 2×2's than in larger tables. In addition to their simplicity, they have interesting and useful properties. Many seemingly different measures of association equal each other in these tables, and many concepts applicable in the dichotomous case readily generalize to higher-dimensional tables.

In spite of these features, there is little advantage in "collapsing" or reducing a larger array into a 2×2 table. Collapsed data frequently introduce distortions. What might be a weak relationship in an $I \times J$ table (where I and J are both greater than 2) could turn out to be a large association if the variables have been dichotomized. The observed relationship would then be more an artifact of one's measurement procedures than a reflection of the true state of affairs (see Section 5.6).

As a general rule, categories should not be collapsed. Of course, if the variables really only have two categories or no other measurement is available, a researcher has little choice. But the widespread practice of uncritically dichotomizing variables risks throwing away valuable information and producing misleading results (see Bishop, 1971; Reynolds, 1976).

2.2.1 Percents. Regardless of the size of a table, one of the easiest ways to measure a relationship between two variables, especially if one is clearly dependent, is to calculate percents. After all, one wants to compare how people in different categories of one variable behave with respect to the classes of another. If the distribution of responses changes from one category to another, there is evidence for a relationship.

Percents are particularly useful in 2×2 tables. A difference in percents (or proportions) is interpretable as a regression coefficient between two dichotomous variables. Look at this very simple 2×2 table of proportions, where raw frequencies are in parentheses:

		B	
		.8	.4
		(40)	(20)
A		.2	.6
		(10)	(30)
		1.0	1.0
		(50)	(50)

Here the difference in proportions (with respect to the first row) between the two columns of B is .4. The same quantity would be obtained if the categories of A and B were coded 0 and 1 and the data substituted into familiar regression formulas. A change in one unit of B (from 0 to 1) produces a change of .4 in A. Given the range of possible values (0 to 1), this result indicates a substantial relationship.

Thus, a difference in percents or proportions has a clear interpretation as a measure of association in a 2×2 table. Furthermore, by virtue of its definition, it is not sensitive to imbalances in the marginal distribution of B.

2.2.2 The Odds Ratio. The odds ratio, often called the cross-product ratio, is surprisingly little known in the social sciences, surprisingly because it actually underlies two popular measures of association and has several useful properties. A thoroughly researched statistic, the odds ratio also provides a very helpful heuristic device for understanding log-linear analysis, a multivariate technique for categorical data described in Chapter 5.

A simplified version of the voting data (Table 1.1) illustrates its meaning and computation. Here, we consider only Democrats and Republicans producing a 2×2 table:[2]

		B: Party Identification	
		Democrat	Republican
A: Vote	Democrat	1103	115
	Republican	207	766
	Total	1310	881

For the moment, the marginal totals pertaining to party are considered fixed.

Obviously the variables are related. The question, however, is how strongly? One answer is given by comparing the *odds* of voting Democratic. For Democrats, the odds are 1103 to 207 or about 5.3 to 1. Now compare these odds to the odds of voting Democratic among Republicans. If partisanship is unrelated to electoral behavior, the odds of voting Democratic should be the same in both groups. If, on the other hand, party identification affects people's preferences, then the odds among Republicans will be different. As it turns out, the odds of a Democratic vote among Republicans is considerably less than 1, namely $115/766 = .15$.

Although the odds differ, it is useful to compare them more explicitly by calculating their ratio:

$$\frac{1103/207}{115/766} = \frac{5.3}{.15} = 35.492.$$

2. An investigator would not normally dichotomize variables in this manner; it is done here for convenience.

The ratio of the odds (the odds ratio) has a simple interpretation. If the odds are the same in both categories of party identification, their ratio will equal 1.0. Hence, 1.0 indicates no relationship. This definition has intuitive appeal because if the odds of voting Democratic are the same in both classes of party identification, it (partisanship) provides very little insight into people's political preference.

Departures in either direction from 1.0 suggest association: the greater the departure, the stronger the relationship. But specific value can only be interpreted as a ratio of odds.

More formally, let $P(A_iB_j) = P_{ij}$ $(i = 1, 2; j = 1, 2)$ be the population probability of being in the ith row and jth column of a 2×2 table relating A and B, where the column totals are fixed. The odds ratio, denoted α, is thus

$$\alpha = \frac{P_{11}/P_{21}}{P_{12}/P_{22}} = \frac{P_{11}P_{22}}{P_{21}P_{12}}. \tag{2.2}$$

The measure is merely the ratio of two ratios and has exactly the same interpretation as already indicated: a value of 1.0 shows no relationship, whereas values greater or less than 1.0 indicate the existence of a relationship. The odds ratio is not a "normed" measure in the sense mentioned in Section 2.1.

The sample estimate of α is

$$\hat{\alpha} = \frac{f_{11}/f_{21}}{f_{12}/f_{22}} = \frac{f_{11}f_{22}}{f_{21}f_{12}}, \tag{2.3}$$

where f_{ij} are observed frequencies in a 2×2 table. This interpretation implicitly assumes fixed marginal totals. But α can actually be calculated when none, one, or both sets of marginals are fixed.

Properties of the Odds Ratio. The odds ratio ranges from 0 to plus infinity with 1.0 indicating statistical independence. Values less than 1.0 imply a "negative" association, whereas values greater than 1.0 mean a positive relationship. In order to see this point, examine these two seemingly different 2×2 tables:

a		b	
200	50	50	200
50	200	200	50
250	250	250	250

The odds ratios for tables a and b are 16.0 and .0625, respectively. But notice the similarities: the second table is obtained from the first by simply rotating the frequencies while maintaining the same underlying strength of association. Most observations in Table a lie in the diagonal running from the upper left to the lower right; in the other table they tend to be in the opposite diagonal. In this sense, the two tables reflect similarity in the magnitude but not in the direction of the relationship.

But also note that $\hat{\alpha}_b = 1/\hat{\alpha}_a$ (that is, $.0625 = \frac{1}{16}$). The upshot is that departures in either direction from 1.0 imply essentially the same thing but are measured on different scales: negative relationships are measured on the interval 0 to 1.0 and positive relationships on the interval 1.0 to plus infinity. Not being symmetric about 1.0 means that two tables with the same degree of association, but in opposite directions, have different $\hat{\alpha}$'s.

The lack of symmetry is easily removed by calculating the natural logarithm[3] of α:

$$\alpha^* = \log \alpha = \log\left(\frac{P_{11}P_{22}}{P_{21}P_{12}}\right)$$
$$= \log P_{11} + \log P_{22} - \log P_{21} - \log P_{12}. \qquad (2.4)$$

The measure α^*, called the log odds, varies from minus to plus infinity, with 0 indicating independence. In the two previous tables $\alpha_a^* = 2.77$ and $\alpha_b^* = -2.77$. Although α^* has the appeal of being symmetric, it is perhaps more difficult to interpret than the simple odds ratio because it involves a logarithm. (Its estimate is obtained by substituting f's for P's.)

Both the odds ratio and its logarithm have several important properties. First, they are invariant under row and column multiplications. To appreciate this feature, consider two hypothetical investigators working on the same problem. Even though their variables are identical, they sample different populations at different rates and thus obtain different marginal distributions (see Table 2.4.)

TABLE 2.4. **Example of the Effect of Changes in Marginal Distributions on Measures of Association**

	a			b	
	B			*B*	
A	75	15	*A*	750	15
	10	100		100	100
Total	85	115	Total	850	115
$\hat{\alpha} = 50$		$\hat{Y} = .75$	$\hat{\alpha} = 50$		$\hat{Y} = .75$
$\hat{\alpha}^* = 3.91$		$\hat{\Phi}^2 = .56$	$\hat{\alpha}^* = 3.91$		$\hat{\Phi}^2 = .36$
$\hat{Q} = .96$		$r = .75$	$\hat{Q} = .96$		$r = .60$
$GFX^2 = 111.65$			$GFX^2 = 348.57$		

---

3. This property of logarithms is discussed briefly in Chapter 5, note 2.

Not only does the first investigator have a smaller sample (200 versus 965), but his cases are relatively more dispersed on B: the proportions in the first column of each table are .43 and .88, respectively. Yet in spite of these differences, the odds ratio and its logarithm are the same in both tables, namely $\hat{\alpha} = 50$ and $\hat{\alpha}^* = 3.91$. Some social scientists find this insensitivity to marginal distributions—a trait not found in many other measures of association—quite useful because the inherent relationships as measured by percents appear equivalent.[4] As a practical matter, this property allows one to compare relationships across tables drawn from different samples. If the basic form of the association is the same in different populations, the $\hat{\alpha}$'s and $\hat{\alpha}^*$'s will be the same (except for sampling error) no matter how much the marginal distributions vary.

A second property is that the odds ratio is also invariant under interchanges of rows *and* columns. (Switching only the rows *or* columns changes α to $1/\alpha$.) In this sense, the odds ratio is a symmetric index.

The odds ratio also attains its upper bound under "weak" perfect association, a fact that some statisticians consider a virtue, others a vice. Certainly the form of association exhibited in the two subtables of Table 2.5 differs substantially.

TABLE 2.5. **Behavior of Measures of Association under Different Definitions of Perfect Relationship**

	a			b	
	B			A	
A	200	0	B	200	0
	0	200		200	200
Total	200	200	Total	400	200

$\hat{\alpha} = +\infty$	$\hat{Y} = 1.0$	$\hat{\alpha} = +\infty$	$\hat{Y} = 1.0$
$\hat{\alpha}^* = +\infty$	$\hat{\Phi}^2 = 1.0$	$\hat{\alpha}^* = +\infty$	$\hat{\Phi}^2 = .25$
$\hat{Q} = 1.0$	$r = 1.0$	$\hat{Q} = 1.0$	$r = .50$

Letting A and B denote the row and column variables, respectively, one sees that in the first table, values of A never occur in the absence of a given value of B, a pattern that does not hold in Table b. There the first column of B is not a good predictor of A; one can only conclude that a person in the second column of B is in the second category of A. In this sense the relationship seems weak.

Yet in the two tables, $\hat{\alpha}$ (and $\hat{\alpha}^*$) equal plus infinity, suggesting an equivalence in relationships. The observed odds ratio equals infinity whenever f_{12} of f_{21} (or both) equal zero. (It equals zero whenever f_{11} or

---

4. Indeed, the second table was obtained from the first by multiplying the entries in the first column by 10.

f_{22} or both equal zero.) A similar principle applies whenever one frequency is very small. Changing the 0 in the second table to 1 means that $\hat{\alpha} = 200$, a value that many social scientists would still consider misleading.

The Variance of the Odds Ratio. Assuming a sufficiently large sample (greater than 25) in which only n is fixed, or in which either the row or column totals are fixed, an estimate of the variance of α is

$$\hat{\sigma}^2_{(\alpha)} = \hat{\alpha}^2 \left(\frac{1}{f_{11}} + \frac{1}{f_{21}} + \frac{1}{f_{12}} + \frac{1}{f_{22}} \right), \tag{2.5}$$

where each f_{ij} must be greater than 0 (Goodman, 1964a, 1964b, 1965c). (Tables with empty cells have to be adjusted, usually by entering a "pseudo-value," before the variance can be calculated. A crude expedient is to add $\frac{1}{2}$ to each frequency; for more sophisticated approaches, see Bishop, Fienberg, and Holland, 1975.)

An estimate of the variance of $\hat{\alpha}^*$ takes a similar form,

$$\hat{\sigma}^2_{(\hat{\alpha}^*)} = \left(\frac{1}{f_{11}} + \frac{1}{f_{21}} + \frac{1}{f_{12}} + \frac{1}{f_{22}} \right), \tag{2.6}$$

where again $f_{ij} > 0$ ($i = 1, 2$; $j = 1, 2$).

Having estimates of the variances of $\hat{\alpha}$ and $\hat{\alpha}^*$ allows one to test hypotheses about the odds ratio or its logarithm, since they are normally distributed with mean α or α^*.

Approximate (large-sample) confidence limits are given by

$$L = \hat{\alpha} + \zeta\hat{\sigma}_{(\hat{\alpha})} \quad \text{and} \quad U = \hat{\alpha} - \zeta\hat{\sigma}_{(\hat{\alpha})}, \tag{2.7}$$

where ζ is an appropriate percentile of the unit normal distribution (Goodman, 1964a, 1964b). Confidence intervals for α for the dichotomous voting data are

$$L = 35.492 - (1.96)(4.453) = 26.765;$$
$$U = 35.492 + (1.96)(4.453) = 44.220;$$

where 1.96 is the 97.5th percentile of the normal distribution and 4.453 is an estimate of the standard error of $\hat{\alpha}$. In view of the large sample size and the magnitude of $\hat{\alpha}$, these limits are not especially informative.

2.2.3 Yule's Q. One of the best-known measures of association in the social sciences, Yule's Q, is a function of the odds ratio and consequently shares most of its strengths and weaknesses. Its definition is

$$Q = \frac{P_{11}P_{22} - P_{12}P_{21}}{P_{11}P_{22} + P_{12}P_{21}} = \frac{\alpha - 1}{\alpha + 1}, \tag{2.8}$$

which can be estimated by

$$\hat{Q} = \frac{f_{11}f_{22} - f_{12}f_{21}}{f_{11}f_{22} + f_{12}f_{21}} = \frac{\hat{\alpha} - 1}{\hat{\alpha} + 1}. \tag{2.9}$$

For the voting data,

$$\hat{Q} = \frac{35.492 - 1}{35.492 + 1} = .945.$$

Unlike α, Q lies between -1.0 and 1.0, with 0 implying statistical independence. Like the odds ratio, however, Q attains its upper limit under strict, implicit, *or* weak perfect association. Thus, as was true of $\hat{\alpha}$, $\hat{Q}$ reaches its maximum, 1.0, in both subtables of Table 2.5. (One readily sees from the appropriate formula that Q is 1.0 whenever P_{12} or P_{21} or both are zero; it is -1.0 whenever P_{11} or P_{22} or both are zero.) For this reason many investigators feel that it overstates the strength of an association. Certainly it gives the largest numerical value of the normed indices usually computed for 2×2 tables, but whether it overstates a relationship depends on one's model of perfect association (Weissberg, 1974).

Since Q equals γ, an ordinal measure of correlation applied to 2×2 tables, its intermediate values are also interpreted in terms of pairs of observations (see Chapter 3).

Q is invariant under row and column multiplications (see Table 2.4) and is symmetric.

Assuming that $f_{ij} > 0$ (for all i and j), its estimated variance,

$$\hat{\sigma}^2_{(\hat{Q})} = \frac{(1 - \hat{Q}^2)^2}{4}\left(\frac{1}{f_{11}} + \frac{1}{f_{21}} + \frac{1}{f_{12}} + \frac{1}{f_{22}}\right), \tag{2.10}$$

can be used to test hypotheses and construct confidence intervals, just as in the case of the odds ratio. For the voting data, the estimated standard error is .007.

2.2.4 Yule's Y. Yule's Y, sometimes called the coefficient of "colligation," is also a simple function of the odds ratio:

$$Y = \frac{\sqrt{P_{11}P_{22}} - \sqrt{P_{12}P_{21}}}{\sqrt{P_{11}P_{22}} + \sqrt{P_{12}P_{21}}} = \frac{\sqrt{\alpha} - 1}{\sqrt{\alpha} + 1}. \tag{2.11}$$

Its sample estimate is

$$\hat{Y} = \frac{\sqrt{f_{11}f_{22}} - \sqrt{f_{12}f_{21}}}{\sqrt{f_{11}f_{22}} + \sqrt{f_{12}f_{21}}} = \frac{\sqrt{\hat{\alpha}} - 1}{\sqrt{\hat{\alpha}} + 1}. \tag{2.12}$$

For the voting data, the estimate is

$$\hat{Y} = \frac{\sqrt{35.492} - 1}{\sqrt{35.492} + 1} = .713.$$

Y has the same properties as Q, although they are by no means equal in most 2×2 tables. In fact, the absolute value of Y is less than the absolute value of Q except when A and B are independent or completely associated.

According to Bishop, Fienberg, and Holland (1975, p. 379), Y can be interpreted as the difference between the probabilities in the diagonal and off-diagonal cells of a standardized table, that is, a table where the marginal probabilities are all $\frac{1}{2}$. This interpretation however, is difficult to translate into substantive or theoretical terms.

The estimated variance of Y, assuming that $f_{ij} > 0$ (for all i, j) is

$$\hat{\sigma}^2_{(\hat{Y})} = \frac{(1 - \hat{Y}^2)^2}{16} \left(\frac{1}{f_{11}} + \frac{1}{f_{21}} + \frac{1}{f_{12}} + \frac{1}{f_{22}} \right). \tag{2.13}$$

For the voting data, $\hat{\sigma}_{(\hat{Y})} = .015$.

2.2.5 A Measure Based on Chi Square, Φ^2.   One reason for not using the goodness-of-fit chi square as a measure of association is that its numerical magnitude depends partly on the size of the sample. Dividing chi square by n corrects for this and leads to a measure of association, phi squared:

$$\hat{\Phi}^2 = \frac{GFX^2}{n}, \tag{2.14}$$

where GFX^2 is the observed goodness-of-fit chi square.

The population definition, a not very informative expression, is

$$\Phi^2 = \frac{(P_{11}P_{22} - P_{12}P_{21})^2}{P_{1+}P_{2+}P_{+1}P_{+2}}, \tag{2.15}$$

where P_{i+} and P_{+j} are row and column marginal probabilities.

In a 2×2 table, $\hat{\Phi}^2$ varies between 0 and 1, obviously equaling zero when the variables are statistically independent. It attains its maximum only under strict perfect association. In Table 2.5, for instance, $\hat{\Phi}^2$ equals 1.0 in the first subtable but not in the second, where it is only .25.

On the other hand, the marginal variation in A or B affects its magnitude. As seen in Table 2.4, the greater the imbalance in the marginal distributions, the lower its value, other things being equal. Using either percents or the odds ratio as the criteria, the form and strength of association are the same in both tables, but $\hat{\Phi}^2_b$ is considerably smaller than $\hat{\Phi}_a^2$. Where one or both marginals are highly skewed, a less sensitive measure may be preferred.

Finally, the computation of Φ^2, a symmetric index, does not depend on which variable is considered dependent.

The interpretation of Φ^2 can be further facilitated by realizing that it is equivalent to ρ^2, the square of the product-moment correlation coefficient, applied to a 2×2 table.

2.2.6 The Correlation Coefficient, ρ. The categories of dichotomous variables can be coded 0 and 1 and used in the (Pearson) product-moment correlation formula. In a 2×2 table, the calculations reduce to

$$\rho = \frac{P_{11}P_{22} - P_{12}P_{21}}{\sqrt{P_{1+}P_{2+}P_{+1}P_{+2}}} \tag{2.16}$$

for the population parameter and

$$r = \frac{f_{11}f_{22} - f_{12}f_{21}}{\sqrt{f_{1+}f_{2+}f_{+1}f_{+2}}} \tag{2.17}$$

for its sample estimate.

Although a symmetric measure, the square of the correlation coefficient is commonly interpreted as the percent of variation in the dependent variable that is "explained" by the independent variable. The estimate of ρ in the 2×2 table of voting data is

$$r = \frac{(1103)(766) - (115)(207)}{\sqrt{(1310)(881)(1218)(973)}} = .702.$$

Since $r^2 = .493$, about 49 percent of the variance in voting is accounted for by party identification. Thus, remembering that statistical explanation is not equivalent to theoretical understanding, ρ has a clear interpretation.

Because ρ^2 is equivalent of Φ^2 in 2×2 tables, they share the same properties. The correlation coefficient is sensitive to skewed marginal distributions (see Table 2.4) but is invariant under interchanges of *both* rows and columns. (It changes sign only when the rows or columns are switched.) It is an appropriate measure when one's definition of perfect is strict perfect association (see Table 2.5).

The value of ρ varies between -1.0 and 1.0. It equals zero if the row and column variables are independent. From the formulas it is apparent that ρ (or r) $= 1.0$ if $P_{12} = P_{21} = 0$ (or $f_{12} = f_{21} = 0$) and ρ (or r) $= -1.0$ if $P_{11} = P_{22} = 0$ (or $f_{11} = f_{22} = 0$). In this sense, the correlation coefficient gives both the direction and strength of association.

In a standardized 2×2 table, where each marginal probability equals $\frac{1}{2}$, $\rho = Y$; otherwise $|\rho| < |Y|$ except when the variables are independent or completely related. Consequently, its numerical value will usually be less than either Y or Q.

The large-sample estimate of the variance of r is

$$\hat{\sigma}_{(r)}^2 = \frac{1}{n} \left[1 - r^2 + \left(r + \frac{r^3}{2} \right) \left(\frac{(f_{1+} - f_{2+})(f_{+1} - f_{+2})}{\sqrt{f_{1+} f_{2+} f_{+1} f_{+2}}} \right) \right.$$
$$\left. - \frac{3r^2}{4} \left(\frac{(f_{1+} - f_{2+})^2}{f_{1+} f_{2+}} + \frac{(f_{+1} - f_{+2})^2}{f_{+1} f_{+2}} \right) \right]. \tag{2.18}$$

Assuming a sufficiently large sample, r is normally distributed with mean ρ and variance $\hat{\sigma}_{(r)}^2$ (Bishop, Fienberg, and Holland, 1975). The estimated standard error of the voting data is $\hat{\sigma}_{(r)} = .015$.

2.3 NOMINAL MEASURES OF ASSOCIATION FOR I × J TABLES

Measuring association in $I \times J$ tables involves many of the same concepts and problems found in the analysis of 2×2 tables. The objective is to find clearly understandable measures, ones that are not confused by marginal distributions or table sizes. Although innumerable approaches exist, many of them can be grouped under five headings: (1) generalizations of the odds ratio, (2) measures based on chi square, (3) "proportional-reduction-in-error" measures, (4) measures of agreement, and (5) a new approach, "prediction logic." These procedures by no means exhaust the alternatives, but they are among the best known.

2.4 THE ODDS RATIO IN I × J TABLES

2.4.1 Definition. The odds ratio or its logarithm readily generalizes to larger tables. An $I \times J$ table, where either I or J or both are greater than 2, contains subsets of 2×2 tables, and an α or α^* can be calculated for each. Looking at several individual odds ratios instead of a single summary index permits one to examine various subhypotheses of interest and, in many instances, to locate the precise source of an association.

Let P_{ij} denote the probability that an observation is in the ijth cell of an $I \times J$ population table. Then a *basic set* of odds ratios is

$$\alpha_{ij} = \frac{P_{ij} P_{IJ}}{P_{iJ} P_{Ij}} \qquad i = 1, 2, \ldots, I-1; \; j = 1, 2, \ldots, J-1. \tag{2.19}$$

Notice that the last (the bottom right) cell of the table is the reference point, although any cell could serve this purpose.

Viewed from this perspective, there are $T = (I-1)(J-1)$ 2×2 tables in an $I \times J$ table, each composed of probabilities from the ith and Ith rows *and* the jth and Jth columns. (There are actually more subtables, but the remainder can be generated from this subset. See Goodman, 1964a, 1964c, 1964d, 1965a, 1969a.) Corresponding to each subtable is an odds ratio which can be estimated from a sample by

$$\hat{\alpha}_{ij} = \frac{f_{ij}f_{IJ}}{f_{iJ}f_{Ij}}, \tag{2.20}$$

where f_{ij} represents the frequency in the ijth cell. Of course, the α's (or their logarithms) have the same interpretation as the odds ratio (or its logarithm) presented earlier.

Using odds ratios to analyze a cross-classification means that an investigator must examine a set of coefficients. In a large table the number of possible α's will be sizeable. In addition, the odds ratio is not normed to lie between 0 and 1.0. Partly for these reasons, social scientists have been reluctant to use it in contingency table analysis.

However, there are several advantages. As already noted, one can thoroughly dissect a cross-classification by looking at the relationships in different parts of the table. For instance, there are $T = (3-1)(3-1) = 4$ basic 2×2 tables in Table 1.3 (see Chapter 1). The corresponding odds ratios are

$$\hat{\alpha}_{11} = \frac{(312)(137)}{(115)(210)} = 1.770 \qquad \hat{\alpha}_{12} = \frac{(34)(137)}{(115)(32)} = 1.266$$

$$\hat{\alpha}_{21} = \frac{(159)(137)}{(110)(210)} = .943 \qquad \hat{\alpha}_{22} = \frac{(24)(137)}{(110)(32)} = .934$$

The strongest relationship, as one might expect, involves liberals versus conservatives in terms of whether they voted mostly Democratic or Republican. On the whole the results agree with voting research and common sense, but ransacking a table in this manner often leads to unexpected and interesting insights.

2.4.2 Simultaneous Confidence Intervals.   One can construct approximate two-sided *simultaneous* confidence intervals for each of the $T\hat{\alpha}$'s. The notion of simultaneous intervals arises because several, interrelated statistics are being computed on the same set of data. It is not legitimate to treat each $\hat{\alpha}$ as though it were independent of the others. Consequently, it is necessary to adjust probability levels to account for the simultaneous calculation of several odds ratios based on the same data.

Assuming a multinomial or product-multinomial sampling where only n or one marginal is fixed, and all $f_{ij} > 0$, approximate confidence limits for $\hat{\alpha}^*$, the log odds, are given by

$$\hat{\alpha}^*_{ij} \pm \chi_T(P)\hat{\sigma}_{(\hat{\alpha}^*_{ij})}, \tag{2.21}$$

where $\chi_T(P)$ denotes the 100 Pth percentile of the chi square distribution with T degrees of freedom and

$$\hat{\sigma}^2_{(\hat{\alpha}^*_{ij})} = \left(\frac{1}{f_{ij}} + \frac{1}{f_{iJ}} + \frac{1}{f_{Ij}} + \frac{1}{f_{IJ}}\right). \tag{2.22}$$

Note that $\chi_T(P)$ is the square root of the appropriate entry in the tabulated chi square distribution presented in Appendix B.

Intervals for the simple odds ratios can be obtained by taking the antilogs of these limits. For the data in Table 1.3, approximate 95 percent simultaneous confidence intervals for the true log odds are

$$.094 \leq \alpha^*_{11} \leq 1.048 \quad -.617 \leq \alpha^*_{12} \leq 1.088$$

$$-.569 \leq \alpha^*_{21} \leq .452 \quad -.989 \leq \alpha^*_{22} \leq .852$$

Taking antilogs of each of the limits yields intervals for the population α's:

$$1.099 \leq \alpha_{11} \leq 2.851 \quad .540 \leq \alpha_{12} \leq 2.700$$

$$.566 \leq \alpha_{21} \leq 1.571 \quad .372 \leq \alpha_{22} \leq 2.345$$

Only the interval pertaining to α_{11} does not contain 1.0, suggesting that this relationship alone is statistically significant. This finding, consistent with the results of the partitioning of this table presented in Chapter 1, shows that differences between liberals and conservatives, as measured by α_{11}, contribute most to the overall relationship.

The investigator is not limited to examining just the T odds ratios. If, on the basis of prior considerations, he specifies a set of S log odds ratios, he can frequently obtain shorter intervals by using

$$\hat{\alpha}^*_s \pm \phi_S(P)\hat{\sigma}_{(\hat{\alpha}^*_s)}, \tag{2.23}$$

where $\hat{\alpha}^*_s$ is the sth log odds ratio, $\phi_S(P)$ is the $100(1 - d/2S)$th percentile of the unit normal distribution, and $d = 1 - P$. [In the previous example where interest is in 95 percent confidence intervals for, say, $S = 3$ log odds ratios, $d = .05$ and $\phi_3(P)$ is 2.40.] One should calculate expression (2.21) instead of (2.23) if $\chi_T(P)$ is less than $\phi_S(P)$ (Goodman, 1964a). [In this case $\chi_3(P)$ is 2.79, so we use (2.23).] Intervals for α^*_{11}, α^*_{12}, and α^*_{22} are

$$.199 \leq \alpha^*_{11} \leq .942 \quad -.429 \leq \alpha^*_{12} \leq .900 \quad -.785 \leq \alpha^*_{22} \leq .649$$

Taking antilogs gives

$$1.221 \leq \alpha_{11} \leq 2.566 \quad .651 \leq \alpha_{12} \leq 2.460 \quad .456 \leq \alpha_{22} \leq 1.914$$

It is apparent that the second set of intervals is slightly shorter than the first. The point is that formula (2.23) is used when the set of odds ratio is selected before examining the data; (2.21) can be used to investigate the full set of odds ratios or odds ratios suggested by the data (Goodman, 1969a).

The odds ratio, incidentally, lends itself very nicely to interpreting log-linear models, a new and important technique for analyzing multidimensional cross-classifications (see Chapter 5).

2.5 MEASURES BASED ON CHI SQUARE

2.5.1 Phi Squared.   As in the 2×2 case, chi square alone is not a good indicator of the form or strength of a relationship in a general table, for its magnitude depends partly on n. Standardizing it by dividing by the sample size is an obvious solution. But the resulting measure, Φ^2, does not have an upper bound except in 2×2 tables. Not being bounded, the measure is difficult to interpret. In Table 1.1, where the goodness-of-fit chi square is 1085.97 with 2 degrees of freedom,

$$\hat{\Phi}^2 = \frac{1085.97}{2843} = .382.$$

How should this number be interpreted? Since Φ^2 equals zero if the variables are independent, the observed value implies at least some degree of association. Without an upper bound, however, one cannot say precisely what .382 means. It is just as hard to do so in tables showing stronger relationships.

Partly for these reasons, a number of normed variations of Φ^2 have been proposed. All of them are symmetric and equal zero when the variables are statistically independent. Two shortcomings are, however, that they frequently cannot attain their maximums and values lying between 0 and 1.0 are hard to interpret.

2.5.2 The Contingency Coefficient.   The contingency coefficient, C, theoretically lies between 0 and 1. For sample data it is estimated by

$$\hat{C} = \sqrt{\frac{\hat{\Phi}^2}{\hat{\Phi}^2 + 1}} = \sqrt{\frac{GFX^2}{GFX^2 + n}}. \tag{2.24}$$

C does not always reach 1.0, even when the variables seem completely associated. In square tables (that is, $I = J$), for instance, its maximum value is $\sqrt{(I-1)/I}$. In this instance one can obtain an "adjusted" C by computing $C_{adj} = C/C_{max}$, where C_{max} is the maximum value of C. In asymmetric tables, such an adjustment is less feasible. In any event, $\hat{C}$ can be less than 1.0 even though there is an implicit perfect association.

2.5.3 Tschuprow's *T.* Another version of Φ^2, Tschuprow's *T*, varies between 0 (for independence) and 1.0 but can only attain its maximum in square tables. When *I* does not equal *J*, *T* will be less than 1.0. The sample estimate of *T* is

$$\hat{T} = \sqrt{\frac{\hat{\Phi}^2}{\sqrt{(I-1)(J-1)}}} = \sqrt{\frac{GFX^2}{n\sqrt{(I-1)(J-1)}}}. \qquad (2.25)$$

2.5.4 Cramér's *V.* Cramér's *V* corrects for some of the deficiencies in *C* and *T*—it achieves its maximum in asymmetric arrays—but is still rather difficult to interpret. The sample estimate is

$$\hat{V} = \sqrt{\frac{\hat{\Phi}^2}{m}} = \sqrt{\frac{GFX^2}{nm}}, \qquad (2.26)$$

where *m* equals the smaller of $(I-1)$ or $(J-1)$. Note that *V* is always at least as large as *T*.

One can test the significance and determine confidence intervals for these measures by calculating their asymptotic variances. (Appropriate formulas are available in Bishop, Fienberg, and Holland, 1975, or Kendall and Stuart, 1966.) As an expedient, however, it is simpler to use the observed chi square statistic as a rough test of significance.

2.6 PROPORTIONAL-REDUCTION-IN-ERROR MEASURES

To avoid weaknesses of indices based on chi square, statisticians have developed a variety of other approaches. Perhaps the most popular alternative is proportional-reduction-in-error (PRE) logic.

PRE measures rest on a simple conception of association. Imagine a game in which one randomly draws people from a population and guesses their scores on *A*, the dependent variable. The predictions are to be made according to two rules. Under the first rule no information is used to predict scores on *A*; the guesses are in a sense blind. According to the second rule, the investigator examines each individual's *B* category and then, based on that information, predicts values on *A*.

It seems natural to compare the probabilities of making misclassification errors under the two rules. Denote the probability of misclassifying a subject on the basis of Rule 1 as $P(1)$ and the probability of error under the second rule as $P(2)$. Then the reduction in error achieved by using Rule 2 as opposed to Rule 1 is

$$\text{PRE Measure of Association} = \frac{P(1) - P(2)}{P(1)}. \qquad (2.27)$$

Note that a PRE measure varies between 0 and 1.0, 0 if the variables are statistically independent, meaning that the probability of misclassifying someone under Rule 1 equals the probability of making an error under Rule 2, and 1.0 if $P(2) = 0$, in which case knowledge of B permits the exact prediction of A. The measure is undefined if $P(1) = 0$. But this contingency will not arise because if there is no possibility of misclassification under 1, all subjects must be in the same category and there would be no variation in A.

Intermediate values are interpreted as the proportional reduction in error in predicting classes of A from Rule 2 as opposed to Rule 1. If the PRE measure is close to its maximum, knowledge of B is being used optimally to predict A; smaller values of the index suggest a weaker relationship in the sense defined here.

Because PRE logic is quite broad, several nominal measures of association are based on it. Their meaning and computation stem from the precise definition of errors.

2.6.1 Goodman and Kruskal's Lambda.

Goodman and Kruskal's (1954) λ rests on very straightforward definitions of prediction error.

According to the first rule, one predicts a randomly selected individual's A class without knowledge of his classification on B. How should the prediction be made? One strategy is always to guess A's modal category, the one with the largest marginal proportion, because most observations belong to it and over the long run fewer errors will be made by picking it.

For an $I \times J$ table, let P_{m+} denote the *maximum* marginal row probability or proportion. Without knowledge of B, one should always guess the category corresponding to the probability P_{m+}. The probability of making accurate predictions is P_{m+}, whereas the probability of error is

$$P(1) = 1 - P_{m+}.$$

According to the second rule, the investigator selects an individual at random, examines his classification on B, and then predicts the A category. Again, exactly how should the prediction be made? Working within each column (i.e., each category of B), the investigator should pick the most probable A category. In other words, given a category on B, pick the A class having the highest proportion. Errors will, of course, be made, but they will be fewer than if some other A classification is guessed.

In an $I \times J$ table, the symbol P_{mj} denotes the *maximum* cell probability or proportion in the jth column. The probability of error under the second rule, $P(2)$, is

$$P(2) = 1 - \sum_j P_{mj}.$$

These steps define a PRE measure, λ:

$$\lambda_A = \frac{(1-P_{m+})-\left(1-\sum_j P_{mj}\right)}{(1-P_{m+})} = \frac{\left(\sum_j P_{mj}\right)-P_{m+}}{(1-P_{m+})}, \qquad (2.28)$$

where the summation is over all J categories of B.

The subscript A indicates that categories of A are being predicted from information about B. Following the same logic but treating B as the dependent variable leads to the definition of λ_B:

$$\lambda_B = \frac{(1-P_{+m})-\left(1-\sum_i P_{im}\right)}{(1-P_{+m})} = \frac{\left(\sum_i P_{im}\right)-P_{+m}}{(1-P_{+m})}, \qquad (2.29)$$

where P_{+m} is the largest column marginal probability or proportion and P_{im} is the largest cell probability in the ith row. (If two or more marginal probabilities are the same, arbitrarily designate one as P_{+m}.)

Note the asymmetry of the measures: λ_A usually does not equal λ_B. One should therefore rely on his substantive knowledge to determine the most appropriate index. If, for instance, the aim of a study is the explanation of variation in A by reference to other variables, λ_A should be computed. Picking whichever coefficient happens to have the largest numerical value would be substantively meaningless.

Sample estimates can be calculated by replacing the population probabilities with estimated probabilities. It is simpler, however, to use raw frequencies and compute the estimate of λ_A from the following formula:

$$\hat{\lambda}_A = \frac{\left(\sum_j f_{mj}\right)-f_{m+}}{(n-f_{m+})}, \qquad (2.30)$$

where f_{m+} represents the largest row marginal total, f_{mj} represents the largest frequency in the jth column, and n is the sample size. The estimate, $\hat{\lambda}_A$, gives the proportional reduction in error for a sample of n observations according to these definitions of errors. The estimate for λ_B is found by replacing f_{m+} with f_{+m} and f_{mj} with f_{im} in (2.28) and summing over the I row categories.

Returning to Table 1.1, the two estimated λ's are

$$\hat{\lambda}_A = \frac{(1103+343+766)-1527}{2843-1527} = .521$$

and

$$\hat{\lambda}_B = \frac{(1103+766)-1310}{2843-1310} = .365.$$

Hence, by taking party identification into account, about a 50 percent reduction in error in predicting voting behavior is achieved; knowledge of how people vote, on the other hand, is of less help in predicting party affiliation.

2.6.2 Variance of Lambda.   It is possible to test the hypothesis that an estimated λ differs significantly from some hypothesized *nonzero* population value. Assuming a sufficiently large sample, a statistic for this purpose is

$$z = \frac{(\hat{\lambda}_A - \lambda_A)}{\hat{\sigma}_{(\hat{\lambda}_A)}},$$ (2.31)

where $\hat{\sigma}_{(\hat{\lambda}_A)}$ is the square root of the estimated variance of $\hat{\lambda}_A$ and z has an approximately unit-normal distribution. The formula for $\hat{\sigma}^2_{(\hat{\lambda}_A)}$ (Goodman and Kruskal, 1963) is

$$\hat{\sigma}^2_{(\hat{\lambda}_A)} = \frac{\left(n - \sum_j f_{mj}\right)\left(\sum_j f_{mj} + f_{m+} - 2\sum_j{}^* f_{mj}\right)}{(n - f_{m+})^3},$$ (2.32)

where $\sum_j{}^* f_{mj}$ denotes the sum of the f_{mj}'s that happen to be in the same row as f_{m+}. For the voting data in Table 1.1, $\hat{\sigma}^2_{(\hat{\lambda}_A)}$ is

$$\hat{\sigma}^2_{(\hat{\lambda}_A)} = \frac{(2843 - 2212)[2212 + 1527 - 2(1103)]}{(2843 - 1527)^3} = .0004.$$

Approximate two-sided confidence intervals for a given level of significance are given by

$$L = \hat{\lambda}_A - \zeta\hat{\sigma}_{(\hat{\lambda}_A)} \quad \text{and} \quad U = \hat{\lambda}_A + \zeta\hat{\sigma}_{(\hat{\lambda}_A)},$$

where ζ is the appropriate percentile of the unit normal distribution. The 95 percent limits for the $\hat{\lambda}_A$ in Table 1.1 are

$$L = .521 - (1.96)(.021) = .481 \quad \text{and} \quad U = .521 + (1.96)(.021) = .561,$$

where 1.96 is the 97.5th percentile of the unit normal distribution and .021 is the estimated standard error, $\hat{\sigma}_{(\hat{\lambda}_A)}$.

The validity of the significance test and the confidence limits holds for random samples. Samples based on fixed marginals require modification of the formula for the standard error (see Goodman and Kruskal, 1963, 1972, for details). The tests apply only in the event that the population value of λ_A does not equal zero or one. To test the hypothesis that $\lambda_A = 0$ (or $\lambda_A = 1$), compute the sample lambda, $\hat{\lambda}_A$, and accept the hypothesis *only if* it equals zero or one. If $\hat{\lambda}_A$ does not equal zero or one, the corresponding hypothesis about the population lambda should be rejected.

2.6.3 Symmetric Version of Lambda. Whether an investigator wants λ_A or λ_B depends on his understanding of the variables: if A depends on B, then λ_A is appropriate; otherwise λ_B is. Occasionally, however, he may not know or may be unwilling to assume any dependency among the variables. In this case he might prefer a "symmetric" coefficient. Fortunately, by slightly modifying the PRE logic, a symmetric version of λ is easily defined.

Symmetric λ combines the logic of computing both λ_A and λ_B. Suppose, for example, that individuals are randomly selected from a population, and half are assigned to A classes and half to B categories.

According to the first rule, these predictions are made without any additional knowledge. In guessing A categories, one would always place individuals in the most probable A class, the one pertaining to P_{m+}, if he wished to minimize the number of errors. On the other hand, when predicting B categories, he would pick the one associated with P_{+m}. During the time A classes are guessed, the probability of a successful prediction is $\frac{1}{2}P_{m+}$ and during the time B categories are assigned, it is $\frac{1}{2}P_{+m}$. A little thought shows that the probability of an *incorrect* guess is

$$P(1) = 1 - \tfrac{1}{2}P_{m+} + \tfrac{1}{2}P_{+m} = 1 - \frac{P_{m+}+P_{+m}}{2}.$$

The factor $\frac{1}{2}$ enters because each probability applies to half of the guesses.

Knowledge of both variables is taken into account under the second rule. For those individuals whose A classes are being guessed, the investigator uses information about their scores on B. The probability of a successful guess is $\frac{1}{2}\sum_j P_{mj}$. This is the same probability as before except that since A classes are being predicted only half of the time, it is multiplied by one-half. For the other individuals, the ones whose B class is being guessed, the probability of a correct prediction knowing A is $\frac{1}{2}\sum_i P_{im}$. The logic is the same as in the calculation of λ_A and λ_B except that one effectively computes one measure half of the time and the other measure the rest of the time. The probability of error under Rule 2 is, then,

$$P(2) = 1 - \frac{1}{2}\sum_j P_{mj} + \frac{1}{2}\sum_i P_{im} = 1 - \frac{\sum_j P_{mj} + \sum_i P_{im}}{2}.$$

PRE logic measures the proportional reduction in error using Rule 2 instead of Rule 1. Hence, symmetric λ is defined as

$$\lambda = \frac{1-(P_{m+}+P_{+m})/2 - 1 - \left(\sum_j P_{mj} + \sum_i P_{im}\right)\Big/2}{1-(P_{m+}+P_{+m})/2},$$

which after algebraic manipulation reduces to

$$\lambda = \frac{\sum\limits_{j} P_{mj} + \sum\limits_{i} P_{im} - P_{+m} - P_{m+}}{2 - P_{m+} - P_{+m}}.$$ (2.33)

The sample estimate, computed from observed frequencies, is

$$\hat{\lambda} = \frac{\sum\limits_{j} f_{mj} + \sum\limits_{i} f_{im} - f_{m+} - f_{+m}}{2n - f_{m+} - f_{+m}}.$$ (2.34)

The estimated λ between party identification and voting (Table 1.1) is

$$\hat{\lambda} = \frac{(2212 + 1869 - 1527 - 1310)}{2(2843) - 1527 - 1310} = .437.$$

Like its asymmetric counterparts, λ has a standard error and a sampling distribution, but since they involve slightly more cumbersome formulas, they are not presented here. The interested reader can consult Goodman and Kruskal (1963).

2.6.4 Goodman and Kruskal's Tau.

Another PRE measure, Goodman and Kruskal's τ, represents a modification of the hypothetical guessing game. As before, randomly selected individuals are assigned to A with and without knowledge of the independent variable. But this time the assignments preserve the original distributions.

Preserving a distribution means that the distribution of assignments is the same as the original distribution. If, for example, f_{1+} and f_{2+} individuals are in the first two categories of A, then the assignment process keeps exactly f_{1+} and f_{2+} people in those categories. When calculating λ, everyone is assigned to A's modal category (under Rule 1) and thus the pattern of guesses is not the same as the observed distribution. For some purposes it is useful to have a measure based on maintaining the original distribution (Goodman and Kruskal, 1954).

The population definition of τ requires making assignments proportional to the number of cases in various classes. Denote the categories of A and B with subscripts: $A_1, A_2, \ldots, A_I$ and $B_1, B_2, \ldots, B_J$. Under Rule 1, one guesses A's first category, A_1, with probability P_{1+}, the second category with P_{2+}, and continues in this manner for all I classes of A. The long-run expected error rate is

$$P(1) = 1 - \sum_{i} P_{i+}^2.$$

Under Rule 2, one guesses A_1 with probability $P_{1j} \mid P_{+j}$ (the conditional probability of A_1 given B_j), A_2 with probability $P_{2j} \mid P_{+j}$, and so forth for all values of I and J. The expected error rate following this method is then

$$P(2) = \frac{1 - \sum_j \sum_i P_{ij}^2}{P_{+j}}.$$

Consequently, the proportional reduction in error, subject to the constraint of preserving the original marginal totals, is, after algebraic manipulation,

$$\tau_A = \frac{\sum_j \sum_i P_{ij}^2 / P_{+j} - \sum_i P_{i+}^2}{1 - \sum_i P_{i+}^2}. \tag{2.35}$$

Like λ, Goodman and Kruskal's τ lies between 0 and 1: it equals zero if the variables are statistically independent and 1.0 under complete association. "Complete" in this context means "strict" or "implied" perfect association. That is, $\tau = 1$ if for each category of the independent variable, j, there is a category of the dependent variable, i, not necessarily unique, such that $P_{ij} = P_{+j}$. And like λ, τ is asymmetric.

The sample estimate, $\hat{\tau}$, involves finding errors from Rules 1 and 2. To compute the expected errors under Rule 1, subject to the constraint that the marginal totals be maintained, one proceeds as follows: For each category of the dependent variable, count the number of observations in the marginal totals not belonging in it, divide by n, and multiply by the category total. Then sum these totals. In symbols,

$$\frac{\text{Total Errors}}{\text{(Rule 1)}} = \sum_i f_{i+} \left[\frac{\left(\sum_{\substack{i' \\ i' \neq i}} f_{i'+} \right)}{n} \right], \tag{2.36}$$

where the notation $\sum_{\substack{i' \\ i' \neq i}}$ means that the summation is carried out for every category except the ith.

To compute the errors under Rule 2, one continues in exactly the same manner except within categories of the independent variable. This amounts to guessing a person's vote while knowing his party affiliation but again subject to the constraint of keeping the original distribution.

Expected errors under the second rule are found by taking each level of the independent variable in turn. Working within successive categories, one counts the number of cases not belonging to a specific category of the dependent variable, say the ith, divides this total by f_{+j}, and then multiplies by f_{ij}. A formula for these operations is

$$\frac{\text{Total Errors}}{\text{(Rule 2)}} = \sum_j \left[\sum_i f_{ij} \frac{\left(\sum_{\substack{i' \\ i' \neq i}} f_{i'j} \right)}{f_{+j}} \right]. \tag{2.37}$$

The two sets of expected errors are substituted into the PRE formula (2.27) to obtain an estimate of the proportional reduction in error, subject to the constraint that the marginal totals be preserved. For Table 1.1 the estimates of τ_A and τ_B are

$$\hat{\tau}_A = \frac{1413.67 - 873.67}{1413.67} = .382 \quad \text{and} \quad \hat{\tau}_B = \frac{1816.84 - 1407.26}{1816.84} = .225.$$

Thus when the marginal totals are kept, we achieve about a 38 percent reduction in error in predicting vote from party identification but only about a 22 percent reduction in predicting party from voting preferences.

2.6.5 An Alternative Interpretation of Tau. Light and Margolin (1971) draw an analogy between measurement of association in a cross-classification and standard analysis of variance. Assume for the moment that the column variable, B, is a factor and the dependent variable, A, is a response (Section 1.1.2). Based on earlier work by Gini, Light and Margolin represent the total sum of squares in A as

$$TSS = \frac{n}{2} - \frac{1}{2n} \sum_i f_{i+}^2.$$

As in one-way analysis of variance, the total sum of squares is partitioned into two parts, the "within" sum of squares (WSS) and the "between" sum of squares (BSS). The within sum of squares is

$$WSS = \frac{n}{2} - \frac{1}{2} \sum_j \frac{1}{f_{+j}} \left(\sum_i f_{ij}^2 \right).$$

Since the components are additive, the between sum of squares can be obtained by subtraction:

$$BSS = TSS - WSS = \frac{1}{2} \left[\sum_j \frac{1}{f_{+j}} \left(\sum_i f_{ij}^2 \right) \right] - \frac{1}{2n} \left(\sum_i f_{i+}^2 \right).$$

A measure of association analogous to the square of the product-moment correlation and that turns out to be equivalent to Goodman and Kruskal's τ is

$$R_A^2 = \frac{BSS}{TSS}$$

$$= \frac{\left[\left(\sum_j 1/f_{+j} \right) \left(\sum_i f_{ij}^2 \right) \right] - \left[(1/n) \left(\sum_i f_{i+}^2 \right) \right]}{n - (1/n) \sum_i f_{i+}^2}. \tag{2.38}$$

Like r^2, R^2_A gives the proportion of variation in A that is "explained" by B. But unlike the correlation coefficient, R^2_A is asymmetric. Because R^2_A and $\hat{\tau}$ are equivalent, the previous computations show that party identification explains about 38 percent of the variation in voting but voting explains only about 22 percent of the variation in partisanship.

Hence, R^2_A provides an alternative interpretation to τ. It has the further advantage of being particularly easy to test for significance. Assuming a sufficiently large random sample, the following statistic has an approximately chi square distribution with $(I-1)(J-1)$ degrees of freedom under the null hypothesis of independence between A and B:

$$M = (n-1)(I-1)\frac{BSS}{TSS} = (n-1)(I-1)R^2_A$$

In Table 1.1, $R^2_A = .382$. Therefore,

$$M = (2843-1)(2-1)(.382) = 1085.64$$

With $(2-1)(3-1) = 2$ degrees of freedom, this value is clearly significant. Note, incidentally, that M is almost the same as the GFX^2 and LRX^2 for these data (see Section 1.2).

Since M is really a test of the hypothesis of independence, it provides an alternative to the usual chi square test. Margolin and Light (1974) give the conditions under which it is advantageous to do so. Bishop, Fienberg, and Holland (1975) also provide an expression for the estimated variance of τ_A when one wants to make inferences about nonzero population values.

2.6.6 Behavior of Measures of Association.   Despite their operational meanings, measures of association discussed so far sometimes mislead as much as they inform. An index's numerical value should, of course, reflect the "true" relationship. But unfortunately, factors having little to do with the intrinsic association may artificially increase or decrease a measure's magnitude. Marginal variation is particularly important in this regard.

Consider the distribution of respondents according to party identification in Table 1.1. The real distribution in the population of adult voters only partly determines the observed distribution. Other elements enter the picture, among them how the investigator chose to word the questions and define the category boundaries. Being to a certain extent arbitrary, these decisions represent the researcher's choices rather than the inexorable workings of nature. Thus, two social scientists studying the same phenomenon can nevertheless obtain different observed marginal distributions. Or, even following the same operational procedures, they may sample populations having different variances. To the extent that their conclusions rest on measures of association that are sensitive to marginal distributions, the results may not be comparable. Consequently, seemingly contradictory findings may be only an artifact of the specific techniques used in the study.

As a general rule, the greater the variation in both the independent and dependent variable, the greater the numerical value of a measure of association, other things being equal. And conversely, limiting variation in one or both variables usually weakens a relationship.

TABLE 2.6. **The Effects of Decreasing Variation in the Independent Variable**

a. Cases Evenly Distributed among B Categories

	B			Total
	600	300	100	1000
A	300	400	300	1000
	100	300	600	1000
Total	1000	1000	1000	3000

$$\hat{\alpha}_{11} = 36 \qquad \hat{\alpha}_{12} = 6.0 \qquad \hat{\lambda}_A = .30$$
$$\hat{\alpha}_{21} = 6.0 \qquad \hat{\alpha}_{22} = 2.67 \qquad \hat{\tau}_A = .13$$
$$\hat{V} = .36 \qquad \hat{T} = .36 \qquad \hat{C} = .45$$
$$\hat{\Phi}^2 = .26$$

b. Uneven Distribution among B Categories

	B			Total
	300	300	50	650
A	150	400	150	700
	50	300	300	650
Total	500	1000	500	2000

$$\hat{\alpha}_{11} = 36 \qquad \hat{\alpha}_{12} = 6.0 \qquad \hat{\lambda}_A = .23$$
$$\hat{\alpha}_{21} = 6.0 \qquad \hat{\alpha}_{22} = 2.67 \qquad \hat{\tau}_A = .10$$
$$\hat{V} = .32 \qquad \hat{T} = .32 \qquad \hat{C} = .41$$
$$\hat{\Phi}^2 = .20$$

c. Extremely Uneven Distribution among B Categories

	B			Total
	150	300	25	475
A	75	400	75	550
	25	300	150	475
Total	250	1000	250	1500

$$\hat{\alpha}_{11} = 36 \qquad \hat{\alpha}_{12} = 6.0 \qquad \hat{\lambda}_A = .16$$
$$\hat{\alpha}_{21} = 6.0 \qquad \hat{\alpha}_{22} = 2.67 \qquad \hat{\tau}_A = .07$$
$$\hat{V} = .27 \qquad \hat{T} = .27 \qquad \hat{C} = .35$$
$$\hat{\Phi}^2 = .14$$

In some tables, for example, λ equals zero even if the variables are not statistically independent. This happens when the modal class of A is so large relative to the others that all f_{mj} are in the same row. Since the maximum cell frequencies in each column lie in the same row, $\sum_j f_{mj} = f_{m+}$ and $\hat{\lambda}_A = 0$. In other tables having a preponderance of cases in one category of A, λ may be quite close to zero, suggesting little or no relationship. τ is less sensitive in this respect and might be used when the dependent variable is highly skewed.

The same principle applies to the independent variable: in general, as the variation in B decreases (that is, as its marginal distribution becomes increasingly uneven), many measures decrease, other things being equal. Looking at the hypothetical data in Table 2.6, one sees that the basic relationship, as measured by percents, stays the same in all three subtables. Indeed, the tables are generated by simply halving the frequencies in the first and last columns while keeping the middle column constant. Although hypothetical, the data could represent three samples drawn from populations having different amounts of variation in B.

Whatever the case, the underlying relationship remains the same. But both PRE and chi square measures decline, indicating that the numerical values depend partly on how the cases are distributed. Note, on the other hand, that the basic sets of odds ratios remain constant. Difficulties of this sort are particularly acute when one is trying to compare tables with unequal marginals.

Standardizing a table often solves problems like this. As noted in Section 2.1.3, standardization refers to the adjustment of frequencies to conform to desired marginal totals. When comparing tables or when variables are skewed, it may be useful to recompute measures of association on standardized data. This should eliminate to a degree the vagaries of marginal totals. In Table 2.2, for instance, most measures of association for the standardized table are larger than those for the unstandardized data. Of course, variation itself may have substantive interest and should also be reported.

These remarks suggest two generalizations.

First, it usually pays to look at a relationship from several points of view, as each measure rests on a slightly different definition of association. Unless one's theory explicitly assumes a particular definition, which is at most never the case, he may overlook important aspects of the data by relying on a single index.

Second, measures of association by themselves do not prove the relative explanatory power of variables. Social scientists commonly ask for the most important explanation of a given dependent variable. After computing coefficients for various independent variables with a given dependent variable, it is tempting to take the variable whose index has the largest numerical value as the best predictor or explanation. But since the coefficients are susceptible to extraneous factors such as marginal distributions, and since they each represent a certain conception of association, these comparisons could be very misleading. In addition, the impact of one variable on another depends partly on its relationship to still other variables, many of which may be unmeasured. For these reasons, using a coefficient of association alone to show explanatory importance seems questionable.

2.7 MEASURES OF AGREEMENT

2.7.1 Unweighted κ. The coefficients presented so far measure association in a rather general sense. Two variables are related to the extent that knowledge of the values of one helps predict values of the other. But association can be defined more narrowly.

Suppose that interest lies in agreement between parents and their children or between husbands and wives on a question measuring attitudes or behavior. Maximum agreement occurs when both members of a pair give the same response. A useful way to assess agreement, then, is to compute the proportion of cases in the main diagonal of a square $I \times I$ table. After all, if husbands and wives agree completely, then all observations would lie in the main diagonal. Let $P_o = \sum_i P_{ii}$ (for $i - 1, \ldots, I$) be the proportion of cases in the main diagonal of a square population table with I rows and columns.

P_o is not a completely satisfactory indicator of agreement, because some cases could be expected to lie in the main diagonal by chance. It is easy to correct for the chance occurrences by taking $P_o - P_c$, where $P_c = \sum_i P_{i+}P_{+i}$ and P_{i+} and P_{+i} are the marginal proportions in the ith row and column, respectively. In other words, P_c is the sum of the proportions expected under the model of independence. This measure, however, depends on the marginal totals. It is normalized by dividing by $1 - P_c$, the maximum possible value of $P_o - P_c$ for given marginal totals, P_{i+} and P_{+i}. The resulting measure, kappa (κ) is

$$\kappa = \frac{P_o - P_c}{1 - P_c}. \tag{2.39}$$

As originally proposed by Cohen (1960), κ measures the proportion of agreement between two groups (e.g., husbands and wives, parents and children) or two judges who are rating or evaluating individuals. It is adjusted for agreement attributable to chance. The value of κ is zero when the observed amount of agreement equals the amount expected by chance alone, it equals 1.0 when the groups or judges agree completely, and it is negative if the observed agreement is less than agreement expected by chance.

Replacing population proportions by their sample equivalent leads to the estimate

$$\hat{\kappa} = \frac{\sum_i f_{ii} - 1/n \sum_i f_{i+}f_{+i}}{n - 1/n \sum_i f_{i+}f_{+i}}. \tag{2.40}$$

Note that the formula applies only to entries in the main diagonal and corresponding marginal totals. For the data in Table 1.6, which compares the voting behavior of husbands and wives, the estimated value of κ is $\hat{\kappa} = .842$, indicating substantial agreement between married couples.

2.7.2 Weighted κ. The value of κ rests on a strict definition of agreement: unless a wife replies exactly as her husband does, her response is considered an error or disagreement. From the point of view of evaluating a theory, however, some disagreements may be less serious than others. A wife whose husband voted for Humphrey might be considered more in agreement if she voted for Nixon than if she voted for Wallace. On the basis of substantive concerns, an investigator may be willing to weight each cell of a table according to the seriousness of the disagreement. In Table 1.6, for example, we could assign the following weights: 1 to the cells on the main diagonal since there is complete *agreement*; 0 to cells $(2, 1)$ and $(2, 3)$; and .5 to the remaining cells. These weights are purely illustrative, but in practice they should be made carefully on the basis of justifiable theoretical considerations. According to Cohen (1968), the weights should be ratio variables so that 1, say, represents twice as much agreement as .5.

Letting w_{ij} be the weight in the ijth cell of a table where $I = J$, weighted κ is

$$\kappa_w = \frac{P'_o - P'_c}{1 - P'_c}, \tag{2.41}$$

where

$$P'_o = \sum_{ij} w_{ij} P_{ij}$$

$$P'_c = \sum_{ij} w_{ij} P_{i+} P_{+j}.$$

(We assume here that the weights lie between 1.0, the maximum, and 0. But other weights can be used.) P'_o and P'_c are thus the observed and expected (under independence) weight proportions of agreement. The sample estimate of κ_w is

$$\hat{\kappa}_w = \frac{\sum_{ij} w_{ij}f_{ij} - 1/n \sum_{ij} w_{ij}f_{i+}f_{+j}}{n - 1/n \sum_{ij} w_{ij}f_{i+}f_{+j}}. \tag{2.42}$$

The weighted agreement in Table 1.6 is $\hat{\kappa}_w = .844$, a figure almost identical to $\hat{\kappa}$. In other tables with different weighting schemes, $\hat{\kappa}$ and $\hat{\kappa}_w$ differ sharply.

2.7.3 The Variance of $\hat{\kappa}_w$. Assuming a sufficiently large sample with only n fixed, drawn from a population having a multinomial distribution, the estimated variance of $\hat{\kappa}_w$ is

$$\hat{\sigma}^2_{(\hat{\kappa}_w)} = \frac{1}{n(1-\hat{P}_c)^4} \left(\left\{ \frac{1}{n} \sum_{ij} f_{ij}[w_{ij}(1-\hat{P}_c) \right. \right.$$
$$\left. \left. -(\bar{w}_{i+} + \bar{w}_{+j})(1-\hat{P}_o)]^2 \right\} - (\hat{P}_o\hat{P}_c - 2\hat{P}_c + \hat{P}_o)^2 \right), \tag{2.43}$$

where the weights w_{ij} are adjusted so that they lie between 0 and 1.0 and

$$\hat{P}_o = 1/n \sum_{ij} w_{ij}f_{ij},$$

$$\hat{P}_c = 1/n^2 \sum_{ij} w_{ij}f_{i+}f_{+j},$$

$$\bar{w}_{i+} = 1/n \sum_j w_{ij}f_{+j},$$

$$\bar{w}_{+j} = 1/n \sum_i w_{ij}f_{i+}.$$

Since the sampling distribution of $\hat{\kappa}_w$ is approximately normal for large n, $\hat{\sigma}^2_{(\hat{\kappa}_w)}$ can be used to set confidence intervals. Under the assumption of independence, the estimated variance reduces to

$$\hat{\sigma}^2_{(\hat{\kappa}_w)} = \frac{1}{n(1-P_c)^2} \left\{ 1/n \sum_{ij} f_{i+}f_{+j}[w_{ij} - (\bar{w}_{i+} - \bar{w}_{+j})]^2 - \hat{P}_c^2 \right\}. \tag{2.44}$$

This quantity is used in testing the hypothesis that $\kappa_w = 0$. For example, $z = \hat{\kappa}_w / \sqrt{\hat{\sigma}^2_{(\hat{\kappa}_w)}}$ has an approximately unit normal distribution.

The estimated large-sample variance of unweighted $\hat{\kappa}$ follows from (2.43) by noting that $w_{ij} = 1$ for $i = j$ and $w_{ij} = 0$ for $i \neq j$. The estimated variance of $\hat{\kappa}_w$ and κ for Table 1.6 are .001 and .0006, respectively. The small values reflect the large sample size.

2.7.4 Extensions. However useful it is, κ is only one method of measuring agreement. Numerous other indices of agreement and disagreement have been proposed (Rae and Taylor, 1970). Furthermore, κ has been extended to measure agreement between more than two judges or groups (Fleiss, 1971) and to a conditional measure of agreement (Light, 1971). Investigators interested in this model of association should find these generalizations quite helpful.

2.8 PREDICTION LOGIC

Hildebrand, Laing, and Rosenthal (1974a, 1975, 1976) have recently developed a "prediction logic" that allows one to state and evaluate scientific predictions. Their approach, as will become apparent, involves some of the same issues as κ. It consists of two parts: a logic for generating propositions and a statistic and a sampling theory for measuring the success of the propositions.

2.8.1 Prediction Logic Propositions. Propositions predict the state of an observation on one variable on the basis of its position on another. The propositions may be quite general, certainly more so than permitted by conventional statistics. Each proposition specifies the events that constitute its success and failure. In the bivariate case where the events are cells in an $I \times J$ table, some cells confirm a proposition whereas others falsify it.

Consider, for example, this proposition, consisting of two parts, for a 2×2 table: given a randomly selected observation, if $B = B_1$, then predict $A = A_1$ or $A = A_2$; if $B = B_2$, then predict $A = A_2$. The set of cells $(1, 1)$, $(2, 1)$, and $(2, 2)$ represent successes for the proposition because if it were true one would expect to find observations in them (see Figure 2.1).

On the other hand, the cell $(1, 2)$ is a falsifying or error cell because the proposition predicts that a person in B_2 will only be in A_2. If the statement is true, one would expect none or at least very few observations in $(1, 2)$. Denote the set of error cells by E.

As statements in prediction logic may be quite general, they can be tailored to any substantive theory or hypothesis. Suppose that one is unable to make a prediction for the full range of values in B. He can still test propositions pertaining to the remaining levels. According to Hilderbrand, Laing, and Rosenthal, this generality does not hold with conventional statistics. The important point, however, is that one may translate verbal propositions about categorical variables into prediction logic statements, assuming that the statements are not tautologies. One simply needs to define the events (i.e., sets of cells) that verify and falsify the proposition.

FIGURE 2.1.   **Example of Cell Invalidating Prediction Logic Proposition**

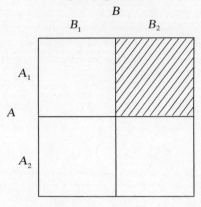

The shaded cell is an error event for the proposition "If $B = B_1$, predict $A = A_1$ or $A = A_2$; if $B = B_2$, predict $A = A_2$."

2.8.2 An Index of Prediction Success.   Prediction logic statements essentially predict that some cells in an $I \times J$ table have zero probabilities. A simple measure of the success of the proposition is

$$\theta_1 = \sum_{ij} w_{ij} P_{ij},$$

where w_{ij} is an indicator variable: $w_{ij} = 1$ if cell (ij) belongs to E, the set of falsifying events, and $w_{ij} = 0$ otherwise. (As with κ, one may generalize the w's to measure the seriousness of the error events. In other words, some cells may represent more serious falsifications of the statement than others. The weights could range from 0 to 1, with $w_{ij} = 1$ meaning a more serious error than, say, $w_{ij} = .7$.) The index θ_1 gives the proportion of observations in the population that falsify the proposition. It varies between 0, for no prediction failures, to 1.0 for complete failure. The statistic

$$1 - \theta_1$$

thus measures the proposition's overall success.

It has a potential drawback, however, of giving misleadingly large values for some statements. A proposition might be expressed in such a way that predictions are made only for a small fraction of the total number of cases. Or the set of error events may be.quite small relative to the successes. In Hildebrand, Laing, and Rosenthal's words, θ_1 does not take account of the "scope" and "precision" of the proposition. Seen from another perspective, θ_1 is sensitive to skewed marginal distributions.

There are two ways of correcting θ_1. Goodman and Kruskal (1974) recommend standardizing the table before computing θ_1. Conceding that this approach has merit, Hildebrand, Laing, and Rosenthal (1974a, 1974b) nevertheless prefer an alternative method. They define

$$\theta_2 = \sum_{ij} w_{ij} P_{i+} P_{+j},$$

where P_{i+} and P_{+j} are the row and column marginal probabilities or proportions, respectively, and w_{ij} is as defined above. The statistic

$$\nabla = 1 - \frac{\theta_1}{\theta_2} = \frac{\theta_2 - \theta_1}{\theta_2} = \frac{\sum\limits_{ij} w_{ij} P_{i+} P_{+j} - \sum\limits_{ij} w_{ij} P_{ij}}{\sum\limits_{ij} w_{ij} P_{i+} P_{+j}} \qquad (2.45)$$

is interpreted as the raw error rate of the proposition adjusted or normalized by its precision. Note, for example, that if the precision is relatively low, the fraction will be large (even greater than 1.0) and ∇ will be small. It equals 1.0 only if errors have zero probability, it equals zero if A and B are statistically independent, and it is less than zero if the total probability of the error event is greater than their probability under statistical independence. For most practical applications, however, where an investigator has a reasonable amount of knowledge about the variables, ∇ ranges between 0 and 1.0.

The sample estimate is

$$\hat{\nabla} = \frac{1/n \sum\limits_{ij} w_{ij} f_{i+} f_{+j} - \sum\limits_{ij} w_{ij} f_{ij}}{1/n \sum\limits_{ij} w_{ij} f_{i+} f_{+j}}. \qquad (2.46)$$

Note once again that $w_{ij} > 0$ for cells in E and $w_{ij} = 0$ otherwise. Usually all error cells are given the same weight ($w_{ij} = 1$) but, as noted above, differential weighting is acceptable.

2.8.3 The Variance of ∇. The variance of ∇ under the assumption of a multinomial distribution is

$$\sigma_{\hat{\nabla}}^2 = \frac{\sum\limits_{ij} w_{ij}^2 P_{ij} - \left(\sum\limits_{ij} w_{ij} P_{ij} \right)^2 + F \left[F \sum\limits_{ij} (\Pi_i + \Pi_{+j})^2 P_{ij} - 2 \sum\limits_{ij} w_{ij} (\Pi_{i+} + \Pi_{+j}) P_{ij} \right]}{(n-1)G^2}$$

$$(2.47)$$

where

$$F = 1 - \nabla,$$

$$\Pi_{i+} = \sum_j w_{ij} P_{+j},$$

$$\Pi_{+j} = \sum_i w_{ij} P_{i+},$$

and

$$G = \sum_{ij} w_{ij} P_{i+} P_{+j}.$$

The estimated variance of $\hat{\nabla}$, $\hat{\sigma}^2_{(\hat{\nabla})}$, is obtained by replacing the appropriate P's with observed proportions. Assuming a sufficiently large n (say, greater than 25), one can compute confidence intervals and test $\hat{\nabla}$ for significance, since it has an approximately normal distribution. (The approximation is improved if the test statistic is corrected for continuity as explained by Hildebrand, Laing, and Rosenthal, 1974a.)

As an example, consider a proposition for the 2×2 voting data given earlier in this chapter: being a Democrat tends to be a necessary and sufficient condition for voting Democratic. The error cells are thus $(2, 1)$ and $(1, 2)$, and the value of $\hat{\nabla} = .699$ suggests that the proposition is highly successful.[5] (In this example, $w_{21} = w_{12} = 1$ and $w_{11} = w_{22} = 0$ are used in formula (2.46).)

2.8.4 Brief Discussion of Prediction Logic.

Hildebrand, Laing, and Rosenthal claim that their approach has unique advantages. For instance, it allows one to make *a priori* predictions in which both successes and errors are unambiguously specified. Therefore, ∇ is really a family of measures. Furthermore, when propositions are stated in certain ways, the resulting index is equivalent to several well-known measures of association such as Goodman and Kruskal's τ. Hence, their method provides a unifying interpretative scheme for such statistics. They also extend it to multivariate tables.

In addition to its meaning as a measure of the adjusted error rate, ∇ has a proportional-reduction-in-error interpretation as well. Contrary to most measures, however, its PRE interpretation does not depend on information about the marginal distribution of the dependent variable. It is in their view a completely *a priori* measure.

Finally, the overall ∇ defined in (2.46) can be partitioned or decomposed into a weighted average of component preductions. As in partitioning chi square, this property allows one to pinpoint the source of a

---

5. The estimated standard error of $\hat{\nabla}$ is .014.

propositions failure. On the other hand, there is no simultaneous inference procedure.

Goodman and Kruskal (1974) have criticized the use of θ_2 in ∇, charging that it is "unwarranted, arbitrary, and inappropriate." They assert, for example, that θ_2 is calculated under the usual assumption of independence when in fact, if a proposition is true, then *quasi-independence* should apply (see Section 1.5). They propose several alternative measures based on quasi-independence.

Hildebrand, Laing, and Rosenthal (1974b) reject this assertion, saying instead that quasi-independence is too restrictive and is itself inappropriate. Both sides make telling points, and the reader will have to judge the merits of the arguments himself. This debate illustrates the fact that the prediction logic, as useful as it seems, has still not won universal acceptance.

3 MEASURES OF ASSOCIATION FOR ORDINAL DATA

3.1 INTRODUCTION

Classification frequently involves much more than simply assigning individuals to groups, for as often as not, the categories contain an implicit order. An investigator recognizing the quantitativeness of a concept may not be able to measure it directly, but can nevertheless construct a variable so that the classes are *ordered*. Belonging to a specific category of an ordinal variable thus implies having an unmeasured amount of the attribute. People ranked "high" on socioeconomic standing presumably have more education, income, or social prestige than those classified "medium" or "low." The numeric magnitude of the difference, however, remains unknown.

Relationships among ordinal variables can, of course, be analyzed with nominal measures of association. One should, however, take advantage of the extra information provided by the ordered classes. In particular, the *form* of a relationship can be specified more precisely: ordering leads to the concept of correlation.

Loosely speaking, two variables are *positively correlated* if observations with low values on one variable tend to have low values on the other and, conversely, observations with high values on the first variable tend to have high values on the second. Increases in A go with increases in B (and vice versa).[1]

Negatively correlated variables show the opposite tendency. High scores on one variable are connected with low scores on the other, whereas low scores on the first are connected with high scores on the second. Increasing values on A implies decreasing values on B (and vice versa).

---

1. Correlation by itself assumes nothing about causal connections between the variables.

Two correlated variables are not necessarily linearly related. In the most general sense, correlation suggests only an increasing or decreasing "monotonic" relationship (see Leik and Gove, 1969).

Ordinal measures of association are designed to measure how strongly two variables are correlated. If A and B are exactly positively correlated according to some standard of perfect correlation, the indices will be 1.0; if they are exactly negatively correlated, the indices will be −1.0. Finally, 0 implies no correlation. Since correlation is a special kind of association, its absence does not mean statistical independence. Therefore, the lack of correlation should not be confused with independence, because the variables may be associated in another way.

3.1.1 Definitions of Perfect Correlation.   The meaning of perfect positive or negative correlation depends on one's point of view. There are at least three definitions of "perfect" (Wilson, 1974c). The analyst should first decide which concept is best suited to his research and then select an appropriate index. As with nominal data, one should note, these definitions make most sense if the underlying variables really are discrete. If they are continuous it may be difficult to frame one's theory in these terms.

Strict Perfect Correlation. Two variables are strictly positively correlated if an increase in one entails an increase in the other and if one does not vary, neither does the other. Consequently, each value of A corresponds to a unique value of B (and vice versa). A strict negative correlation means that the values of A and B are related in a one-to-one but decreasing fashion: as B increases, A decreases; if B does not change, then neither does A (see Tables 3.1a and 3.1b for examples). Clearly, the number of rows and columns must be equal for this condition to hold.

Asymmetric Perfect Correlation. If perfect positive asymmetric correlation holds, increases in B always produce increases in A, but increasing A does not necessarily increase B. In other words, the categories of A and B are not uniquely associated, although there is a tendency for high and low values of A to be connected to high and low values of B (see Table 3.1c). Similarly, a negative asymmetric correlation means that increases in B lead to decreases in A, but changing A does not necessarily affect B (see Table 3.1d).

This definition has two versions, depending on which variable is dependent. This definition of perfect correlation will be most appropriate for many problems because dependencies among variables is known ahead of time and because the number of rows and columns do not have to equal each other.

Weak Perfect Correlation. A weak positive correlation exists when increases in B mean only that A does not decrease. That is, as B increases, A may increase or stay the same. Perfect negative correlation

TABLE 3.1. **Examples of Different Definitions of Perfect Positive and Negative Correlation**

a. Strict Positive Correlation					b. Strict Negative Correlation			

			B					B	
		L	M	H			L	M	H
	L	50	0	0		L	0	0	50
A	M	0	50	0	A M	0	50	0	
	H	0	0	50		H	50	0	0
	Total	50	50	50		Total	50	50	50

$\hat{\tau}_a = .671$ $\hat{\tau}_b = 1.0$ $\hat{\tau}_c = 1.0$ $\hat{\tau}_a = -.671$ $\hat{\tau}_b = -1.0$ $\hat{\tau}_c = -1.0$
$\hat{\gamma} = 1.0$ $\hat{d}_{AB} = 1.0$ $\hat{d}_{BA} = 1.0$ $\hat{\gamma} = -1.0$ $\hat{d}_{AB} = -1.0$ $\hat{d}_{BA} = -1.0$
$\hat{e} = 1.0$ $\hat{e} = -1.0$

c. Asymmetric Positive Correlation					d. Asymmetric Negative Correlation			

			B					B	
		L	M	H			L	M	H
	L	50	0	0		L	0	0	50
A	ML	0	50	0	A ML	0	50	0	
	MH	0	50	0	MH	0	50	0	
	H	0	0	50		H	50	0	0
	Total	50	100	50		Total	50	100	50

$\hat{\tau}_a = .628$ $\hat{\tau}_b = .913$ $\hat{\tau}_c = .937$ $\hat{\tau}_a = -.628$ $\hat{\tau}_b = -.913$ $\hat{\tau}_c = -.937$
$\hat{\gamma} = 1.0$ $\hat{d}_{AB} = 1.0$ $\hat{d}_{BA} = .833$ $\hat{\gamma} = -1.0$ $\hat{d}_{AB} = -1.0$ $\hat{d}_{BA} = -.833$
$\hat{e} = .833$ $\hat{e} = -.833$

e. Weak Positive Correlation					f. Weak Negative Correlation			

			B					B	
		L	M	H			L	M	H
	L	50	50	0		L	0	0	50
A	M	0	50	50	A M	0	50	50	
	H	0	0	50		H	50	50	0
	Total	50	100	100		Total	50	100	100

$\hat{\tau}_a = .482$ $\hat{\tau}_b = .750$ $\hat{\tau}_c = .720$ $\hat{\tau}_a = -.482$ $\hat{\tau}_b = -.750$ $\hat{\tau}_c = -.720$
$\hat{\gamma} = 1.0$ $\hat{d}_{AB} = .750$ $\hat{d}_{BA} = .750$ $\hat{\gamma} = -1.0$ $\hat{d}_{AB} = -.750$ $\hat{d}_{BA} = -.750$
$\hat{e} = .600$ $\hat{e} = -.600$

Key: L = Low, ML = Medium Low, M = Medium, MH = Medium High, H = High.

in this sense means that increases in B produce decreases or no change in A (Table 3.1f). Again, there are two versions of this definition.

One ordinal index (γ) reaches its maximum value under this definition of perfect correlation. But in many respects the definition conveys very little information about the relationship. Variables can be perfectly correlated by this criterion when by other standards they would be at best weakly related. For example, the data in Table 3.2 fit the model of weak positive correlation. Most social scientists, however, would hesitate to call the relationship perfect. Knowledge of B reveals very little about A. And, in fact, most measures of association, nominal or ordinal, indicate at most a moderate relationship. Still, in some research contexts this definition of perfect correlation may be justified (Weisberg, 1974).

TABLE 3.2. **Behavior of Various Measures under Weak Perfect Correlation**

		B			
		L	M	H	Total
	L	10	0	0	10
A	M	10	0	0	10
	H	10	1	1	12
	Total	30	1	1	32

$$\hat{\lambda}_A = .000 \qquad \hat{\tau}_A = .059 \qquad \hat{\gamma} = 1.0$$
$$\hat{\tau}_a = .081 \qquad \hat{\tau}_b = .278 \qquad \hat{\tau}_c = .117$$
$$\hat{d}_{AB} = .656 \qquad \hat{d}_{BA} = .118 \qquad \hat{e} = .111$$

In short, ordinal correlation coefficients lie between -1.0 (for perfect negative correlation) and 1.0 (for perfect positive correlation), with 0 indicating no correlation (zero does *not* imply statistical independence). All except one are symmetric, because their values do not depend on which variable is dependent. And like nominal measures, they are affected by the amount of variation in the variables.

Unlike nominal indices, however, their definition and interpretation rest on *pairs* of observations rather than single cases. Hence, it is necessary to describe various types of pair.

3.1.2 The Concept of Pairs of Observations. The basic building blocks of most ordinal measures are pairs of observations. Consider Table 3.3, containing ten individuals jointly distributed on A and B. The entries in each cell have been named to help clarify terms. There are $N = n(n-1)/2$ total pairs in a collection of n objects. (Here $N = 10(9)/2 = 45$.) The N pairs can be partitioned or divided into several types.

Concordant Pairs. Randomly select two people from the table and denote their values on A and B as $(A_l B_l)$ and $(A_m B_m)$, respectively. (That is, A_l and B_l represent the lth person's scores on A and B; A_m and B_m stand for the corresponding scores for the mth person.)

A pair is said to be concordant if one person in the pair is higher (or lower) on *both* A and B than the other person. More precisely, if $A_l > A_m$ *and* $B_l > B_m$ or $A_l < A_m$ *and* $B_l < B_m$, the pair $(A_l B_l)(A_m B_m)$ is concordant. John and Kathy, for example, are concordant because Kathy's

TABLE 3.3.   **Examples of Pairs of Observations**

		B			
		L	M	H	Total
A	L	John Barbara		Diane	3
	M	Alan	Kathy Lisa Anne	Phil	5
	H			Tim Kevin	3
	Total	3	3	4	10

scores on A and B are higher than John's. (Or, seen from the opposite side of the coin, John's scores are both lower than Kathy's.) Among other concordant pairs are John and Anne, John and Phil, Barbara and Kathy, Barbara and Phil, Kathy and Tim, and Alan and Kevin.

The easiest way to calculate the total number of concordant pairs, N_c, is to multiply each cell frequency, f_{ij}, by the total number of observations in cells lying to the right and below it and sum the results. In Table 3.3 the total number of concordant pairs is

$$N_c = 2(6) + 0(3) + 1(0) + 1(2) + 3(2) + 1(0) + 0(0) + 0(0) + 2(0) = 20$$

A somewhat complicated general formula but still useful for computer programs and the calculation of standard errors is

$$N_c = \frac{\sum\limits_{i=1}^{I} \sum\limits_{j=1}^{J} f_{ij} C_{ij}}{2}, \tag{3.1}$$

where

$$C_{ij} = \sum_{i'=1}^{i-1} \sum_{j'=1}^{j-1} f_{i'j'} + \sum_{i'=i+1}^{I} \sum_{j'=j+1}^{J} f_{i'j'}. \tag{3.2}$$

Discordant Pairs. Other pairs—Diane and Kathy, for instance—have a different relationship with respect to A and B. If for a randomly drawn pair, $A_l > A_m$ and $B_l < B_m$ or $A_l < A_m$ and $B_l > B_m$, the pair is discordant. In short, as with Kathy and Diane, discordance occurs when one member of a pair is higher (or lower) on A but is lower (or higher) on B. The other discordant pairs in Table 3.3 are Diane and Lisa, Diane and Anne, and Diane and Alan.

The total number of discordant pairs in a table, N_D, is most easily found by multiplying each cell frequency, f_{ij}, by the sum of the observations in the cells lying to the left and below it and then summing the results. In Table 3.3, N_D is

$$N_D = 1(4) = 4.$$

Once again, the computing formula is more complicated than following the verbal algorithm, but is helpful later on:

$$N_D = \frac{\sum\limits_{i=1}^{I} \sum\limits_{j=1}^{J} f_{ij} D_{ij}}{2}, \tag{3.3}$$

where

$$D_{ij} = \sum_{i'=1}^{i-1} \sum_{j'=j+1}^{J} f_{i'j'} + \sum_{i'=i+1}^{I} \sum_{j'=1}^{j-1} f_{i'j'}. \tag{3.4}$$

There is an affinity between the concepts of concordance and discordance on the one hand and correlation on the other. Generally speaking, a preponderance of concordant over discordant pairs suggests positive correlation. If the probability that a randomly drawn pair of observations exhibits concordance, P_c, is large compared to P_D, the probability that a randomly drawn pair is discordant, the variables are positively correlated, other things being equal. Similarly, an excess of discordant pairs implies negative correlation.

These ideas are reflected in Table 3.3, where concordant outnumber discordant pairs. Notice, in addition, that most observations lie in or near the main diagonal, indicating a correspondence between the different values of A and B. Hence, concordance and discordance are useful in defining measures of correlation. But before presenting these indices, the remaining kinds of pairs have to be explained.

Pairs Tied Only on A. Having the same A attribute, John and Diane are neither concordant nor discordant with respect to each other but are tied on A only. A pair is tied on A only if $A_l = A_m$ and $B_l < B_m$ or $B_l > B_m$. Among other pairs tied only on A are Barbara and Diane, Alan and Kathy, Alan and Phil, and Lisa and Phil. The total number of tied pairs is

$$N_A = \frac{\sum\limits_{i=1}^{I} \sum\limits_{j=1}^{J} f_{ij} T_{A_{ij}}}{2}, \tag{3.5}$$

where

$$T_{A_{ij}} = f_{i+} - f_{ij}. \tag{3.6}$$

Following this formula, N_A for Table 3.3 is

$$N_A = \frac{\left[\begin{array}{l} 2(3-2)+0(3-0)+1(3-1)+1(5-1)+ \\ +3(5-3)+1(5-1)+0(2-0)+0(2-0)+2(2-2) \end{array} \right]}{2} = 9.$$

Pairs Tied Only on B. A pair (such as Phil and Tim) are tied only on B if $B_l = B_m$ and $A_l > A_m$ or $A_l < A_m$. The total number of pairs tied only on B is

$$N_B = \frac{\sum_{i=1}^{I} \sum_{j=1}^{J} f_{ij} T_{B_{ij}}}{2}, \tag{3.7}$$

where

$$T_{B_{ij}} = f_{+j} - f_{ij}. \tag{3.8}$$

In Table 3.3, N_B is

$$N_B = \frac{\begin{bmatrix} 2(3-2) + 1(3-1) + 0(3-0) + 0(3-0) + \\ + 3(3-3) + 0(3-0) + 1(4-1) + 1(4-1) + 2(4-2) \end{bmatrix}}{2} = 7.$$

Pairs Tied on Both A and B. Finally, some pairs in a contingency table are tied on both A and B because $A_l = A_m$ and $B_l = B_m$. Their number is

$$N_{AB} = \frac{\sum_{i=1}^{I} \sum_{j=1}^{J} f_{ij} T_{AB_{ij}}}{2}, \tag{3.9}$$

where

$$T_{AB_{ij}} = n_{ij} - 1. \tag{3.10}$$

But N_{AB} can be determined more simply by noting that the total number of pairs, N, must equal the sum of the different kinds:

$$N = N_C + N_D + N_A + N_B + N_{AB}. \tag{3.11}$$

Thus, N_{AB} is easily obtained by subtraction. In Table 3.3, for example,

$$N_{AB} = 45 - 20 - 4 - 9 - 7 = 5.$$

Formula (3.11) provides a means for checking the accuracy of one's calculations: the sum of the various types of pairs should equal N, the total number of pairs.

3.2 ORDINAL CORRELATION COEFFICIENTS

3.2.1 Kendall's Tau *a*.   The value of τ_a is at once the easiest measure to compute and understand but the least helpful in practice. It measures the difference in the probabilities that randomly drawn pairs are concordant or discordant:

$$\tau_a = P_C - P_D, \tag{3.12}$$

where P_C and P_D are the population probabilities of observing concordance and discordance, respectively.[2] Clearly, τ_a varies between -1.0 and

---

2. The subscript a distinguishes this measure from τ_A, Goodman and Kruskal's τ, with A considered the dependent variable.

1.0. If the probability of discordance is nil, it equals 1.0, meaning the variables are perfectly positively correlated; it is −1.0 if P_C is zero; and it equals zero if a randomly drawn pair is as likely to be concordant as discordant. (Note that $\tau_a = 0$ does not imply statistical independence.) Since concordance and discordance do not depend on which variable is dependent, τ_a is symmetric.

It is reasonable to estimate P_C and P_D by computing the proportions of concordant and discordant pairs in a sample. Taking their difference gives an estimate of τ_a:

$$\hat{\tau}_a = \frac{N_C}{N} - \frac{N_D}{N} = \frac{N_C - N_D}{N}. \tag{3.13}$$

For Table 1.1, where party identification and vote for Senate are now treated as ordinal variables, $\hat{\tau}_a = .330$; for Table 3.3,

$$\hat{\tau}_a = \frac{20 - 4}{45} = .356.$$

Despite its easy computation and interpretation, τ_a is not used much in practice. For one thing, it is not really appropriate for any of the three models of perfect correlation (see Table 3.1). All pairs, whether tied or not, enter its denominator. Consequently, whenever there are ties on either variable (or both), it cannot attain it maximum even if the remaining pairs display only concordance or discordance.

Actually, cross-classifications normally contain a large number of ties. One might consider the ties a penalty for the imprecise classifications: to the extent that ties occur, the absolute value of τ_a is small. In Table 3.1a, for example, where about 33 percent of the pairs are tied, τ_a turns out to be

$$\hat{\tau}_a = \frac{N_C - N_D}{N} = \frac{N_C - N_D}{N_C + N_D + N_{AB}} = \frac{7500 - 0}{7500 + 0 + 3675} = .671.$$

Were more refined variables available, these ties might be resolved into concordant and discordant pairs and the value of $\hat{\tau}_a$ could increase. Indeed, it might be 1.0 if all the ties became concordant pairs. In this sense, low (absolute) values are ambiguous because they may result either from weak correlations or from the crudity of the measurement, or both.

Be that as it may, τ_a treats the data as given. From this point of view it is a conservative measure. It makes no assumption about the disposition of ties with better measurement. In fact, as Goodman and Kruskal (1959 p. 141) point out, one can argue that

> a measure of association for cross-classifications should not be able to attain the value unity, because while complete dependence might exist between the two polytomies it could well be the case that a finer cross-classification would show that within the original cells complete association did not exist.

But from another perspective, τ_a understates, in some instances drastically, the true relationship. When the number of ties is large, its absolute value can be misleadingly low. As a result, social scientists have turned to indices that handle tied pairs differently.

3.2.2 Goodman and Kruskal's Gamma.

A much more popular measure, Goodman and Kruskal's γ (Goodman and Kruskal, 1954) is a *conditional* index: it gives the difference in probabilities of concordance and discordance among untied pairs. In symbols,

$$\gamma = P_{C|\text{no ties}} - P_{D|\text{no ties}}, \qquad (3.14)$$

where $P_{C|\text{no ties}}$ means that the probability of finding concordance given that the pair is not tied. ($P_{D|\text{no ties}}$ has a similar definition.) A reasonable estimate is

$$\hat{\gamma} = \frac{N_C}{N_C + N_D} - \frac{N_D}{N_C + N_D} = \frac{N_C - N_D}{N_C + N_D}. \qquad (3.15)$$

In Table 1.1, $\gamma = .840$, whereas in Table 3.3,

$$\hat{\gamma} = \frac{20 - 4}{20 + 4} = .667.$$

Although it is not clear from the formula, γ in 2×2 tables equals Yule's Q (Section 2.2.3) and can thus be interpreted from two perspectives.

Eliminating tied pairs solves the problem posed by τ_a. The value of γ reaches its maximum under all three definitions of perfect correlation. If substantive research considerations point to weak perfect correlation as the most appropriate model, γ should be used because only it achieves its maximum value for hypotheses of this kind (see Tables 3.1e and 3.1f).

Many social scientists, however, consider this virtue a vice. Return to Table 3.2. Technically, the data fit the weak perfect correlation model, but how informative is it to say that the two variables are perfectly related? Perhaps a bit extreme, the example nevertheless demonstrates that γ equals 1.0 (or has a high absolute value) in many tables that by other, more customary standards would not represent strong association.

As a consequence of ignoring ties, γ is affected by the table size. The number of tied pairs, whether on A, B, or both, increases markedly as the number of categories declines, provided that n remains constant. Since these pairs are excluded from the denominator, the absolute value of γ increases. And conversely, as categorization becomes more refined, the absolute value of γ decreases, other things being equal.

Furthermore, Wilson (1969, p. 341) has criticized γ on the grounds that it throws away information:

> The position taken here is that even if ordinal variables are taken to be crude representations of underlying continua, pairs so close together as to appear

tied on one variable should, if there is a strong relation, be close enough together · · · to appear tied on the other, provided, of course, that the "level of crudeness" of measurements on the two variables are roughly the same. On this assumption, ignoring ties amounts to ignoring evidence against the hypothesis that the two variables vary exactly together.

Therefore, in spite of its clear interpretation and easy calculation, γ has serious drawbacks. To avoid overstating a relationship, one should probably compute and report other coefficients unless the hypothesis specifically asserts weak positive correlation.

3.2.3 Asymmetric Measures, d_{AB} and d_{BA}.   Somers (1962) has defined an asymmetric measure of ordinal correlation. It, too, is a conditional measure:

$$d_{AB} = P_{\substack{C|\text{no ties on}\\ \text{independent}}} - P_{\substack{D\,\text{no}|\text{ties on}\\ \text{independent}}}, \tag{3.16}$$

where $P_{\substack{C|\text{no ties on}\\ \text{independent}}}$ denotes the conditional probability that a randomly drawn pair will be concordant given that it is not tied in any way on the independent variable, although it may be tied on the dependent variable. (The other probability has a similar definition.) Unlike γ, d_{AB} includes certain tied pairs, as is evident from its sample estimate

$$\hat{d}_{AB} = \frac{N_C}{N_C + N_D + N_A} - \frac{N_D}{N_C + N_D + N_A} = \frac{N_C - N_D}{N_C + N_D + N_A}. \tag{3.17}$$

The sample estimate of d_{AB} in Table 3.3 is

$$\hat{d}_{AB} = \frac{20 - 4}{20 + 4 + 9} = .485,$$

and in Table 1.1, $\hat{d}_{AB} = .516$.

It is an obviously asymmetric measure because its numerical value depends on which ties are included in the denominator. If A is the dependent variable, N_A appears in the denominator; if B is dependent on A, then

$$\hat{d}_{BA} = \frac{N_C - N_D}{N_C + N_D + N_B}. \tag{3.18}$$

Since N_A rarely equals N_B, $\hat{d}_{AB} \neq \hat{d}_{BA}$. The formulas can be kept straight by remembering that pairs tied on the independent variable are excluded.

Somer's measures are appropriate for asymmetric hypotheses (see Tables 3.1c and 3.1d). The number of categories on the dependent variable has to be at least as large as the number on the independent variable for the measure to achieve its maximum value.

Since d_{AB} and d_{BA} are easily calculated, are generally not misleadingly high or low, and can be interpreted in several other interesting ways, they are among the most valuable indices for the analysis of cross-classifications, especially if the dependent variable has been clearly identified.

3.2.4 Wilson's *e*.   Wilson (1974c) has recently proposed an index somewhat akin to d_{AB}. Like both γ and the asymmetric coefficient, it measures the differences in conditional probabilities of concordance and discordance, the condition being that pairs tied on both A *and* B are excluded:

$$e = P_{C|\text{no ties on } A \text{ and } B} - P_{D \text{ no}|\text{ties on } A \text{ and } B}, \qquad (3.19)$$

where $P_{C|\text{no ties on } A \text{ and } B}$ represents the conditional probability that a randomly drawn pair is concordant with respect to A and B, given that it is not tied on both.

An estimate is

$$\hat{e} = \frac{N_C}{N_C + N_D + N_A + N_B} - \frac{N_D}{N_C + N_D + N_A + N_B} = \frac{N_C - N_D}{N_C + N_D + N_A + N_B}. \qquad (3.20)$$

The sample estimate in Table 3.3 is

$$\hat{e} = \frac{20 - 4}{20 + 4 + 9 + 7} = .400,$$

whereas in Table 1.1, $\hat{e} = .443$.

Wilson's *e* is appropriate for measuring the extent to which data fit a model of strict correlation. It is not quite as useful in the other two cases, since it cannot achieve its maximum if there are pairs tied only on A or only on B, which is usually the case in nonsquare tables.

To compensate partly for the fact that *e* does not achieve its maximum value in nonsquare tables, it is first necessary to find a table in which N_{AB}, the number of pairs tied on A and B, is a maximum given the original marginal totals. Note that maximizing N_{AB} effectively minimizes N_A and N_B and one can thus determine the largest value of e (or d_{AB}) for the particular marginals. Finally, the observed coefficient, e, is divided by its maximum value to obtain an "adjusted" measure.

Finding the table with the largest N_{AB} involves five steps (Leik and Gove, 1971, p. 296):

Step 1. List both sets of marginal frequencies in their proper order.
Step 2. Create a set of cell frequencies, n_i $(i = 1, \ldots, IJ)$, that will be the entries in the new "adjusted" table. (At the outset, let $i = 1$.)
Step 3. Find the first nonzero marginal in both sets of marginal totals. Let n_i equal the smaller of the two and subtract it from each of these two marginal frequencies. Note that the marginals must be taken in the order in which they appear.

Step 4. Continue Step 3 (incrementing i by 1 each time) until all the marginals in both sets equal zero.

Step 5. Set the remaining n_i equal to zero.

The numbers n_i constitute the frequencies in a table with minimum ties on A only (N_A) and B only (N_B). In other words, the n_i are arranged in a table having the same dimensions and marginal totals as the original one but in which N_A and N_B are a minimum. Maximum versions of e (or d_{AB}) are then calculated and used to find the adjusted values.

The data in Table 3.4 provide an example. In the first panel, where $\hat{e} = .527$ and $\hat{d}_{AB} = .564$, an investigator might wonder if the relationship is not bigger. There are, after all, relatively few discordant pairs. Furthermore, A's marginals are skewed, possibly because it was not measured as precisely as B. It would be useful, he concludes, to see how large the coefficients could be, given these marginal distributions.

The calculation of the adjusted tables proceeds as follows:

Step 1. $\{65, 65, 65\} \{125, 70\}$

Step 2. Create n_i for $i = 1, \ldots, 6$

Step 3. $n_1 = 65$
$\{0, 65, 65\} \{60, 70\}$

Step 4. $n_2 = 60$
$\{0, 5, 65\} \{0, 70\}$
$n_3 = 5$
$\{0, 0, 65\} \{0, 65\}$
$n_4 = 65$
$\{0, 0, 0\} \{0, 0\}$

Step 5. $n_5 = n_6 = 0$

The numbers n_i ($i = 1, \ldots, 6$) are entries in the adjusted table (panel b of Table 3.4). For these data, $\hat{e}_{(max)} = .651$ and $\hat{d}_{AB(max)} = .667$. As it turns out, the observed coefficients are not too numerically discrepant with the

TABLE 3.4. **Adjusting Data to Compute Maximum d_{AB} and e**

		a. Original Table						**b. "Maximum" Table**			
			B						*B*		
		L	M	H	Total			L	M	H	Total
A	L	60	60	5	125	*A*	L	65	60	0	125
	H	5	5	60	70		H	0	5	65	70
	Total	65	65	65	195		Total	65	65	65	195

$\hat{\tau}_b = .517 \qquad \hat{d}_{AB} = .564 \qquad \hat{e} = .527$

$\hat{\tau}_{b(max)} = .802 \qquad \hat{d}_{AB(max)} = .667 \qquad \hat{e}_{(max)} = .651$

$\hat{\tau}_{b(adj)} = .644 \qquad \hat{d}_{AB(adj)} = .846 \qquad \hat{e}_{(adj)} = .809$

maximums. The adjusted values are

$$\hat{e}_{(adj)} = \frac{.527}{.651} = .809 \quad \text{and} \quad \hat{d}_{AB_{(adj)}} = \frac{.564}{.667} = .846$$

Of course, in reporting adjusted values, one would also report the original values and tables because they too would normally be of interest.

3.2.5 Kendall's τ_b. The discussion has not presented the measure's chronological development. When Kendall first proposed τ_a, it was clear that tied rankings could confuse its interpretation. He therefore introduced a correction factor to remove the effect of the ties (Kendall, 1970). The resulting measure, τ_b, has turned out to be one of the most widely used and popular coefficients in statistics. Unfortunately, it is not interpreted in terms of the probabilities of concordance and discordance, but it can be understood in other ways (see Section 3.4).

Its sample estimate is

$$\hat{\tau}_b = \frac{N_C - N_D}{\sqrt{N_C + N_D + N_A}\sqrt{N_C + N_D + N_B}} \tag{3.21}$$

The estimate in Table 3.3 is

$$\hat{\tau}_b = \frac{20 - 4}{\sqrt{20 + 4 + 9}\sqrt{20 + 4 + 7}} = .500$$

and in Table 1.1, $\hat{\tau}_b = .585$.

Like other measures, τ_b does not always attain its maximum, as for example in nonsquare tables. (See Table 3.4, for example, where the adjusted value is .644.) Because of this sensitivity, it is common to compute an alternative measure, τ_c.

3.2.6 τ_c. The measure τ_c was developed explicitly for contingency tables and avoids some of the problems raised by τ_a and τ_b. Being a rather *ad hoc* measure, designed to achieve its maximum in nonsquare tables, it does not have a straightforward population interpretation. In fact, it is used mainly as a descriptive index to summarize the amount of correlation in rectangular tables.

For tables where m is the number of rows or columns (whichever is smaller), the sample estimate is

$$\hat{\tau}_c = \frac{(N_C - N_D)}{n^2[(m-1)/2m]}. \tag{3.22}$$

In Table 3.3

$$\hat{\tau}_c = \frac{(20 - 4)}{10^2(2/6)} = .480.$$

The sample estimate in Table 1.1 is $\hat{\tau}_c = .659$.

3.2.7 Relationships among the Measures. As a practical matter, the numerical values of most ordinal measures turn out to be quite similar. Relying solely on τ_a or γ might cause one's conclusions to depart from what they might otherwise be, but other measures applied to the same data generally produce similar results.

That the measures agree is not surprising, in view of their definitions. Their numerators, $N_C - N_D$, are, of course, the same. They differ only in the denominator, which incorporates tied pairs in different ways. For example, τ_a, τ_b, and γ have an obvious relationship to each other:

$$|\tau_a| \leq |\tau_b| \leq |\gamma|, \tag{3.23}$$

with the equality holding only if there are no ties whatever. Similarly, if $N_A = N_B$, then

$$d_{AB} = d_{BA} = \tau_b, \tag{3.24}$$

and, if, say, $N_B = 0$,

$$d_{AB} = e. \tag{3.25}$$

Furthermore, Stuart (1953) points out that

$$\tau_c = \left(\frac{n-1}{n}\right)\left(\frac{m}{m-1}\right)\tau_a,$$

where n is for the moment considered the total for a population table.

What these and many other relationships mean is that in spite of their diverse formulations they generally have the same empirical behavior. For instance, the relative variation in B, the independent variable, affects their magnitudes, as Blalock (1975) has shown. Consider the data sets in Table 3.5. Following the ideas presented in the previous chapter, the frequencies in the first and last columns have been successively doubled. Since these are ordinal variables, most variation in B occurs in Table 3.5e, the least in Table 3.5a. (The indices of qualitative variation presented in the last chapter are not really applicable here because they do not use the ordering among the classes.) Yet even though the variation in B increases, the basic relationship, as measured by percents or odds ratios, remains constant.

As with the nominal indices, however, the ordinal coefficients become numerically larger. This is true for all the measures, including d_{AB} and d_{BA}, statistics that some social scientists believe are analogous to regression coefficients (see Section 3.3). Unstandardized regression parameters do not depend on the amount of variation in the independent variable. If d_{AB} and d_{BA} behaved like b's in regression analysis, they would keep the same value in all the tables.

The point is that an investigator must pay attention to the variation in A and B. For if the observations are highly skewed or are concentrated in one category, the true relationship is easily understated. Similarly, it will

TABLE 3.5. **The Effects of Decreases in Variation on Measures of Ordinal Correlation**

a

		B			
		L	M	H	Total
	L	150	300	25	475
A	M	75	400	75	550
	H	25	300	150	475
Total		250	1000	250	1500

$\hat{\tau}_a = .192$ $\hat{\tau}_b = .332$ $\hat{\tau}_c = .288$
$\hat{\gamma} = .561$ $\hat{d}_{AB} = .383$ $\hat{D}_{BA} = .288$
$\hat{e} = .233$

b

		B			
		L	M	H	Total
	L	300	300	50	650
A	M	150	400	150	700
	H	50	300	300	650
Total		500	1000	500	2000

$\hat{\tau}_a = .256$ $\hat{\tau}_b = .397$ $\hat{\tau}_c = .384$
$\hat{\gamma} = .591$ $\hat{d}_{AB} = .410$ $\hat{d}_{BA} = .385$
$\hat{e} = .299$

c

		B			
		L	M	HH	Total
	L	600	300	100	1000
A	M	300	400	300	1000
	H	100	300	600	1000
Total		1000	1000	1000	3000

$\hat{\tau}_a = .300$ $\hat{\tau}_b = .450$ $\hat{\tau}_c = .450$
$\hat{\gamma} = .634$ $\hat{d}_{AB} = .450$ $\hat{d}_{BA} = .450$
$\hat{e} = .349$

d

		B			
		L	M	H	Total
	L	1200	300	200	1700
A	M	600	400	600	1600
	H	200	300	1200	1700
Total		2000	1000	2000	5000

$\hat{\tau}_a = .320$ $\hat{\tau}_b = .490$ $\hat{\tau}_c = .480$
$\hat{\gamma} = .685$ $\hat{d}_{AB} = .500$ $\hat{d}_{AB} = .480$
$\hat{e} = .381$

e

		B			
		L	M	H	Total
	L	2400	300	400	3100
A	M	1200	400	1200	2800
	H	400	300	2400	3100
Total		4000	1000	4000	9000

$\hat{\tau}_a = .326$ $\hat{\tau}_b = .519$ $\hat{\tau}_c = .489$
$\hat{\gamma} = .733$ $\hat{d}_{AB} = .550$ $\hat{d}_{BA} = .489$
$\hat{e} = .450$

Source: Blalock (1975).

also be difficult to compare data based on populations with varying degrees of variation on *A* and *B* or collected at different times. Although considerable research has been conducted on the subject, no completely satisfactory solution has as yet been found (see Blalock, 1975). One could, of course, standardize or smooth the table using the procedures described in Section 2.1.3.

Agresti (1976) has recently compared these measures from another perspective. He constructs bivariate normal distributions in which two continuous variables are correlated to varying degrees. These correlations are the standard for judging the behavior of the ordinal statistics. He then categorizes the data to produce cross-tabulations with different dimensions and marginal proportions. This method compares the magnitude of the ordinal coefficients with the "true" correlations.

According to this criterion, τ_b is most satisfactory because it provides the best approximation to the correlation in the ungrouped data. Ironically, γ, which is one of the most popular measures in the social sciences, is least satisfactory. τ_c is in between. Agresti does not consider d_{AB} or e, although they presumably behave more like τ_b than γ.

If an investigator believes that the underlying variables are continuous, he ought to rely on τ_b rather than γ. This also applies to discrete variables that have been collapsed into dichotomies and trichotomies. Although Agresti's work is limited to bivariate normal distributions and his particular categorizations, the principle probably holds for most situations encountered by social scientists. His work also reemphasizes an earlier point: keep as many categories in each variable as possible.

3.3 ALTERNATIVE INTERPRETATIONS

As well defined as these measures appear, there still exists considerable controversy about their interpretation and application. On one side, some social scientists (e.g., Hawkes, 1971; Somers, 1974; Smith, 1974) believe that these measures can be interpreted and manipulated in the same framework as parametric statistics such as correlation and regression analysis. Others (Wilson, 1974a, 1974b; Kim, 1975) contest this point of view, saying that such interpretations are highly misleading. It is worth pausing briefly to examine the arguments, since they arise later in conjunction with multivariate analysis.

3.3.1 A Parametric Interpretation of Ordinal Correlation. Daniels (1944) introduced a generalized correlation coefficient,

$$\Gamma = \frac{\sum\limits_{i=1}^{n} \sum\limits_{j=1}^{n} a_{ij} b_{ij}}{\sqrt{\sum\limits_{i=1}^{n} \sum\limits_{j=1}^{n} a_{ij}^2} \sqrt{\sum\limits_{i=1}^{n} \sum\limits_{j=1}^{n} b_{ij}^2}}. \tag{3.26}$$

(Note that in this section the subscripts i and j refer to individuals, not cells.)

This measure is based on comparing all n^2 pairs of observations (the pairs will not necessarily be distinct or distinguishable and hence n^2 does not equal N). For any two observations, say the ith and jth, scores a_{ij} and

b_{ij} are assigned subject only to the provision that $a_{ij} = -a_{ji}$ and $b_{ij} = -b_{ji}$. By properly defining a_{ij} and b_{ij}, one can show that the product-moment correlation, r, Spearman's ρ, and Kendall's τ_b (or τ_a if there are no ties) are all special cases of Γ.

Suppose, for example, that a_{ij} is the arithmetic difference $A_i - A_j$, the difference between individuals i and j on A. Letting b_{ij} be similarly defined for B, Γ turns out to be the familiar correlation coefficient, r. Or let a_{ij} be the difference in ranks on A between the ith and jth observations. Under this scoring system, Γ is Spearman's ρ, the correlation between two sets of ranks.

Alternatively, define a_{ij} as follows. For a pair of randomly drawn subjects, let

$$a_{ij} = \begin{cases} 1 \text{ if } A_i > A_j, \\ 0 \text{ if } A_i = A_j, \\ -1 \text{ if } A_i < A_j. \end{cases}$$

Since A consists of ordered categories containing implicit magnitudes, these comparisons seem reasonable and justified. Furthermore, the sum of squares of all such comparisons, $\sum_{i=1}^{n} \sum_{j=1}^{n} a_{ij}^2$, equals the total number of pairs (not necessarily distinct or nonredundant) that differ on A.

If b_{ij} is defined in a similar fashion, the sum of the products $a_{ij}b_{ij}$ equals the number of concordant minus discordant pairs. When all these quantities are substituted into equation (3.26), Γ becomes Kendall's τ_b. (The redundant and nondistinct pairs effectively get cancelled.) Hence, $\hat{\tau}_b$ is directly analogous to r, the product-moment correlation.

Actually, "analogous" may be too weak for Hawkes (1971), who writes (pp. 913–14, italics added):

> It seems that the interpretation of the measures of variation and covariation of ordinal variables is not as strained as [might have been believed]. The only difference between them and the familiar variance and covariance of interval variables is the rule which assigns numbers to the differences between pairs.... In a strong sense, the variance and covariance "analogs" of ordinal variables are variances and covariances.
>
> Since the variances and covariances of interval measures may be defined in terms of differences between pairs, it follows that the product-moment system of measures of zero-order, multiple, and partial association may be similarly defined. It further follows that, in the general case, the product-moment system is applicable to comparisons of pairs, *regardless of how values are assigned to paired differences* as long as [$a_{ij} = -a_{ji}$].

From these arguments an unwary but enthusiastic researcher might conclude that he can analyze ordinal data with the same precision attained in the analysis of continuous variables. It would be especially easy to believe this because Hawkes and others (e.g., Somers, 1974; Smith, 1974) produce formulas for ordinal multiple and partial correlation coefficients that are identical to their product-moment counterparts. With these tools, it might seem, one could perform sophisticated causal or path analyses on ordinal data.

Yet some social scientists vigorously criticize this perspective. Wilson (1974a, 1974b), Kim (1975), and Allan (1976) provide a statistical critique. The scoring system, they say, may distort reality because all differences are coded 1 or -1, no matter how different the observations. In Table 3.3, the pairs John and Lisa and John and Diana both generate $a_{ij} = -1$, even though the difference between the members of the last pair is greater than that between the members of the first pair. Alternatively, consider two marginal distributions, {100, 300, 500, 500, 300, 100} and {500, 300, 100, 100, 300, 500}. Both sets of marginals would produce equal variances, but the variation on the second set seems greater than on the first. Wilson (1974b, p. 247) also criticizes the logic of the product-moment analogy on the grounds that Γ, the generalized coefficient, has no general interpretation:

> No model for interpretation [of correlation] is presented that holds for both the ordinal and interval cases and from which Daniels' general formula can be derived. Thus, the measures obtained from Daniels' formula by various assignments of pair scores cannot be given an interpretation by virtue of being special cases of Daniels' general coefficient; for the general coefficient has no independently established interpretation. Rather, among the special cases that do have meaning, such as [r], each has its own specific interpretation that apparently does not generalize to all cases.

Others argue that an uncritical acceptance of the parametric interpretation can mislead as much as it informs. Blalock (1975) and Reynolds (1971, 1973, 1974a, 1974b) show that ordinal measures, however conceived, do not behave in the same fashion as interval-level statistics applied to interval data. The data presented in Table 3.5 provide a case in point. One hopes that the slope analogues, d_{AB} and d_{BA}, would remain invariant in the face of changes in marginal distributions, especially since the distributions often reflect only happenstance choices of cutpoints. As is apparent, however, that the terms behave similarly to the other measures of association.

Considering τ_b, or any other index, as a correlation coefficient applied to pair differences could be equally misleading. It would be deceptive if a researcher thought τ_b^2 actually measured the percent of variation in A explained by B. After all, one should ask, has the variation in A and B been fully measured? What changes in τ_b would another set of categories produce? Unless questions like these are answered adequately, it seems premature to think in terms of the variance explained in ordinal variables.

Paradoxically, there might be a mathematical justification, as Hawkes asserts, but resulting conclusions could be vacuous.

In view of this continuing debate, the reader ought to consider carefully the appealing practice of extending ordinal data into the realm of interval-level statistics.

3.3.2 Proportional-Reduction-in-Error Interpretations.

Ordinal measures of correlation can also be given PRE interpretations (see Chapter 2). Since the advantages of doing so seem limited, however, only a bare outline is presented.

A PRE measure, remember, has the general form:

$$\frac{\text{PRE}}{\text{Measure}} = \frac{(\text{Expected Errors by Rule 1}) - (\text{Expected Errors by Rule 2})}{\text{Expected Errors by Rule 1}}$$

where predictions made according to Rule 1 do not take the independent variable into account, whereas they do in Rule 2.

For γ, a PRE interpretation is as follows: randomly draw a pair of observations and under Rule 1 always predict that the first observation is larger on A than the second. Because only untied pairs are considered, disregard pairs tied on A or B. The probability of error under this rule is $\frac{1}{2}$, because the two observations are drawn randomly (that is, the ith is as likely as the jth to be selected first).

According to the second rule, where knowledge of B is used, one predicts the same order on the dependent variable as exists on the independent variable if $P_C > P_D$; if $P_C < P_D$, predict the pair that will have the opposite order on A as it has on B; and if $P_C = P_D$, predict the same order half of the time and the opposite order half of the time. To make these predictions, one has to know or estimate the probabilities. The probability of error following this model turns out to be $.5 + |\gamma|/2$. Therefore,

$$\text{PRE Measure for } \gamma = \frac{.5 - (.5 + |\gamma|/2)}{.5} = |\gamma|.$$

The absolute value of γ gives the reduction in error in predicting the order of a pair of randomly selected observations, the reduction resulting from the use of B to make the prediction.

Somers' d_{AB} has a similar interpretation, provided that Rule 2 is suitably modified (Somers, 1968). Now only pairs tied on A and B and pairs tied only on B are ignored. Rule 2 stays the same except that if a pair is tied on A, it is counted as an error half of the time. The probability of an erroneous prediction is $.5 + |d_{AB}|/2$. Since Rule 1 is unchanged,

$$\text{PRE Measure for } d_{AB} = \frac{.5 - (.5 + |d_{AB}|/2)}{.5} = |d_{AB}|.$$

Like γ, the absolute value of d_{AB} has a PRE interpretation: it is the reduction in error in predicting the order on *A* of a pair of observations when the pair's order on *B* is known as opposed to when it is not known.

Social scientists have developed parallel interpretations for other measures such as τ_b and τ_c (e.g., Wilson, 1969, 1974c; Leik and Gove, 1969, 1971; Kim, 1971; Ploch, 1974). Wilson (1971), however, has criticized these efforts, arguing among other things that such interpretations occasionally lead to negative values. (This means that knowledge of *B* is less helpful than knowing nothing at all.)[3] Still, as a heuristic device the PRE framework may be helpful in augmenting the other interpretations.

3.4 STANDARD ERRORS AND STATISTICAL TESTS

Until relatively recently, significance tests for ordinal measures posed problems. Kendall (1970) originally presented a rather cumbersome formula for the variance of $(N_C - N_D)$ that allowed a test of $\tau_b = 0$, assuming a sufficiently large sample. But it was really oriented to measuring association among ranked data, rather than among variables in contingency tables, although it could be used for that purpose. Goodman and Kruskal (1963, 1972) have given formulas for the standard error of gamma under various sampling conditions, but they too are rather awkward.

Quade (1974), on the other hand, provides an asymptotic sampling theory covering most ordinal measures of association. He first defines a general index of correlation

$$\hat{\theta} = \frac{\sum\limits_{i=1}^{n} W_i}{\sum\limits_{i=1}^{n} R_i}, \tag{3.27}$$

where for each i $(i = 1, \ldots, n)$, R_i is the number of "relevant" pairs that include that observation. (Note that i refers to individuals, not cells.) "Relevant" depends on a particular measure, but in general it refers to pairs appearing in the denominator of different measures. For τ_a, all pairs are relevant since each kind enters the denominator. For γ, on the other hand, only untied pairs are relevant. For *e*, all relevant pairs are those not tied on *both* A and B, whereas for d_{AB} they are all pairs untied on *B*.

R_i, then, is simply the number of relevant pairs that include the *i*th individual. In Table 3.3, for example, let $i = 1 =$ John. For τ_a, where all pairs are relevant, $R_1 = 9$ since he can be paired with nine other people

---

3. It should be pointed out that Wilson's critique has been challenged; see Mayer and Good (1974).

and all these pairs enter τ_a's calculation. For γ, R_1 equals 5, the number of untied pairs involving John. The sum $\sum R_i$ equals the total number of relevant pairs for the statistic in question. For τ_a, γ, d_{AB}, and e, $\sum R_i$ is $2N$, $2(N_C + N_D)$, $2(N_C + N_D + N_A)$, and $2(N_C + N_D + N_A + N_B)$, respectively. Every pair is counted twice, hence the factor 2.

W_i is the number of the relevant pairs that are concordant minus the number that are discordant. Continuing with the previous example, W_1 is 5 in the case of τ_a because, of the nine relevant pairs involving John, he is concordant on five and discordant one none. (He tied with the remaining observations on at least one variable.) Similarly, for γ, $W_1 = 5$; John is concordant on all five of the relevant pairs. The sum $\sum_{i=1}^{n} W_i$ is simply the total number of concordant pairs (among those that are relevant) minus the number of discordant pairs. For all of the bivariate ordinal measures of association $\sum W_i = 2(N_C - N_D)$, the factor 2 again being a consequence of counting each pair twice.

Thus, θ is a general expression with a specific meaning for each definition of R_i. When R_i includes all pairs, $\theta = \hat{\tau}_a$, as noted above. By the same token, $\theta = \hat{\gamma}$ when R_i includes only untied pairs; $\theta = \hat{d}_{AB}$ when R_i includes pairs not tied on A, and $\theta = \hat{e}$ when R_i includes all pairs not tied on A and B.

An advantage of θ is that Quade has found its asymptotic (i.e., large-sample) standard error:

$$\hat{\sigma}_{(\theta)} = \frac{2}{(\sum R_i)^2} \sqrt{\sum W_i^2 (\sum R_i)^2 - 2 \sum R_i \sum W_i \sum R_i W_i + (\sum W_i)^2 \sum R_i^2}.$$

$$(3.28)$$

(Here the summation is over all n individuals.)

For contingency tables where many observations have the same R_i and W_i, the expressions for θ and σ_θ can be calculated more conveniently by

$$\hat{\theta} = \frac{\sum f_{ij} W_{ij}}{\sum f_{ij} R_{ij}}, \qquad (3.29)$$

and

$$\hat{\sigma}_{(\theta)} = \frac{2}{\{\sum f_{ij} R_{ij}\}^2}$$

$$\sqrt{\sum f_{ij} W_{ij}^2 (\sum f_{ij} R_{ij})^2 - 2 (\sum f_{ij} R_{ij})(\sum f_{ij} W_{ij})(\sum f_{ij} W_{ij} R_{ij}) + (\sum f_{ij} W_{ij})^2 (\sum f_{ij} R_{ij}^2)},$$

$$(3.30)$$

where the summations in both expressions are now understood to be over all IJ cells and f_{ij} is the observed frequency in the ijth cell. In addition,

$$W_{ij} = C_{ij} - D_{ij},$$

and R_{ij} depends on the particular statistic. For τ_a,

$$R_{ij} = C_{ij} + D_{ij} + T_{A_{ij}} + T_{B_{ij}} + T_{AB_{ij}}.$$

For γ,

$$R_{ij} = C_{ij} + D_{ij}.$$

For d_{AB},

$$R_{ij} = C_{ij} + D_{ij} + T_{A_{ij}}.$$

For e,

$$R_{ij} = C_{ij} + D_{ij} + T_{A_{ij}} + T_{B_{ij}}.$$

Each term, C, D, T_A, T_B, and T_{AB}, has been defined in Section 3.1.2. Note that the subscripts i and j now refer to *cells*, not individuals.

Examples of these computations for the data in Table 1.1 appear in Table 3.6. (For simplicity, only the calculations involving τ_a and γ are reported.) Several points are worth noting. The column labeled f contains the frequencies from the appropriate cells of Table 1.1. These entries are multiplied by W_{ij}, R_{ij}, and so forth, and summed to obtain the necessary quantities. As is apparent, the numbers can become quite large, so it is usually necessary to work with scientific notation.

TABLE 3.6. **Calculation for Variances for $\hat{\tau}_a$ and $\hat{\gamma}$ for Data in Table 1.1**

Cell									$\hat{\tau}_a$	$\hat{\gamma}$
i	j	f	C	D	T_B	T_A	T_{AB}	W	R	R
1	1	1103	1109	0	207	424	1102	1109	2842	1109
1	2	309	766	207	343	1218	308	559	2842	973
1	3	115	0	550	766	1412	114	−550	2842	550
2	1	207	0	424	1103	1109	206	−424	2842	424
2	2	343	1103	115	309	973	342	988	2842	1218
2	3	766	1412	0	115	550	765	1412	2842	1412

$$\sum fW = 2{,}665{,}416 \qquad \sum fW^2 = 3{,}387{,}141{,}800 \qquad \left(\sum fW\right)^2 = 7.104442453 \times 10^{12}$$

Calculations for $\hat{\tau}_a$

$$\sum fR = 8{,}079{,}806 \qquad \sum fR^2 = 2.296{,}280{,}865 \times 10^{10} \qquad \left(\sum fR\right)^2 = 6.5283265 \times 10^{13}$$

$$\sum fWR = 7{,}575{,}112{,}272$$

$$\hat{\theta} = \hat{\tau}_a = .330 \qquad \hat{\sigma}_{(\hat{\tau}_a)} = .0074$$

Calculations for $\hat{\gamma}$

$$\sum fR = 3{,}174{,}268 \qquad \sum fR^2 = 3{,}757{,}155{,}722 \qquad \left(\sum fR\right)^2 = 1.007597734 \times 10^{13}$$

$$\sum fWR = 3{,}392{,}593{,}490$$

$$\hat{\theta} = \hat{\gamma} = .840 \qquad \hat{\sigma}_{(\hat{\gamma})} = .0116$$

Note: Subscripts (i, j) have been omitted for clarity.

More important, this computing algorithm leads to the same estimates as did the formulas presented earlier. Here, for example, $\sum f_{ij} W_{ij} = 2(N_C - N_D)$ and in the case of τ_a, $\sum f_{ij} R_{ij} = 2N$. The procedure may be computationally cumbersome but, as Quade points out, it can readily be programmed for a computer. Its major advantage, however, is that it provides a common framework for calculating a variety of ordinal measures and their standard errors, including several multivariate measures (see Chapter 4).

The variable

$$z = \frac{(\hat{\theta} - \theta)}{\hat{\sigma}_{(\theta)}} \tag{3.31}$$

has an approximately unit (standard) normal distribution for large random samples. Furthermore, approximate two-sided confidence intervals can be obtained from

$$\theta \pm \zeta \hat{\sigma}_{(\theta)}, \tag{3.32}$$

where ζ is the appropriate percentile of the unit normal distribution. Approximate 95 percent confidence intervals for τ_a and γ in Table 1.1 are $(.316 - .344)$ and $(.817 - .863)$, respectively.

A quick but rough method for making inferences about τ_b or τ_c is to calculate

$$\hat{\sigma}^2_{(\hat{\tau}_b)} \leq \frac{2}{n(1 - \hat{\tau}_b^2)}, \tag{3.33}$$

which gives a conservative upper bound for the estimated variance of τ_b (Kendall, 1970; Stuart, 1953.) For τ_c, relationship (3.34) must be modified:

$$\hat{\sigma}^2_{(\hat{\tau}_c)} \leq \frac{2}{n} \left[\left(\frac{n}{m-1} \right)^2 - \hat{\tau}_c^2 \right]. \tag{3.34}$$

This is a conservative procedure because the variance of $\hat{\tau}_b$ or $\hat{\tau}_c$ will be no larger than the expressions in (3.33) or (3.34). Since the distribution of these measures tends to be normal for large n, with mean τ_b or τ_c it is possible to set conservative confidence limits. Stuart (1953) notes the crudeness of these upper bounds. But for large n they nevertheless provide a fast and reasonably accurate method for many practical purposes.

The development of a sampling theory for ordinal measures is, of course, welcome. Yet most social scientists should, no doubt, be most concerned with the estimation and interpretation of the measures. Statistical significance is usually of secondary interest, especially since many samples are so large that even trivial associations are significant. It is well known but perhaps worth reemphasizing that statistical significance is not at all synonymous with substantive importance.

4 MULTIVARIATE ANALYSIS
OF CROSS-CLASSIFICATIONS

4.1 INTRODUCTION

The fact that party identification and voting are correlated is of course interesting. Facts, however, do not speak for themselves but must be interpreted. For although discovering an association between two variables is an important step, it is equally important to know why and how they are related.

After all, one variable may be related to another purely by chance. Or knowledge of the connection may convey very little real information. Birth rates and stork populations are correlated in some countries. Yet would anyone seriourly contend that the understanding of either variable is advanced by this information?

No, what is required is more precise data about the conditions, the times and places, under which variables are related. That Democrats vote for Democrats seems sensible enough. Superficially, no further explanation is needed. But for years much to-do has been made about the decline in party voting. Furthermore, party identification develops in adolescence, presumably long before current issues and candidates become salient. What, then, causes Democrats to continue voting for Democratic candidates? Is it blind party loyalty? habit? shared interests? Is such allegiance to a party rational? What thought processes, in short, are involved that make the relationship so strong and enduring? Few political scientists are content with simply knowing that party identification and voting are related; instead, they want to know why.

Traditionally, social scientists explain a relationship by introducing additional variables. All the variables constitute a model that essentially describes how and under what conditions the original relationship holds.

Explaining a relationship by adding more variables can be looked at from two broad perspectives. The first is the effect of controlling for one or more variables. Suppose, for example, that we examine the impact of party identification within categories of partisan attitude. Referring to the respondents' general attitudes toward the parties as managers of government, the attitude scale is based on answers to open-ended questions and ranges from pro-Democratic to pro-Republican with neutrals in between. Consequently, there are three separate tables depending on the level of partisan attitude, as in Table 4.1.

Why should data be organized in this fashion? A major concern in any cross-sectional study such as a sample survey is the avoidance of spurious associations. There may be factors creating a relationship between party and voting. The analyst's task is to discover and control for these causes.

This job has traditionally been accomplished in three ways. First, one can simply restrict the study to respondents who are homogeneous on the extraneous factors. In the present context this requires looking only at nonpartisans or pro-Democrats or pro-Republicans. A second method is matching. A Democrat with pro-Democratic attitudes is paired with a Democrat having pro-Republican feelings.

Both methods have advantages and disadvantages. A third and more common approach is to adjust for possible spurious causes by literally holding them constant. This necessitates subclassifying the respondents on the control factors. The result is a multidimensional cross-classification. Arrayed in this manner, however, the data raise several questions.

4.1.1 Interaction. Is the strength and direction the same in all levels of the control variable? Generally speaking, if the association between A and B varies from one category of C to another, *interaction* exists. Figure 4.1a presents an intuitive example. There the impact of B on A (or vice versa) depends on the value of C: at C_1 there is no relationship; at C_2 it is quite strong; whereas at C_3 it is moderate.

Obviously, its definition and measurement must be more precise than this. As a matter of fact, the study of statistical interaction among categorical variables has been the object of a vast amount of research. Among many works are those of Simpson (1951), Kastenbaum and Lamphiear (1959), Lewis (1962), Darroch (1974), Goodman, (1963, 1964b, 1964c, 1969b, 1970), Birch (1963, 1964, 1965), Bhapkar and Koch (1968a, 1968b), Gart (1972) and Berkson (1968). For now, however, the concept means simply that the form of a relationship between two variables is *not* the same within the classes of a third variable.[1]

4.1.2 Partial Associations. Assuming that interaction is not present—that is, the AB relationship remains the same at all levels of C—how

---

1. Actually, the concept extends to higher-dimensional tables, making it necessary to specify the "order" of the interaction (see Chapter 5 for details).

TABLE 4.1. **Vote for U.S. Senator by Party Identification within Categories of Partisan Attitude**

| | Pro-Democratic | | | | C: Attitude Neutral | | | | Pro-Republican | | | |
| | B: Party | | | | B: Party | | | | B: Party | | | |
A: Vote	D	I	R	Total	D	I	R	Total	D	I	R	Total
D	89% (620)	74% (89)	19% (13)	(722)	85% (367)	50% (151)	21% (52)	(570)	65% (116)	31% (69)	9% (50)	(235)
R	11% (80)	26% (40)	81% (55)	(175)	15% (64)	50% (150)	79% (200)	(414)	35% (63)	69% (153)	91% (511)	(727)
Total	100% (700)	100% (129)	100% (68)	(897)	100% (431)	100% (301)	100% (252)	(984)	100% (179)	100% (222)	100% (561)	(962)

Note: Numbers in parentheses are number of cases.   Key: D = Democrat, I = Independent, R = Republican.

Source: Cowart (1973), p. 841, table 2.

Figure 4.1.   **Example of Interaction***

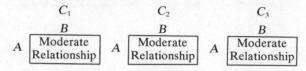

a. Interaction Present

	C_1		C_2		C_3
	B		B		B
A	No Relationship	A	Strong Relationship	A	Moderate Relationship

b. No Interaction (Partial Correlation Not Equal to Zero)

	C_1		C_2		C_3
	B		B		B
A	Moderate Relationship	A	Moderate Relationship	A	Moderate Relationship

c. No Interaction (Zero Partial Association)

	C_1		C_2		C_3
	B		B		B
A	No Relationship	A	No Relationship	A	No Relationship

* Each box can be thought of as a contingency table between A and B for a given level of C.

strongly are the variables related? In many instances, C has no bearing on either A or B, meaning that the connection between them is unaffected by controlling for it. In other cases, holding C constant will increase or decrease the strengths of the relationships. In any event, however, each *partial association* has the same form and magnitude (Figure 4.1b).

It is frequently useful to have a summary measure of the partial associations. Indices of partial association or correlation serve this purpose.

4.1.3 Zero Partial Association.   Occasionally the introduction of a control variable causes the original relationship to vanish. Then the partial associations are all zero (Figure 4.1c). Zero partial associations naturally imply that interaction does not exist. Knowing whether or not the partial associations are zero (except for sampling error) is important because it permits one to distinguish among various models (see Section 4.2).

It is difficult to detect interaction from a cursory inspection of Table 4.1. Party affiliation has a strong impact on voting in all three subtables—hence, the partial associations are not zero—but its effects are less pronounced among pro-Republicans. Clearly, what is needed is a systematic method for examining these relationships.

4.1.4 Multiple Relationships. The second general aspect of multivariate analysis concerns the cumulative impact of adding variables. The concern is somewhat analogous to the issue raised in multiple regression analysis: how much variance in a dependent variable does a set of independent variables explain? With categorical variables the easiest but perhaps least satisfactory solution is to combine the independent variables into a joint variable and then measure its relationship to the dependent variable, using any appropriate bivariate measure of association or correlation.

As an example, one can treat the combined categories of party and attitude in Table 4.1 (e.g., pro-Democratic Democrats) as categories of a single [joint] variable and then compute indices of association between that variable and voting. In this instance, most measures that are interpretable as analogues to multiple correlation coefficients are only slightly larger than the bivariate measures computed for Table 1.1. (The multiple $\hat{\lambda}_A$ in Table 4.1, for example, is .563, whereas in Table 1.1 it is .521.) For other data, however, the increases may be larger.

Unfortunately, the comparison to multiple regression is weak at best. Since there is no objective way to combine the categories, "multiple" ordinal measures may be numerically smaller than their original versions. Moreover, variation in variables such as voting is not really defined, making the analogy with explained variation seem tenuous indeed. Still, except for this rather *ad hoc* procedure, there is no totally satisfactory solution. Goodman (1972a) proposes a summary measure somewhat similar to a multiple correlation coefficient, but it rests on log-linear models, a topic covered in the next chapter.

The issues raised by multivariate categorical analysis—the definition and measurement of interaction and partial and multiple association— have led to much research by statisticians and social scientists. As techniques have evolved over the past two decades, they have become highly sophisticated. Many of the basic ideas are quite simple, however, and are easily grasped by briefly considering one of the earlier approaches.

4.2 TEST-FACTOR STRATIFICATION

Test-factor stratification, one of the earliest forms of multivariate categorical data analysis, tries to explain relationships by controlling for one or more variables, often called test factors (Lazarsfeld, 1955; Hyman, 1955; Rosenberg, 1968). The analysis proceeds in three steps.

1. Propose a model that might account for the observed data. The model states how the variables are interconnected.

2. Determine a set of predictions for the model. In other words, if the model is true, the observations should exhibit certain patterns of association, except for sampling error.
3. Examine the contingency tables formed by controlling for the test factor to see how closely the data agree with the predictions.

In these respects, test-factor stratification parallels most model-building procedures, including the causal analysis of interval-scale variables. The main objective is to see which of several competing models is most compatible with the observed data. Figure 4.2 shows some common three-variable models.

In the first model, a spurious association, the covariation between A and B is due solely to C. A change in C produces changes in both A and B, but changing A or B has no effect on C. More important, since there is no direct link between them, changing B does not affect A.

The model predicts that if C is held constant, the relationship between A and B will disappear. (Actually, in most presentations of test-factor stratification (Hyman, 1955; Rosenberg, 1968), the prediction is less precise: if spurious correlation exists, controlling for the test factor, C, considerably weakens the relationship but does not necessarily cause it to vanish.) If, for example, partisan attitudes cause a spurious connection between party identification and voting, the three relationships in Table 4.1 should, on the whole, be smaller than the original, uncontrolled association (Table 1.1).

Of course, this prediction assumes that variables not included in the model have essentially random effects. It would not hold if an unmeasured variable, say C', was also a spurious cause (Figure 4.2b). Testing that model would require explicitly taking account of C'. The model also assumes the causal priority among the variables. Presumably, C temporally precedes both A and B, but this cannot be demonstrated from the data.

Given these kinds of simplifying assumptions, one can determine

FIGURE 4.2. **Simple Three-Variable Models**

---

a. Spurious Association   **b. Double Spurious Association**

          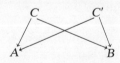

c. Developmental Sequence   **d. Alternative Developmental Sequence**

$$B \longrightarrow C \longrightarrow A \qquad\qquad C \longrightarrow B \longrightarrow A$$

---

whether an observed cross-classification conforms to the model's predictions. The method is straightforward. One controls for the test factor with K classes by dividing the data into K subgroups. The members of the first subgroup belong to C_1, the first category of C; the members of the second subgroup belong to C_2, and so on. (C may actually be multivariate—that is, a composite formed by combining two or more variables.) One then examines the *contingent* or *conditional* associations between A and B within each level of C. As a typical layout, Table 4.1 shows the party identification by vote relationship for each of the $K = 3$ subgroups of partisan attitude.

In traditional test-factor stratification, percentage distributions are the standard for measuring the strength of the relationship. If spurious correlation holds, the percents in each column of a subtable should be about the same, indicating that A does not vary by B.

Another model, one that leads to the same prediction as a spurious correlation, is a *developmental sequence* (Figure 4.2c). Here, A is indirectly linked to B through C. A change in B produces changes in C, which in turn affects A. Inasmuch as the model assumes that no other variables are operative, holding C constant should substantially weaken the AB relationship, if not eliminate it altogether. The only way of distinguishing this model from the previous one is to know on some other grounds that C temporally or causally follows B.[2]

If the contingent or partial associations do not vanish and yet if their magnitudes vary from one category to another, interaction exists. The presence of interaction requires, in Hyman and Rosenberg's words, the specification of the relationship. Specification is part and parcel of theory building, because it is a statement of the conditions under which A and B are related.

Stratifying relationships by a test factor yields insights into the data's structure. In spite of its usefulness, the technique, especially in its early development, had a number of shortcomings.

---

2. There is a possible ambiguity here because the model shown in Figure 4.1d is also a developmental sequence, but one in which C causes B. Now, controlling for C will not cause the AB relationship to vanish. On the other hand, C produces variation in B, which produces variation in A. Hence, holding C constant limits the variation in B, although B's variation will not completely disappear since it probably has other causes. Still, the net effect will be a weaker AB relationship.

With interval-level data and statistics, one could easily sort out these models, provided that the assumptions regarding causal priorities and outside variables were met. Model 4.1c predicts that $r_{AB.C} = 0$ and $|r_{AC.B}| < |r_{AC}|$, except for sampling error; model 4.1d predicts that $r_{AC.B} = 0$ and $|r_{AB.C}| < |r_{AB}|$. With test-factor stratification, however, the predictions are more ambiguous. The original proponents, Lazarsfeld, Hyman, and Rosenberg, asserted that the controlled relationships between A and B (with C held constant) should be weaker than the original relationship. There was no stipulation that they had to vanish totally, as in regular causal analysis. But by that criterion, either model 4.1c or 4.1d would be acceptable. Consequently, it is especially important to know which variable precedes which.

4.2.1 The Limitations of Test-Factor Stratification. The principal difficulty with test-factor stratification is the absence of an easy and objective way of judging by how much the original relationship has been reduced. As Table 4.1 makes clear, one has to scan several contingent relationships. If C is multivariate or has a large number of categories, the number of partial associations is also large. This places a burden on the investigator, who must decide if all the subtables display the same relationships and if as a whole they are weaker than the original one. Furthermore, the method requires a large number of cases, since percents are the basis of judgement.

4.2.2 Test-Factor Standardization.   Partly as a reaction to these limitations, Rosenberg (1962) suggested an alternative, *test-factor standardization*. The goal is the removal of the effects of the test factor on the AB relationship. Standardizing the test factor provides a summary table containing the frequencies or proportions that would be expected if relevant background characteristics are held constant. Basically, one reconstructs the original table by weighting the observed proportions according to the distribution of cases on the test factor. The method consists of four parts.

First, form the partial or contingent subgroups, just as in the usual test-factor analysis except that it is now more convenient to work with percents or proportions rather than frequencies. Next, compute the proportion of cases (designated w_k) in each level of C. The w_k are multiplied by each conditional observed proportion, p_{ijk}, to obtain adjusted or standardized proportions, p'_{ijk} (for $i = 1, \ldots, I$; $j = 1, \ldots, J$; $k = 1, \ldots, K$). Finally, the standardized proportions can be added to obtain the reconstructed table in which the proportions have been standardized on the control variables. The resulting table, which implicitly assumes that all of C's categories contain the same number of cases, is usually easier to read and interpret than the initial array.

In order for this procedure to be valid, one should note, interaction must not be present. The objective is to summarize the contingent relationships. But if doing so obscures different associations, one is effectively throwing away information. Hence, it is assumed that the investigator has already ruled out interaction.

Table 4.2 illustrates the technique for hypothetical data in which C causes A and B. It is, of course, apparent from the contingent relationships that A and B are spuriously related. But when the variables have more than two categories and the relationships are not so clearcut, the method helps clarify the patterns of association. Applied to the data in Table 4.1, for example, test-factor standardization indicates that controlling for partisan attitude does not weaken the impact of party affiliation on voting.

TABLE 4.2. **Example of Test-Factor Standardization**

a. Original Relationship

		B	
	A	.690	.090
		.310	.910
Total		1.000	1.000
		(292)	(445)	$n = 737$

b. Conditional Proportions

	C_1				C_2	
		B				B
A	.800	.800		A	.050	.050
	.200	.200			.950	.950
Total	1.000	1.000		Total	1.000	1.000
	(250)	(25)	$f_{++1} = 275$		(42)	(420)	$f_{++2} = 462$
	$w_1 = 275/737 = .373$				$w_2 = 462/737 = .627$	

c. Standardized Conditional Proportions

	C_1				C_2	
		B				B
A	.298	.298		A	.031	.031
	.075	.075			.596	.596
Total	.373	.373		Total	.627	.627

d. Standardized Proportions

		B	
	A	.329	.329
		.671	.671
Total		1.000	1.000

Note: Data are proportions.

Rosenberg's approach has another advantage. Standardizing the proportions partly corrects for random fluctuations arising from an uneven distribution of cases on C (Rosenberg, 1962, p. 59). Most partial associations do not contain the same number of observations; some, in fact, may have relatively few, particularly if K is large. If one treats each subgroup equally, then some contingent associations contribute disproportionately to the analysis. Standardization mitigates the disparities by differentially weighting the proportions. In other words, C_1 in Table 4.2 contains fewer cases than C_2, therefore $w_1 < w_2$ and the entries in C_1 contribute less to the final table than the entries in C_2.

In spite of its advantages, the method has a few problems. Test-factor standardization involves weighted sums or means. But it is not obvious that the weights, w_k, are always the most appropriate. Kalton (1968) discusses the procedure in detail, showing that for some purposes different weights are more useful.

More important, standardization as a variation of test-factor stratification still depends on a sizeable n, and the adjusted proportions can be difficult to interpret if I and J are large. It does not provide a single summary index of the strength of partial association. Finally, it is perhaps best viewed as a heuristic device for which no adequate sampling theory has been developed (Boyle, 1966).

For these reasons, social scientists have long sought analogues to partial and multiple regression coefficients, numbers that summarize multivariate relationships.

4.3 COEFFICIENTS OF PARTIAL ASSOCIATION FOR NOMINAL AND ORDINAL DATA

Faced with nominal and ordinal variables, a social scientist might resort to one of two devices for measuring partial association.

4.3.1 Treating Ordinal as Interval Scales. One widespread and appealing approach to the problem is to treat ordinal variables as if they were interval. This has been a common practice in sociology, political science, and other disciplines. If the underlying variables are continuous, not discrete, the important question is whether or not the practice leads to erroneous conclusions.[3]

Many investigators think that it does not. They argue that statistics such as tests of significance or measures of association apply to numbers as numbers and do not depend for their validity on the measurement model. Burke (1953), for example, claims that "a statistical technique begins and ends with the numbers and with statements about them" (p. 74). He continues, "the properties of a set of numbers as a measurement scale should have no effect upon the choice of statistical techniques for representing and interpreting the numbers" (p. 75).

Buttressing this position is empirical evidence that violations in measurement assumptions usually do not cause many mistakes in significance tests or parameter estimation. Similarly, Labovitz (1967, 1970) asserts that correlation coefficients are more or less unaffected by applying them

---

3. If all the variables are truly discrete and have relatively few categories, one would probably be better off analyzing them by the methods described below.

to ranked instead of numeric data. He concludes that parametric statistics can be given their "interval interpretation" with only negligible errors when used on ordinal data. Echoing this position, Boyle (1970, p. 479) writes:

> The theoretical analysis concluded that regression and path coefficients are generally quite stable no matter what the interval scale, because appreciable distortion depends not on the magnitude of error, but on special coincidences between more than one kind of error.[4]

From these arguments, one might conclude that the simplest way to analyze multivariate ordinal scales is simply to put the category scores in the usual parametric formulas, pretending all the while that the data are truly numeric.

But this position has critics. Although statistical formulas deal only with numbers regardless of their source, the results must be interpreted in substantive terms. Senders (1953) illustrates the point. Suppose that families are grouped on income as follows:

Limits	Category Score
$5,000–100,000	5
$3,000–5,000	4
$2,000–3,000	3
$1,000–2,000	2
$0–1,000	1

A family in the $5,000–100,000 bracket, for example, is coded 5. Now, if the families in Town A fall in category 3 while half the families in Town B are in category 1 and half are in category 5, both towns will have a mean of 3. Yet Town B is undoubtedly richer than Town A. Relying solely on the category scores could thus be quite misleading.

Hays (1963, p. 74) summarizes the problem:

> It seems, ..., that statistics qua statistics is quite neutral on the issue. In developing procedures, mathematical statisticians have assumed that techniques involving numerical scores, orderings or categorizations are to be applied where these numbers of classes are appropriate and meaningful.... If the statistical method involves the procedures of arithmetic used on numeric scores, then the numerical answer is formally correct. Even if the numbers are the purest nonsense, having no relation to real magnitudes or the properties of real things, the answers are still right as numbers. *The difficulty comes with the interpretation of these numbers back into statements about the real world. If nonsense is put into the mathematical system, nonsense is sure to come out.* [Italics added.]

---

4. Besides Burke, Labovitz, and Boyle, see McNemar (1969), Baker et al. (1966), and Anderson (1961) for related remarks.

This is a crucial point.[5] The techniques discussed throughout this volume assume the meaningfulness of the data however they are represented or coded. One should not let either the simplicity of treating ordinal as interval scales or the mathematical elegance of techniques described later beguile him into thinking that the level of measurement does not matter. The coding system must correspond in a reasonably approximate way to the underlying variables. Otherwise, no method can be expected to yield accurate information about the real world. In the end, mathematical sophistication cannot compensate for weak measurement.

In view of these comments, using ordinal scales in interval-level statistics is risky. Assuming that the variables are really continuous, one should be able to determine the underlying structure of the data if they all have at least five categories. With 10 categories, the substantive conclusions will probably be the same no matter what method is used.

When variables have fewer than five categories, however, the analyst must be particularly careful because it is extremely difficult, sometimes impossible, to detect the true pattern of associations. This conclusion has particular relevance for model testing. In most circumstances, for example, it will be hard to discern a spurious correlation from some other model if the variables are dichotomies and trichotomies and the regular product-moment partial correlation is used.[6]

4.3.2 Coefficients of Partial Association and Correlation.

Since many social scientists hesitate to ignore the level of measurement, they have turned to measures developed specifically for ordinal and nominal scales. They are on safe ground in this respect, but as will be seen shortly, even these measures do not have ideal properties.

Goodman and Kruskal's Partial Lambda. Goodman and Kruskal (1954) propose a method for measuring partial association among nominal or ordinal variables. Using the PRE logic (see Chapter 2), they

---

5. Hays's views have been supported by numerous statisticians and social scientists. Wilson (1971, pp. 436–37), speaking particularly about Labovitz and Boyle's work, comments: "The major import of these results is that the interpretation of data relative to an interval-variable model will be ambiguous so long as measurement is limited to the ordinal level. . . . This conclusion is not altered by suggestions that in some situations it may make little practical difference what scoring procedure is used. . . . For, in any given situation, one would have to show that the scoring procedure actually employed makes little difference in the particular situation at hand in order to justify faith in the conclusions of an analysis in that situation. Such a demonstration, however, requires either knowing the 'real' underlying variable . . . or knowing that the situation in question falls into a class of situations for which the scoring system is known to be irrelevant. . . ."

6. See Kim (1975) and Reynolds (1971, 1973, 1974a, 1974b) for a discussion of the difficulties of testing causal models with ordinal data.

suggest predicting B in two ways: (1) knowing only the individual's scores on C, the control variable, and (2) knowing their scores on both C and B, the independent variable. The measure, merely an extension of the bivariate λ in which only B is used, is defined as

$$\lambda_{AB.C} = \frac{\sum_k \sum_j P_{mjk} - \sum_k P_{m+k}}{1 - \sum_k P_{m+k}}, \tag{4.1}$$

where P_{m+k} is the largest row marginal probability in the kth subtable and P_{mjk} is the largest probability in the jth column of the kth subtable (for $i = 1, \ldots, I$; $j = 1, \ldots, J$; $k = 1, \ldots, K$). As always, C might be multivariate.

Partial lambda gives the relative decrease in the probability of making an error when B is known, as opposed to when it is unknown, given that C is always known. If A and B are spuriously related because of C, then within classes of C, B should not be associated with A, at least in the present sense. If they are related, then B will help predict A's categories. These ideas are exemplified by the data in Table 4.2. After converting the conditional proportions in Table 4.2b to proportions, $P_{ijk'}$ we find that $\lambda_{AB.C} = 0.0$, as expected. Consequently, if the true system of variables are discrete, $\lambda_{AB.C}$ is useful in distinguishing among the models in Figure 4.2.

The sample estimate is

$$\hat{\lambda}_{AB.C} = \frac{\sum_k \sum_j f_{mjk} - \sum_k f_{m+k}}{n - \sum_k f_{m+k}}, \tag{4.2}$$

where f_{m+k} is the largest row marginal frequency in the kth subtable and f_{mjk} is correspondingly the largest frequency in the jth column of the kth subtable. An estimate of the asymptotic variance of $\hat{\lambda}_{AB.C}$ is

$$\hat{\sigma}^2_{(\hat{\lambda}_{AB.C})} = \frac{\left(n - \sum_k \sum_j f_{mjk}\right)\left(\sum_k \sum_j f_{mjk} + \sum_k f_{m+k} - 2\sum_k \sum_j{}^* f_{mjk}\right)}{\left(n - \sum_k f_{m+k}\right)^3}, \tag{4.3}$$

where $\sum_k \sum_j{}^* f_{mjk}$ is the sum of those f_{mjk}'s that happen to be in the same row as f_{m+k}, for all k. Since $\hat{\lambda}_{AB.C}$ is approximately normally distributed with mean $\lambda_{AB.C}$, expression (4.3) is used in testing significance and constructing confidence intervals, provided that $\lambda_{AB.C}$ is not 0 or 1 and n is a random sample. For the data in Table 4.1, $\hat{\lambda}_{AB.C} = .295$ and $\hat{\sigma}_{(\hat{\lambda}_{AB.C})} = .023$.

Partial Association Viewed as an Average. Although the measurement of partial association has been approached from many directions, the layout in Table 4.1 suggests a straightforward definition. A measure of partial association can be viewed as an average of the relationships between A and B within each of the K subtables. In other words, one may compute some measure of association for each subtable and then calculate their average, the average being interpreted as a partial correlation coefficient. There are several possibilities, of course, depending on the specific measure and type of average.

This approach to the problem of measuring partial association has several advantages. With various measures of association, an investigator may choose the one that best serves his research interests and data. In addition, for many kinds of statistics and weighting schemes, a well-developed sampling theory exists. Finally, this interpretation parallels some definitions of parametric partial correlation. Blalock (1972), for example, writes: "The partial correlation coefficient can also be interpreted as a *weighted average* of the correlation coefficients that would have been obtained had the control variable been divided into very small intervals and separate correlations computed ˙ within each of these categories" (p. 436).[7]

To illustrate the idea, suppose that an investigator wanted to measure the partial association in Table 4.1, treating each variable as nominal. At the outset, he must test for interaction. Its presence would preclude computing a partial because an average of the contingent relationships would obscure the differences among them. If neutrals behave differently than pro-Democrats and pro-Republicans, one ought to at least investigate the differences before submerging them in an average. These are innumerable methods for testing and measuring interaction. A general framework is given in the next chapter.

Assuming no interaction, the investigator next chooses a measure of association relevant to his hypotheses. Selecting, say, Goodman and Kruskal's τ, he computes an estimate for each subtable and then takes their average. It can be a simple average or preferably a weighted average, the weight again depending on the situation. If the cases are unevenly distributed on C, weighting by f_{++k} would be appropriate. A weighted average of $\hat{\tau}$ in Table 4.1 is

$$\hat{\tau}_{AB.C} = \frac{(897)(.222) + (984)(.287) + (962)(.246)}{867 + 984 + 962} = .250$$

Other weighted averages can be computed similarly.[8]

---

7. As Blalock (1972, chap. 19) indicates, there are other, more widely known definitions of partial correlation.

8. For a method of analyzing K 2×2 tables that somewhat resembles this approach to partialling, see Fleiss (1973, chap. 10).

Quade's Index of Matched Correlation. Instead of using a nominal measure, one can calculate an average of an ordinal coefficient, provided, of course, that A and B are ordinal variables. (The control variable need not be ordinal.) A strategy that turns out to be very useful is to select an index and weight it by its denominator (Quade, 1971, 1974).

Taking τ_a, for example, the weighted average across all K subtables is

$$\hat{\bar{\tau}}_a = \frac{\sum\limits_{k} N_k \hat{\tau}_{a_k}}{\sum\limits_{k} N_k} = \frac{\sum\limits_{k}(N_{C_k} - N_{D_k})}{\sum\limits_{k} N_k}, \tag{4.4}$$

where N_{C_k}, N_{D_k}, and N_k are the number of concordant, discordant, and total pairs in the kth subtable, respectively, and

$$\hat{\tau}_{a_k} = \frac{N_{C_k} - N_{D_k}}{N_k}.$$

Obviously, N_k, the weight, is the denominator of τ_a in the kth subtable. Note that $\sum\limits_{k} N_k$ does not equal N, the number of pairs in a sample of n. On the contrary, $\sum\limits_{k} N_k$ is the sum of all the pairs tied on C, since N_k is the number of tied pairs at the kth level of C. As with the nominal indices, $\hat{\bar{\tau}}_a$ can be interpreted as an overall measure of the correlations between A and B, controlling for C.

Similar weighted averages are computed by choosing appropriate statistics and weights. A partial γ, for example, is

$$\bar{\gamma} = \frac{\sum\limits_{k}(N_{C_k} + N_{D_k})\hat{\gamma}_k}{\sum\limits_{k}(N_{C_k} + N_{D_k})} = \frac{\sum\limits_{k}(N_{C_k} - N_{D_k})}{\sum\limits_{k}(N_{C_k} + N_{D_k})}. \tag{4.5}$$

Here, $(N_{C_k} + N_{D_k})$, the denominator of γ, is the weight. (This measure, incidentally, is equivalent to Davis' (1967) partial γ.)

Using terms from the denominator as weights is advantageous because the resulting averages are special cases of Quade's index θ, defined in expression (3.30), Chapter 3. In a three-dimensional table, $\hat{\theta}$ is

$$\hat{\theta} = \frac{\sum\limits_{k}\sum\limits_{i}\sum\limits_{j} f_{ijk} W_{ijk}}{\sum\limits_{k}\sum\limits_{i}\sum\limits_{j} f_{ijk} R_{ijk}} \tag{4.6}$$

where for an individual in the ijkth cell, R_{ijk} is the number of relevant pairs that include that person and W_{ijk} is the number of these pairs that are concordant minus the number that are discordant. Depending on how one defines "relevant," $\hat{\theta}$ is equivalent to a weighted average of various ordinal measures of correlation.

For τ_a, a relevant pair is one tied on C. In this case the total number of such pairs equals $2\sum_k N_k$; that is,

$$\sum_k N_k = \frac{\sum_k \sum_i \sum_j f_{ijk} R_{ijk}}{2}.$$

(The factor 2 enters because each relevant pair is counted twice; see Section 3.4.) By the same token, the number of relevant concordant minus discordant pairs equals $2\sum_k (N_{C_k} - N_{D_k})$ or

$$\sum_k (N_{C_k} - N_{D_k}) = \frac{\sum_k \sum_i \sum_j f_{ijk} W_{ijk}}{2}.$$

It is clear from these considerations that $\hat{\theta}$ is equivalent to a weighted average τ_a, assuming that "relevant" means pairs tied on C. Relevant could be defined differently, however. Suppose that it means "tied on C but untied on A and B." The total number of relevant pairs in this case is $\sum_k (N_{C_k} + N_{D_k})$, and $\hat{\theta}$ is a weighted average γ as in expression (4.5). Alternatively, a relevant pair might be one that is tied on C but untied on B. According to this definition, $\hat{\theta}$ would be equivalent to a weighted average d_{AB} with weights $(N_{C_k} + N_{D_k} + N_{A_k})$.

An equivalent interpretation of θ is based on conditional probability. Let $(A_l B_l C_l)$ and $(A_m B_m C_m)$ be a pair of randomly drawn individuals from a population where A and B are ordinal variables and C is either nominal, ordinal, or interval. (As always, C may be multivariate.) Establish a rule for deciding when a pair is relevant or *matched*. In subgroup analysis (e.g., Table 4.1), a pair is matched if each member has the same value on C. But the concept of match is quite general. A pair could be considered relevant if it was matched on C in some designated manner. For instance, two individuals could be considered matched if their absolute difference on C, a continuous variable, is less than a specified amount (as when a pair has approximately the same income or IQ). Thus, if a pair is matched in some way on C, the pair is considered relevant.

Let R be the event that a pair of observations is relevant (i.e., matched on the control variable); let C be the event that they are concordant; and let D be the event that they are discordant. Then θ, which Quade calls the index of matched correlation, is also defined as

$$\theta = P(C\,|\,R) - P(D\,|\,R), \tag{4.7}$$

where $P(C\,|\,R)$ is the conditional probability that a pair of randomly selected observations is concordant with respect to A and B, given that the pair is relevant (i.e., matched on C, the control variable) and $P(D \mid R)$ is the conditional probability of discordance. The index can be estimated by

$$\hat{\theta} = \frac{N_{CR}}{N_R} - \frac{N_{DR}}{N_R} = \frac{N_{CR} - N_{DR}}{N_R}, \tag{4.8}$$

where N_R is the number of relevant pairs in the sample, N_{CR} is the concordant pairs among them, and N_{DR} is the number of discordant pairs. Formula (4.8), as another way of writing expression (4.6), merely provides an alternative interpretation.

$\hat{\theta}$ is calculated in two ways. The easiest perhaps is to compute the individual coefficients, say $\hat{\gamma}_{k'}$ and average them across the K subtables, using the appropriate weights. Alternatively, one can apply formula (4.6) directly, as is done in Table 4.3. This involves more computations but

TABLE 4.3.   **Example of Computations for Index of Matched Correlation and Its Standard Error**

Control	Cell									$\hat{\tau}_a$	$\hat{\gamma}$
k	i	j	f	C	D	T_A	T_B	T_{AB}	W	R	R
1	1	1	620	95	0	102	80	619	95	896	95
1	1	2	89	55	80	633	40	88	−25	896	135
1	1	3	13	0	120	709	55	12	−120	896	120
1	2	1	80	0	102	95	620	79	−102	896	102
1	2	2	40	620	13	135	89	39	607	896	633
1	2	3	55	709	0	120	13	54	709	896	709
2	1	1	367	350	0	203	64	366	350	983	350
2	1	2	151	200	64	419	150	150	136	983	264
2	1	3	52	0	214	518	200	51	−214	983	214
2	2	1	64	0	203	350	367	63	−203	983	203
2	2	2	150	367	52	264	151	149	315	983	419
2	2	3	200	518	0	214	52	199	518	983	518
3	1	1	116	664	0	119	63	115	664	961	664
3	1	2	69	511	63	166	153	68	448	961	574
3	1	3	50	0	216	185	511	49	−216	961	216
3	2	1	63	0	119	664	116	62	−119	961	119
3	2	2	153	116	50	574	69	152	66	961	166
3	2	3	511	185	0	216	50	510	185	961	185

$\sum fW = 580{,}218 \qquad \sum fW^2 = 256{,}746{,}672 \qquad (\sum fW)^2 = 3.366529275 \times 10^{11}$

Calculations for Partial τ_a

$\sum fR = 2{,}695{,}466 \qquad \sum fR^2 = 2{,}559{,}381{,}530 \qquad (\sum fR)^2 = 7.265536957 \times 10^{12}$

$\sum fWR = 556{,}490{,}300$

$\hat{\theta} = \hat{\tau}_{aAB.C} = .215 \qquad \hat{\sigma}_{(\hat{\tau}_{aAB.C})} = .0086$

Calculations for Partial γ

$\sum fR = 758{,}694 \qquad \sum fR^2 = 291{,}219{,}140 \qquad (\sum fR)^2 = 5.756165856 \times 10^{11}$

$\sum fWR = 250{,}942{,}810$

$\hat{\theta} = \hat{\gamma}_{AB.C} = .765 \qquad \hat{\sigma}_{(\hat{\gamma}_{AB.C})} = .0173$

leads to an estimate of the standard error of $\hat{\theta}$. (Formula (3.31) for the standard error still applies, except that summations are now taken over an additional dimension.) Table 4.3 illustrates the computations for τ_a and γ. (The various quantities W_{ijk}, R_{ijk}, C_{ijk}, D_{ijk}, are merely extensions of the definitions given in Chapter 3.) For example, C_{ijk} means C_{ij} in the kth subtable.

Since the original relationships in Table 1.1 (that is, $\hat{\tau}_a = .330$ and $\hat{\gamma} = .840$) hardly decline (that is, $\hat{\hat{\tau}}_a = .215$ and $\hat{\hat{\gamma}} = .765$), there does not seem to be a spurious relationship between voting and party identification, a conclusion that is consistent with other findings reported in this chapter.

The Ordinal Analogue to Parametric Partial Correlation. Somers (1974), Hawkes (1971), and Smith (1974) conceptualize ordinal measures as special cases of a generalized product-moment system. Their thinking rests on the scoring system described in Chapter 3. There, it will be recalled, a pair of randomly selected observations is compared on A. If $A_l > A_m$, $a_{lm} = 1$; if $A_l < A_m$, $a_{lm} = -1$; and if $A_l = A_m$, $a_{lm} = 0$. Following this system for the other variables, they argue, leads to ordinal coefficients, τ_a and γ, which, as special cases of Daniels' generalized correlation, are interpretable along the same lines as interval-level correlation and regression coefficients. By simply extending the logic, it follows that measures of multiple and partial correlation can be obtained from the usual parametric formulas. Hawkes (1971) presents a first-order partial for *Kendall's* τ_b:

$$\tau_{AB.C} = \frac{\tau_{AB} - \tau_{AC}\tau_{BC}}{\sqrt{1 - \tau_{AC}^2}\sqrt{1 - \tau_{BC}^2}}. \tag{4.9}$$

where τ is τ_b. This formula is identical to regular partial correlation except that τ's replace r's.

Along with Hawkes, Somers (1970, 1974) presents a partial $d_{AB.C}$ having the same form as a partial regression coefficient. (Somers, however, provides an extended interpretation and regards it mostly as an ordinal partial correlation coefficient.) By this "straightforward generalization," Hawkes maintains, other higher-order partials and multiple regression coefficients can be obtained.

The crucial assertion in their arguments is that because of the scoring system, ordinal bivariate and multivariate measures ought not to be considered analogues but rather special cases of the product-moment system. One is therefore justified in manipulating them in the same manner as interval-level statistics are handled.

Wilson (1974a, 1974b), among others, has vigorously taken issue with this position. (See Chapter 3 for a summary of his remarks.) But whatever one's position, nonparametric partial correlation, however defined, has a major practical weakness. This weakness should be taken into consideration so that the analyst will not be misled by this results.

4.3.3 A Shortcoming of Measures of Nominal and Ordinal Partial Association. If one can assume that his variables have a fixed number of categories or that the observed categorizations are reasonably representative of the underlying categorizations in the population, the various measures of partial association should accurately indicate the pattern of relationship. In other words, they assume discrete data and ought to work if that assumption holds. If, on the other hand, the observed variables have been collapsed or combined from variables having numerous categories, serious difficulties arise. Although the hypothetical data in Table 4.4 are certainly not definitive, they are nevertheless suggestive in this respect.

TABLE 4.4.   **Nonparametric Partial Correlations Applied to a Developmental Sequence**

a. Original AB Relationship

	B	
A	320	167
	187	326
Total	507	493

$$\hat{\tau}_A = .086 \quad \hat{\tau}_a = .146$$
$$\hat{d}_{AB} = .298 \quad \hat{\gamma} = .539$$
$$\hat{e} = .205$$

b. Partial Relationships

C_1			C_2		
	B			B	
A	219	110	A	101	57
	59	109		128	217
Total	278	219	Total	229	274

$$\hat{\tau}_{A_1} = .090 \quad \hat{\tau}_{a_1} = .141 \qquad \hat{\tau}_{A_2} = .063 \quad \hat{\tau}_{a_2} = .116$$
$$\hat{d}_{AB_1} = .286 \quad \hat{\gamma}_1 = .575 \qquad \hat{d}_{AB_2} = .233 \quad \hat{\gamma}_2 = .501$$
$$\hat{e}_1 = .203 \qquad\qquad\qquad \hat{e}_2 = .166$$

Quade's Index of Matched Correlation: $\hat{\bar{\tau}}_a = .128$, $\hat{\bar{\gamma}} = .537$, $\hat{\bar{d}}_{AB} = .259$, $\hat{\bar{e}} = .184$.
Hawkes's Partial $\hat{\tau}_b$ (formula (4.9)): .275.
Simple average of Goodman and Kruskal's $\hat{\tau}_A$: .076.

The data for this table were generated by a computer program that created a developmental sequence: B causes C, which in turn causes A (Figure 4.2c). A sample of $n = 1000$ was drawn from this population. Since the scores were originally continuous, the model was tested using the criterion that $r_{AB.C}$ should equal zero except for sampling error. The observed value met this standard: $r_{AB.C} = -.046$. Thus, the data conformed to the model's prediction.

Then each variable was dichotomized at approximately the mean, producing the subtables shown in Table 4.4. This operation reflects what presumably happens in actual practice when social scientists for one reason or another classify subjects into two or three large categories.

None of the ordinal partials, neither Quade's nor Hawkes's, comes close to being zero. What would an investigator conclude from these findings? If he wanted to test for a developmental sequence he could be badly misled, for without additional information he would probably reject the model. Note in particular that the partials are only slightly lower than the original correlations.

In several works (Reynolds, 1971, 1973, 1974a, 1974b), I have studied the behavior of ordinal partial correlation. Looking at a variety of circumstances, I conclude that if each variable has at least five categories, but preferably more, one can generally obtain good approximations to the behavior of product-moment measures. With fewer categories, however, it is difficult to detect underlying models, especially if the intercorrelations are strong.

The behavior of nominal measures of partial association has not been extensively studied. It is interesting to find that partial λ (expression (4.2)) equals zero, whereas a simple average of Goodman and Kruskal's τ does not. This topic needs to be investigated further.

In addition to this work, Kim (1975) has discussed the problem at a more theoretical level. He compares and evaluates the Hawkes-Somers strategy with the practice of treating ordinal variables as if they were interval. Kim does not recommend the former approach, since it "involves measurement assumptions that are not supported by the ordinal scale" (p. 293). His endorsement of using ordinal variables in parametric formulas must be tempered by the realization that, unless these are a sufficient number of categories, the results can be equally unsatisfactory.[9]

The conclusion, to reemphasize an earlier point, is that social scientists should strive for as much precision in measurement as possible. It is tempting, and occasionally necessary, to lump subjects together into common groups. Yet the analyses can become seriously distorted. Furthermore, these dangers remain in spite of recent advances, many of them highly sophisticated, in multivariate categorical data analysis.

---

9. Kim (1975, p. 279) also briefly discusses weighted averages of ordinal correlations, finding them useful expedients until better measures of partial correlation are developed.

5 LOG-LINEAR MODELS

5.1 INTRODUCTION

Social science research ultimately involves three interrelated objectives. The most important, perhaps, is the explanation of variation in dependent variables. Variation is, after all, what makes life interesting. People have different political preferences. Some vote for Republicans; others prefer Democrats. Why?

Explaining variation leads to the investigation of causal relationships, the mechanisms that relate one variable to another. Although many analysts deny a concern with causality, everyone works within a theoretical framework that explicitly or implicitly contains causal assumptions. Sooner or later, directly or indirectly, the results of any serious empirical research must be related to the underlying theoretical context.

Finally, social scientists face practical problems. They may have to predict some aspects of behavior on the basis of limited knowledge. Knowing only a person's party preference or his attitude on a single issue, they may still be asked to predict his vote. Along with the first two objectives, estimation and prediction are fundamental activities.

Common to all of these efforts is the need to impose order on data. Many statistical procedures seem ideally suited for this purpose. Regression analysis, for example, begins with a dependent variable and a set of possible explanatory or predictor variables. The goal of the analysis is to account for variation in the dependent variable. Ideally, the final model is both simple and consistent with the observed data. But what is really important is that the underlying structure among the variables be identified. For without this understanding, one cannot make sense of the phenomenon under investigation.

Log-linear analysis has the same general purpose: it attempts to identify the structure underlying a set of categorical variables. It tries, in

109

other words, to discover the essential features of an observed cross-classification. Like a regression equation, a log-linear model eliminates "noise" or extraneous variation by summarizing and, in a way, simplifying the table. In applying the technique, the investigator hopes to explain variation, to explore causal relationships, and to make predictions.

Unlike most statistical procedures, however, log-linear analysis deals only with categories or groups of observations. The unit of analysis is not individual scores, but rather cell probabilities or functions of cell probabilities. In a regression equation, for example, Y_i is the dependent variable, where i runs from 1 to n, the number of cases.

In log-linear analysis, by contrast, the "dependent variable" is not a variable at all, but a cell probability, P, the probability that a randomly selected individual from some population has a particular combination of characteristics. The probabilities, or some function of them, serve as the dependent variable.

In most respects, however, log-linear analysis proceeds as do other statistical procedures. The goal is to build a model that in some sense accounts for or explains variation in cell probabilities. Moreover, assuming that the observed table has been sampled from a population, one also wants to estimate its parameters. The process of finding a satisfactory model entails several steps.

1. *Propose a model that might account for the observed data.* A model is really a hypothesis about how a set of variables are distributed and interrelated. A model, in other words, represents an investigator's beliefs about the data's underlying structure. If, for example, a group of variables were mutually independent, the observed cell probabilities should reflect this independence.

2. *Derive a set of expectations under the assumption that the model is true.* One asks, in effect, what a set of data would look like if the model were true. These expectations have to be estimated. Suppose, as before, that one believes that the variables are mutually independent. Under this assumption the observed table should exhibit certain characteristics except for sampling error.

3. *Decide whether or not the model is acceptable.* If the cross-classification is indeed drawn from a population for which the model holds, then any discrepancies between expected and observed data should result only from sampling error. At this stage an analyst asks if the departures are small enough that they can reasonably be attributed to chance or if the model must be rejected as untenable.

4. *If the discrepancies are sufficiently small, retain the model; otherwise return to Step 1.* Presumably the new model is a refinement of the previous one. One cannot proceed efficiently by blindly proposing

models. Instead he should look for the reasons why a model fails and then attempt to improve it.

5. *Having accepted a model, seek further refinements.* As in regression analysis, many models superficially fit the data but can be further refined and simplified. Rather than accepting the first well-fitting model encountered, the investigator should develop a complete yet parsimonious explanation for the data, as it is often possible to eliminate superfluous or redundant variables.

6. *Estimate parameters.* Since a model contains parameters linking variables, one tries to make good estimates of them. The parameters in turn are translated into substantive conclusions and used to make predictions.

Although it may not be apparent, the familiar chi square test for independence in an $I \times J$ table actually involves many of these steps. The model underlying the chi square test, statistical independence, leads to estimated expected frequencies which are compared to observed values. The magnitude of the departures from independence, measured by the chi square statistic, indicates the model's acceptability. If the statistic is significantly large, the model is rejected and one concludes that the variables are related; otherwise, independence is accepted as an adequate description of the population.[1]

In this sense, the basic ideas of log-linear analysis should be familiar to most social scientists. What remains is to describe in detail the meaning of the models, the estimation of expected values, and procedures for refining and interpreting the results.

5.2 LOG-LINEAR MODELS FOR TWO-WAY TABLES

A log-linear model for a two-dimensional $I \times J$ table pertains to P_{ij}, the population proportion or probability of being in the ith row and jth column of an $I \times J$ table. (Note that the P's sum to 1.0.) Instead of probabilities, one may also analyze expected frequencies, F_{ij}, the expected number of observations in the ijth cell of a population table, or for reasons to be seen shortly, the natural logarithm[2] of the expected frequencies, $L_{ij} = \log F_{ij}$. (Taking logarithms requires that $F_{ij} > 0$ for all i, j.) Whether a model is for probabilities, expected frequencies, or the logarithm of expected frequencies is mainly a matter of taste and convenience, since a model for one can easily be translated into models for the others.

---

1. Whatever the decision, one can further refine the model using techniques akin to those presented in Chapter 1 (see Goodman, 1968, 1969a, 1972c).

2. Throughout this book, "log" refers to natural logarithms or logarithms to the base e. As a reminder to the reader I state without proof some properties of logarithms.

Being considered as dependent variables, the F's or L's are expressed as functions of a set of parameters. The parameters pertain to *main* and *interaction* effects. (Readers familiar with analysis of variance will soon recognize the resemblance between these parameters and treatment and interaction effects in ANOVA models.)

Social scientists typically have two uses for these effects. First, and probably most important, their presence or absence in a model tells him about the structure of the data. An interaction effect, for instance, indicates a relationship between two variables. Second, he may be interested in estimates of their numerical values. Although they do not have the same easily grasped meaning as regression coefficients, they still indicate the strength of relationships among variables.

5.2.1 No Effects Model. The simplest model for an $I \times J$ table also happens to be the least plausible. It states that all cell probabilities, expected frequencies, or logarithms of expected frequencies equal a constant. In symbols, the no effects model is

$$F_{ij} = \mu' \tag{5.1a}$$

or

$$L_{ij} = \mu. \tag{5.1b}$$

The parameters μ' and μ, analogous to a grand mean, indicate that each cell frequency in the population equals a constant. Except for sampling error, a sample cross-classification drawn from such a population would have the same frequency in each cell.

Under this model, the variables A and B are statistically independent *and* both the row and column variables are *equally probable*. Equally probable means that the categories of each variable are equally likely to occur. If B is trichotomous, then the probability of being in B_1 equals the probability of being in B_2 equals the probability of being in B_3, which

---

For positive numbers a and b:

$$\log(ab) = \log(a) + \log(b),$$
$$\log(a/b) = \log(a) - \log(b),$$
$$\log(a^b) = b \log(a).$$

The inverse of the logarithmic function, often called the antilogarithm (denoted exp) is used frequently. For any real number c, $\exp(c) = e^c$, where e is $2.718282\ldots$. The relationship between log and exp functions is made clear by $\exp(\log(a)) = a$, where a is a positive number. Thus, if one takes the log of a number, the exponential or antilogarithm returns that number.

In addition, we exploit the fact that $\exp(a + b) = \exp(a) \exp(b)$.

Tables of natural logarithms and antilogarithms are widely available, and even many inexpensive pocket calculators compute them automatically. Their presence, therefore, in the ensuing analyses should cause no problems.

equals one-third. If A, a dichotomy, is equally probable, the probability of being in A_1 or A_2 is one-half.

5.2.2 Model Containing Only Row Effects. A more realistic model contains *row effects*, showing the amount of departure from equiprobability in the row variable. Row effect parameters may be interpreted as a measure of skewness: if people are more likely to belong to A_1 than to A_2, then the distribution of A will be uneven.

The row effects model is written mathematically as

$$F_{ij} = \mu' \mu_i'^A \qquad (5.2a)$$

or

$$L_{ij} = \mu + \mu_i^A. \qquad (5.2b)$$

The notation reveals several aspects of log-linear models. First, a superscript corresponding to the appropriate variable denotes an effect. The coefficients are thus referred to by either $\mu_i'^A$ (or μ_i^A) or, more simply, by the letter of the variable itself.

The presence of a subscript points to the fact that the row effects are a set of parameters, one for each level of the variable. Thus, μ_i^A pertains to the ith effect of A. (The parameters differ in this respect from usual regression terms.)

Finally, and perhaps most important, notice that the first model is multiplicative whereas the second is additive. It is mathematically awkward and undesirable to construct linear models for F_{ij} (or P_{ij}). Instead, multiplicative models have more desirable properties. But one can obtain an additive model by taking (natural) logarithms. Relying on the basic principles of logarithms,[3] the change to an additive model is

$$\log(F_{ij}) = \log(\mu' \mu_i'^A) = \log(\mu') + \log(\mu_i'^A).$$

Then, letting $L_{ij} = \log(F_{ij})$, $\mu = \log(\mu')$, and $\mu_i^A = \log(\mu_i'^A)$, one obtains an additive model for the cell frequencies. Naturally, it is easy to switch back from the logs to the frequencies themselves by taking antilogarithms. Therefore, after finding a model for L_{ij}, one can quickly convert it to a model for the expected frequencies. In order to simplify the presentation, only models for L_{ij} are described, but they are easily changed to their multiplicative form by taking antilogarithms (for example, $\exp(L_{ij}) = F_{ij}$).

Whatever perspective is taken, the model still asserts statistical independence between A and B *and* that the categories of the column variable (but not the row variable) are equally probable. For most social science data, this model does not seem realistic, so consider an alternative.

---

3. See note 2.

5.2.3 Independence Model. The model, stating only independence between A and B, contains both row and column effects as well as a grand mean:

$$L_{ij} = \mu + \mu_i^A + \mu_j^B. \tag{5.3}$$

The model's most important assertion obviously is that A and B are not associated. It does, however, allow for both row and column effects. It is convenient, especially in later sections, to denote this model $[A \otimes B]$, read simply, "A is statistically independent of B."

According to the model, the logarithm of the cell frequencies in the population can be written as the sum of a grand mean, μ, a set of row effects μ_i^A, and a set of column effects μ_j^B.

The grand mean in any model is defined as the average of all the logarithms of the frequencies:

$$\mu = \frac{\sum_{ij} L_{ij}}{IJ} = \frac{L_{++}}{IJ}, \tag{5.4}$$

where the plus signs denote summation over the appropriate subscript and of course $L_{ij} = \log(F_{ij})$. To obtain a sample estimate of any parameter, replace the L's with the logarithms of the *estimated* expected frequencies. The parameter has no other meaningful interpretation and is seldom found in substantive work.

The main effects, μ_i^A and $\mu_{j'}^B$ are defined as departures from the grand mean. In this respect, they resemble "treatment" effects in analysis of variance. The effect of the ith category is defined as the difference between the mean of the logged frequencies in that class and the grand mean:

$$\mu_i = \frac{\sum_j L_{ij}}{J} - \mu = \frac{L_{i+}}{J} - \mu, \tag{5.5}$$

where L_{i+} is the sum of the logged frequencies in the ith row of an $I \times J$ table.

The corresponding formula for column effects is, naturally enough,

$$\mu_j^B = \frac{\sum_i L_{ij}}{I} - \mu = \frac{L_{+j}}{I} - \mu.$$

Although the definition of effects is intuitively appealing and is analogous to similar definitions in analysis of variance, the interpretation of their numerical values is less meaningful because there is no underlying physical scale. If, for example, the row categories are equally probable, then the average of the logged frequencies in a row would be the same as in any other row and would consequently equal the grand mean. In this case, each μ_i^A would equal zero. But if more cases belong in, say, the first row than in the second or third, then the average of the logarithms in that row would also be larger than the mean and the effect would be positive. The greater the number of cases relative to the other categories, the greater the numerical value of the corresponding effect. The presence of the coefficients in a model has meaning—it indicates nonequi-probability—but the numerical values are somewhat difficult to interpret.

Further insight into the parameters can be gained, however, by substituting their values into the equation to obtain predicted frequencies, a point discussed later.

The model's key feature does not lie in the presence of main effects but rather in the absence of interaction terms. This model underlies the chi square test for independence in a two-way table. Estimated expected frequencies for that test are computed under the hypothesis that only row and column effects (as well as a grand mean) are present. Thus, except for the fact that the parameters are not estimated, the common goodness-of-fit chi square test can be viewed as a test of the fit of the independence model.

5.2.4 Saturated Model. It is easy to expand the previous model to allow for a relationship between A and B:

$$L_{ij} = \mu + \mu_i^A + \mu_j^B + \mu_{ij}^{AB}. \tag{5.6}$$

The model is *saturated* because it contains as many *independent* parameters as there are cells in the table. ("Independent" will be defined shortly.) No more parameters can be added, and a saturated model always fits the observed data in the sense that the expected frequencies estimated under it equal the observed frequencies.

The mean (μ) and main effects (μ_i^A, μ_j^B) have the same meaning. The only new components, μ_{ij}^{AB} (usually called first-order or two-factor interactions), measure the $A-B$ association. Their presence, therefore, implies an absence of statistical independence.

The formal definition of the interaction terms is

$$\mu_{ij}^{AB} = L_{ij} - \frac{\sum_j L_{ij}}{J} - \frac{\sum_i L_{ij}}{I} + \frac{\sum_{ij} L_{ij}}{IJ}$$

$$= L_{ij} - \frac{L_{i+}}{J} - \frac{L_{+j}}{I} + \mu. \tag{5.7}$$

These parameters, it should be noted, are functions of the odds ratios (see Section 2.2.2). If the basic set of odds ratios in an $I \times J$ table equals 1.0, then the interaction terms will equal zero; and conversely, if some of the odds ratios do not equal 1.0, then at least some of the μ^{AB}'s will not be zero.

The use of μ terms as measures of association has advantages and disadvantages. On the positive side, their presence can be quite informative because they show how and where the variables are related. Moreover, like other indices, they increase in absolute value with increases in the strength of the association. If a set of μ^{AB}'s tends as a whole to be close to zero, one would infer a weak relationship and, similarly, large values would suggest a stronger connection. Being functions of the odds ratio, moreover, they are insensitive to the marginal variation in A and B.

On the negative side, each cell of the tables has its own interaction term. So instead of a single summary index, one is left with a matrix of measures. When I and J each have several categories, the number of coefficients to calculate and interpret is quite large. Further compounding the problem is the fact that they are not bounded. In practice, their absolute value usually falls between 0 and 1.0, but not always. Finally, one cannot give them a clear physical or statistical meaning such as the proportion of variance explained.

5.2.5 The Hierarchy Principle. Is it possible to develop a model containing two-factor interactions (μ_{ij}^{AB}) but with no row or column effects? In principle, yes, but the mathematics are more difficult. Therefore, permissible log-linear models are limited by the *hierarchy principle*:

> *If a μ term in a model contains in its superscript a set of letters, S, representing different variables, then the model must also contain μ terms corresponding to all subsets of these letters.*

As an illustration, if μ_{ij}^{AB} is included, $S = \{AB\}$ and the model must also contain μ_i^A and μ_j^B since A and B are subsets of S. Or seen from the opposite direction, if μ_i^A is *not* included in the model, then neither is μ_{ij}^{AB}. Models following this principle are called *hierarchical*. Nonhierarchical models are not considered here.[4] Adherence to the hierarchy principle, incidentally, simplifies notation. Instead of writing out all the parameters in a model, one can more succinctly describe it by listing only the higher-order terms, realizing that their lower-order relatives are included as well. Thus, for a two-dimensional table, the notation μ_{ij}^{AB}—or even more simply, the set of letters $\{AB\}$—implies a model having μ, $\mu_{i'}^A$ μ_j^B, as well as μ_{ij}^{AB}. The notation $\{S\}$, where S is a set of letters representing variables, is used extensively throughout.

---

4. The hierarchy principle means that some models of potential interest cannot be explored. Occasionally a hierarchical model does not fit the data when a nonhierarchical one does. Although this is a potentially serious drawback (Evers and Namboodiri, 1976), hierarchical models ought to be satisfactory for many purposes. Chapter 7 describes a technique for analyzing both types of model.

5.3 MODELS FOR THREE-WAY TABLES

Three-variable models pertain to $L_{ijk'}$ the natural logarithms of the expected frequencies, in an $I \times J \times K$ table. One might consider models having no effects or having only effects for the row, column, or layer variables. But these models have little practical value because social scientists seldom study variables with equally probable classes. A more interesting case is mutual independence.

5.3.1 Mutual Independence Model.   The mutual independence model contains only main effects along with a grand mean:

$$L_{ijk} = \mu + \mu_i^A + \mu_j^B + \mu_{k'}^C \qquad (5.8)$$

where L_{ijk} is the natural logarithm of the expected frequency F_{ijk} in the ijkth cell of an $I \times J \times K$ table.

The model asserts mutual independence among the three variables. It states, in other words, that by most standards all pairs of variables are unrelated. For instance, the basic sets of odds ratios between A and B all equal 1.0 except for sampling error in all levels of C, the control variable. Following previous practice, we denote the model $[A \otimes B \otimes C]$ and describe it by the set of letters $\{A\}$, $\{B\}$, $\{C\}$ since there are no higher-order terms present.

Tables satisfying this standard have an important property. Suppose that one creates a marginal table between, say, A and B, denoted $\{AB\}$, by adding over the levels of C. Then, with regard to A and B, the marginal table has the same characteristics as the full table. Specifically, A and B are statistically independent *and* the row and column effects μ_i^A and μ_j^B have the same numerical value as they do in the full table. (The grand mean does change, however.)

The upshot is that under this model, ignoring variable C does not affect the relationship between A and B. Hence, it is immaterial whether A and B are analyzed in the full or reduced table. This result not only simplifies the analysis but means that even if one had inadvertently not measured C, the conclusions about A and B would still be valid.[5]

The main effects are calculated in the same general way as in two-dimensional tables except for an additional dimension to sum over. For instance,

$$\mu_i^A = \frac{\sum\limits_{jk} L_{ijk}}{JK} - \frac{\sum\limits_{ijk} L_{ijk}}{IJK} = \frac{L_{i++}}{JK} - \mu, \qquad (5.9)$$

---

5. This applies to any pair of variables, since they are all mutually independent.

where $\sum\limits_{ijk}$ means summation over all IJK cells and, as before, the $+$ signs mean summation over the appropriate subscript.

5.3.2 Model with One Two-Factor Interaction.

Suppose a researcher feels, on the one hand, that A and B are related, but on the other that neither is related to C. Therefore, he proposes a model having a single set of two-factor interactions:

$$L_{ijk} = \mu + \mu_i^A + \mu_j^B + \mu_k^C + \mu_{ij}^{AB}. \tag{5.10}$$

This model asserts, among other things, that (1) A and B are related, and (2) this relationship does *not* depend in any way on C because (3) A and B are not related to C. It also states that the classes of A, B, and C are not equally probable.[6]

Perhaps a concrete example at this point would be helpful. Consider the hypothetical data in Table 5.1 as *population* cross-classification between (A) vote for Senate, (B) party identification, and (C) partisan attitude. The numbers have been contrived to fit the single two-factor interaction model (5.10).

Computing the basic odds ratios within each subtable, one finds that voting and party identification are related and, perhaps just as important, that the form and strength of the association is the same in each subtable. Hence, there is *no higher-order interaction* in this model.

The lack of a higher-order interaction can be started more formally. Let $\alpha_{ij(k)}$ be the ijth odds ratio in the kth subtable:

$$\alpha_{ij(k)} = \frac{F_{ijk}F_{IJk}}{F_{Ijk}F_{iJk}} \qquad (i = 1, \ldots, I-1; \, j = 1, \ldots, J-1). \tag{5.11}$$

Then the absence of higher-order interactions implied by model (5.10) means that the $\alpha_{ij(k)}$, serving as measures of association between A and B, are the same in each level of C:

$$\alpha_{ij(k)} = \alpha_{ij*} \qquad \text{for} \qquad k = 1, \ldots, K. \tag{5.12}$$

This property holds exactly for the data in Table 5.1 except for rounding errors produced in the generation of the data.[7] For example, α_{11} is approximately 35 in all three tables, and it is easy to verify that the

---

6. Since the μ_{ij}^{AB} term is present, main effect parameters for A and B must be included, too. In this respect, μ_k^C is optional but is added for realism. Removing it would not alter the model's key features.

7. Note, incidentally, that this is not the only way to define interaction. For further discussion, see Bhapkar and Koch (1968a, 1968b), Birch (1963), Darroch, (1974), Gart (1972), Lewis (1962), and Plackett (1974), as well as Goodman's articles cited above.

TABLE 5.1. **Example of Data Fitting the Model*** $\mu + \mu_i^A + \mu_j^B + \mu_k^C + \mu_{ij}^{AB}$

		Pro-Democratic			*C: Attitude* Neutral			Pro-Republican		
		B: Party			*B: Party*			*B: Party*		
		D	I	R	D	I	R	D	I	R
A: Vote	D	348	97	36	382	107	40	373	105	39
	R	65	108	243	72	119	264	70	116	259
Total		413	205	279	454	226	304	443	221	298

*Hypothetical data.   Key: D = Democrat, I = Independent, R = Republican.

remaining basic odds ratios are the same across subtables. With sample data one has to estimate how well this condition is satisfied.[8]

Since both *A* and *B* are independent of *C*, they can be considered as a joint variable unrelated to attitude. Combining *A* and *B*, in other words, leads to an $IJ \times K$ two-dimensional table in which the joint variable (*AB*) is statistically independent of *C*. Continuing with the independence notation, let $[AB \otimes C]$ denote this model.

As a consequence of the independence of *A* and *B* from *C*, collapsing or combining the categories of the control variable does not change the nature of their interrelationship. The {*AB*} marginal table derived from Table 5.1 is

		B: Party		
		Dem.	Ind.	Rep.
A: Vote	Dem.	1103	309	115
	Rep.	207	343	766
		1310	652	881

Here, the *AB* relationship, as measured either by odds ratios or by μ terms, has the same magnitude as in each subtable of Table 5.1.

According to the model, furthermore, *A* and *C* are independent. They stay independent even in the $I \times K$ marginal {*AC*} table formed by adding over the categories of *B*. Similarly, collapsing *A* does not create an association between *B* and *C* in the $J \times K$ marginal {*BC*} table. In this model, as in the previous one, collapsing any variable, whether intentionally or not, does not affect the form and strength of relationships, at least as

8. Goodman, among others, has developed numerous methods for testing differences between observed odds ratios (Goodman, 1963, 1964a, 1964b, 1964c, 1964d, 1965c, 1969b).

measured by odds ratios or two-factor μ parameters. This imperviousness of the relationships does not hold for all models, however.

5.3.3 A Note on Calculating Parameters.

Two-factor interactions can be computed just as in the $I \times J$ table, except that the calculation involves another dimension.[9] The parameter μ_{ij}^{AB} is defined as

$$\mu_{ij}^{AB} = \frac{L_{ij+}}{K} - \frac{L_{i++}}{JK} - \frac{L_{+j+}}{IK} + \frac{L_{+++}}{IJK}, \tag{5.13}$$

where, as always, $+$ denotes summation and $L_{ijk} = \log(F_{ijk})$. For example, $L_{ij+} = \sum_k \log(F_{ijk})$.

In Table 5.1,

$$\mu_{11}^{AB} = \frac{L_{11+}}{3} - \frac{L_{1++}}{9} - \frac{L_{+1+}}{6} + \frac{L_{+++}}{18}$$

$$= \left[\frac{\log(348) + \log(382) + \log(373)}{3} \right]$$

$$- \left[\frac{\log(348) + \log(97) + \cdots + \log(39)}{9} \right]$$

$$- \left[\frac{\log(348) + \log(65) + \log(382) + \cdots + \log(70)}{6} \right]$$

$$+ \left[\frac{\log(348) + \log(97) + \cdots + \log(259)}{18} \right]$$

$$= .891.$$

The two-factor interactions, calculated in a similar way, are

$$\mu_{11} = .891 \qquad \mu_{12} = .002 \qquad \mu_{13} = -.894$$
$$\mu_{21} = -.891 \qquad \mu_{22} = -.002 \qquad \mu_{23} = .894$$

Perhaps a clearer interpretation of two-factor interactions is as the average of the two-factor μ's in a set of subtables. Viewing Table 5.1 as three separate 2×3 tables, one computes the two-factor interaction in each, using formula (5.7) (Section 5.2.4), and then takes their average. More formally,

$$\mu_{ij}^{AB} = \frac{\sum \mu_{ij(k)}^{AB}}{K},$$

where $\mu_{ij(k)}^{AB}$ denotes the interaction term in the kth subtable. In Table 5.1, $\mu_{11(1)}^{AB}$, $\mu_{11(2)}^{AB}$, and $\mu_{11(3)}^{AB}$ are all .891, and naturally their average is

---

9. Calculation of main effects and the grand mean is given by equation (5.9).

.891, as it should be. The three terms equal each other because there is no *three*-factor interaction.

5.3.4 Model with Two Two-Factor Interactions.

A model with two two-factor interactions is a straightforward extension of the previous one:

$$L_{ijk} = \mu + \mu_i^A + \mu_j^B + \mu_k^C + \mu_{ik}^{AC} + \mu_{jk}^{BC}. \tag{5.14}$$

Now, only *A* and *B* remain unrelated. More precisely, there is no *direct* relationship between them but they are indirectly or spuriously related because both are connected to *C*. From another perspective, someone examining the {*AB*} marginal table alone might be misled into thinking that they are associated. The association, however, is due solely to their connection with *C*. In causal terms, assuming that no other variables are operative, a change in *C* produces changes in both *A* and *B* and thus the latter two variables seem to co-vary. Only when *C* is explicitly taken into account does the independence between *A* and *B* become evident. For this reason, the model asserts *conditional* independence, denoted $[A \otimes B \mid C]$.

Consequently, if this model holds, it is inappropriate—very misleading, in fact—to analyze the collapsed {*AB*} marginal table. It would be equally fallacious to combine some of *C*'s categories. That is, one might find a relationship between *A* and *B* in an $I \times J \times K'$ table, where $K' < K$, even though *A* and *B* are independent in the full $I \times J \times K$ table. We return to this point shortly.

Models obeying conditional independence have noteworthy properties. Although *A* and *B* may be related in the marginal {*AB*} table, the relationship disappears in the three-way table where *C* is explicitly controlled. There is, in other words, no higher-order interaction; in terms of equation (5.12),

$$\alpha_{ij(k)} = 1.0 \qquad \text{for } i = 1, \ldots, I-1; \ j = 1, \ldots, J-1; \text{ and all } k.$$

On the other hand, there are direct relationships between *A* and *C* and *B* and *C*. Suppose that one arranged the data so that *B* was the control variable. Then the nature of the *AC* association would be the same within each level of *B*. (This is also true when *A* is held constant.)

It should be noted here that models with one and two two-factor interactions have different versions, depending on which relationships are excluded. The previous model has three versions, since either μ_{ij}^{AB}, μ_{ik}^{AC}, or μ_{jk}^{BC} could be left out.

5.3.5 Model with All Pairwise Interactions.

To allow for the third set of two-factor interactions, simply add μ_{ij}^{AB} to the previous model:

$$L_{ijk} = \mu + \mu_i^A + \mu_j^B + \mu_k^C + \mu_{ij}^{AB} + \mu_{ik}^{AC} + \mu_{jk}^{BC}, \tag{5.15}$$

The interpretation if straightforward. The model, denoted $[ABC = 0]$, asserts that every variable is directly associated with every other variable. The presence of a two-factor μ term implies a direct connection. Controlling or holding one variable constant does not wipe out the relationship between the other two. For this reason, the model is a bit more complex but also more general and perhaps more realistic for many situations.

In one way the model is quite simple. The form and strength of the relationship as measured by the odds ratio between any two variables is the same in all levels of the control variable. That is, for example,

$$\alpha_{ij(k)} = \alpha_{ij*} \qquad \text{for } i = 1, \ldots, I-1; \, j = 1, \ldots, J-1; \text{ and all } k.$$

Similar remarks apply to the other sets of odds ratios, $\alpha_{(i)jk}$ and $\alpha_{i(j)k}$.

This phenomenon, called *no three-factor interaction*, or more simply, *no interaction*, was described in Chapter 4 (see Figure 4.1b). It is easier to explain a relationship that does not depend on the level of a third variable than to account for one that depends on other variables. Therefore, social scientists usually look first for the presence of three-factor interactions.

If this model holds, one cannot collapse or combine the categories of a variable without changing, often in a striking manner, the association between the other two. The AB relationship, for instance, is almost always noticeably different in the $\{AB\}$ marginal table than it is in the full cross-tabulation. I mention this point with every model because of its critical importance in analyzing and interpreting multidimensional tables.

5.3.6 Saturated Model.
A three-variable model containing a three-factor interaction term is saturated because the number of *independent* parameters (explained below) equals the total number of cells in the cross-classification. The model,

$$L_{ijk} = \mu + \mu_i^A + \mu_j^B + \mu_k^C + \mu_{ij}^{AB} + \mu_{jk}^{BC} + \mu_{ik}^{AC} + \mu_{ijk}^{ABC}, \qquad (5.16)$$

states many of the things the previous one did. It asserts, in particular, that all three variables are interrelated. And by the hierarchy principle the model also contains all main effects.

The new elements, μ_{ijk}^{ABC}, called three-factor interactions, are defined as

$$\mu_{ijk}^{ABC} = L_{ijk} - \frac{L_{ij+}}{K} - \frac{L_{i+k}}{J} - \frac{L_{+jk}}{I} + \frac{L_{i++}}{JK} + \frac{L_{+j+}}{IK} + \frac{L_{++k}}{IJ} - \frac{L_{+++}}{IJK}. \qquad (5.17)$$

The presence of three-factor interactions means that the association between any two variables changes with changes in the level of the third variable. According to this model, the relationship between, say, A and B must be "specified" for each level of C. Figure 4.1 presents intuitive examples of both the presence and absence of three-factor interactions.

The important point, the figure reveals, is that interaction implies different relationships within categories of the control variable. The more formal definition of interaction implies, for example, that

$$\alpha_{ij(k)} \neq \alpha_{ij*} \quad \text{for } i = 1, \ldots, I-1; \; j = 1, \ldots, J-1; \text{ and } k = 1, \ldots, K.$$

The μ_{ijk}^{ABC} terms are also interpretable as measures of the magnitude of the differences among two-factor interactions. Suppose that one computes μ_{ij}^{AB} for each category of C and then obtains their average. Denote the individual terms $\mu_{ij(k)}^{AB}$ and their averages by μ_{ij}^{AB}, as in Section 5.3.3. The three-factor interaction measures the difference between an individual $\mu_{ij(k)}^{AB}$ and the average:

$$\mu_{ijk}^{ABC} = \mu_{ij(k)}^{AB} - \mu_{ij}^{AB}.$$

The larger the discrepancies, the larger μ_{ijk}^{ABC} will be. This in turn means that each subtable has its own level of relationship.

A specific example may again be helpful. Think for a moment of the data in Table 4.1 as a population cross-classification relating voting to party identification within categories of partisan attitude. These data illustrate some of the model's features.

The calculation of the main effects, the two-factor and the three-factor interactions, is performed according to formulas (5.9), (5.13), and (5.17), respectively. For example,

$$\mu_{111}^{ABC} = \log(620) - \frac{\log(620) + \log(367) + \log(116)}{3}$$

$$- \frac{\log(620) + \log(89) + \log(13)}{3} - \frac{\log(620) + \log(80)}{2}$$

$$+ \frac{\log(620) + \cdots + \log(50)}{9} + \frac{\log(620) + \cdots + \log(63)}{6}$$

$$+ \frac{\log(620) + \cdots + \log(55)}{6} - \frac{\log(620) + \cdots + \log(511)}{18}$$

$$= .017.$$

The 18 three-factor interaction terms, written without superscripts, are

$\mu_{111} = .017$	$\mu_{113} = -.049$	$\mu_{212} = -.033$
$\mu_{121} = .125$	$\mu_{123} = -.020$	$\mu_{222} = .105$
$\mu_{131} = -.142$	$\mu_{133} = .070$	$\mu_{232} = -.072$
$\mu_{112} = .033$	$\mu_{211} = -.017$	$\mu_{213} = .049$
$\mu_{122} = -.105$	$\mu_{221} = -.125$	$\mu_{223} = .020$
$\mu_{132} = .072$	$\mu_{231} = .142$	$\mu_{233} = -.070$

Notice that the sum of these parameters equals zero when added over any subscripts. The same is true of two- and one-factor terms. For instance, $\mu_1^A = -.039$ whereas $\mu_2^A = .039$. This property, analogous to analysis of variance effects, holds for *all* models and reduces the number of parameters that have to be calculated because the remainder are obtained by subtraction (see the next section).

One can also determine that the effect of party identification on voting varies within categories of attitude. This is clear from the μ_{ij}^{AB} terms or the odds ratios. For instance, $\alpha_{11(1)} = 32.79$ whereas $\alpha_{11(2)} = 22.05$ and $\alpha_{11(3)} = 18.82$. Any rearrangement of the table produces similar results: the nature of the relationship between any two variables depends on the level of the third.

Finally, as in the previous model, collapsing a variable affects the association between the other two. In the two-way $\{AB\}$ marginal table, for example, $\mu_{11}^{AB} = .891$, whereas in the full array $\mu_{11}^{AB} = .773$. From another point of view, $\alpha_{11} = 35.492$ in the marginal table, a different value from those reported in the previous paragraph. A stronger interaction would make the differences even greater.

5.3.7 Independent Parameters.   All μ terms in log-linear models sum to zero over any of their subscripts; that is, for example,

$$\sum_i \mu_i^A = \sum_j \mu_j^B = \sum_i \mu_{ij}^{AB} = \sum_j \mu_{ij}^{AB} = \sum_i \mu_{ijk}^{ABC} = \sum_j \mu_{ijk}^{ABC} = \sum_k \mu_{ijk}^{ABC} = 0.$$

This property, similar to the behavior of treatment or experimental effects in the analysis of variance, results from their being deviations from means. These constraints lead to a practical advantage. Once all but one member of a set have been determined, the last one can be calculated automatically by subtraction. (See the previous section for examples.) Consequently, not all of the parameters are independent.

The number of independent parameters pertaining to an effect is less than the full set. For an $I \times J$ table, the numbers of *independent* parameters associated with the row, column, and interaction effects are $I - 1$, $J - 1$, and $(I - 1)(J - 1)$, respectively.

The *total* number of independent parameters for a specific model is 1 (for the grand mean) plus the number of *independent* μ terms included in that model. For the independence model in an $I \times J$ table, the total is

Grand Mean:	1
Row Effects:	$I - 1$
Column Effects:	$J - 1$
Total:	$1 + (I - 1) + (J - 1) = I + J - 1$

For the $I \times J \times K$ table with no three-factor interactions (model 5.15), the total is

Grand Mean:	1
Row Effects:	$I-1$
Column Effects:	$J-1$
Layer Effects:	$K-1$
$A \times B$ Interaction:	$(I-1)(J-1)$
$A \times C$ Interaction:	$(I-1)(K-1)$
$B \times C$ Interaction:	$(J-1)(K-1)$
Total:	$IJ + IK + JK - I - J - K + 1$

The constraints thus reduce the coefficients needed to describe a model. If the variables are dichotomous, only a single parameter for each type of effect is required.

5.4 MODELS FOR HIGHER-DIMENSIONAL TABLES

The basic ideas of log–linear analysis—mutual independence, conditional independence, equiprobability, interaction—readily extend to tables consisting of more than three variables. Additional variables merely increase the variety of types and versions of models. There are altogether eight basic models for three-dimensional tables, although many of them (for example, $L_{ijk} = \mu$) are trivial. With four variables, the number rises to 27 and, again, many have several variations.

Their meaning is easily determined from an inspection of the included and excluded μ parameters. I present a few four-variable models simply to reemphasize the general principles.

5.4.1 Mutual Independence Model. Mutual independence, denoted $[A \otimes B \otimes C \otimes D]$, means that the variables in four-way, $I \times J \times K \times L$ tables are unrelated:

$$L_{ijkl} = \mu + \mu_i^A + \mu_j^B + \mu_k^C + \mu_l^D, \tag{5.18}$$

where, for example,

$$\mu_i^A = \frac{\sum\limits_{jkl} L_{ijkl}}{JKL} - \frac{\sum\limits_{ijkl} L_{ijkl}}{IJKL} = \frac{L_{i+++}}{JKL} - \frac{L_{++++}}{IJKL} = \frac{L_{i+++}}{JKL} - \mu. \tag{5.19}$$

Everything said about mutual independence among three variables applies here as well. Independence implies that collapsing over any variable or group of variables does not alter the relationships among the remaining variables.

5.4.2 Model with All Two-Factor Interactions.   As opposed to mutual independence, this model asserts that all pairs of variables are related:

$$L_{ijkl} = \mu + \mu_i^A + \mu_j^B + \mu_k^C + \mu_l^D + \mu_{ij}^{AB} + \mu_{ik}^{AC} + \mu_{il}^{AD} + \mu_{jk}^{BC} + \mu_{jl}^{BD} + \mu_{kl}^{CD}.$$

$$(5.20)$$

The two-factor parameters, which measure the relationship between two variables, are calculated like the two-factor μ terms in a three-variable model. For example,

$$\mu_{il}^{AD} = \frac{L_{i++l}}{JK} - \frac{L_{i+++}}{JKL} - \frac{L_{+++l}}{IJK} + \mu.$$

Alternatively, one may view it as an average two-factor term across all JK levels of variables B and C:

$$\mu_{il}^{AD} = \frac{\sum_{jk} \mu_{il(jk)}^{AD}}{JK},$$

where $\mu_{il(jk)}^{AD}$ is the two-factor interaction between A and D in the jkth subtable.

Since this model contains all pairwise interactions, it is not possible to collapse completely or partially any variable. On the other hand, the nature of the association between any two variables stays exactly the same at each level of the remaining variables.

5.4.3 A Model with One Three-Factor Interaction.   Consider the following model:

$$L_{ijkl} = \mu + \mu_i^A + \mu_j^B + \mu_k^C + \mu_l^D + \mu_{ij}^{AB} + \mu_{ik}^{AC} + \mu_{jk}^{BC} + \mu_{ijk}^{ABC}, \quad (5.20)$$

where

$$\mu_{ijk}^{ABC} = \frac{L_{ijk+}}{L} - \frac{L_{ij++}}{KL} - \frac{L_{i+k+}}{JL} - \frac{L_{+jk+}}{IL} + \frac{L_{i+++}}{JKL} + \frac{L_{+j++}}{IKL} + \frac{L_{++k+}}{IJL} - \mu. \quad (5.21)$$

It is easiest to demonstrate the model's characteristics with hypothetical data. Table 5.2 cross-tabulates (A) voting, (B) party identification, (C) partisan attitudes, and (D) "incumbency," a variable indicating whether or not the election involved an incumbent.

Model (5.20) really consists of two submodels. Since elections involving incumbents were more prevalent than those with no incumbent, a main effect for D is included. But otherwise D is unrelated to A, B, and C. Denote this submodel as $[D \otimes ABC]$, which means that D is independent of the joint variable, ABC.[10] As a result, D is "collapsible" with respect to the other variables.[11]

---

10. The reader can verify this for himself by rearranging Table 5.2 into an $L \times IJK$ table and testing for independence.

11. The reader can also verify this by combining the two portions of Table 5.2 into a $2 \times 3 \times 3$ marginal table where both the μ terms and odds ratios pertaining to A, B, and C are the same as in the full table. But it is *not* possible to collapse the table further.

TABLE 5.2. **Example of Data Fitting the Model**

$$\mu + \mu_i^A + \mu_j^B + \mu_k^C + \mu_l^D + \mu_{ij}^{AB} + \mu_{ik}^{AC} + \mu_{jk}^{BC} + \mu_{ijk}^{ABC}$$

		D_1: Incumbent								
						C: Attitude					
		Pro-Democratic			Neutral			Pro-Republican		
		B: Party			*B: Party*			*B: Party*		
		D	I	R	D	I	R	D	I	R
A: Vote	D	481	285	90	69	117	54	10	40	39
	R	62	50	49	31	116	119	43	155	396
	Total	543	335	139	100	233	173	53	195	435

$\alpha_{11(11)} = 4.23$	$\alpha_{11(21)} = 4.91$	$\alpha_{11(31)} = 2.36$
$\alpha_{12(11)} = 3.10$	$\alpha_{12(21)} = 2.22$	$\alpha_{12(31)} = 2.62$

		D_2: No Incumbent								
						C: Attitude					
		Pro-Democratic			Neutral			Pro-Republican		
		B: Party			*B: Party*			*B: Party*		
		D	I	R	D	I	R	D	I	R
A: Vote	D	139	82	26	19	34	15	3	12	11
	R	18	14	14	9	34	34	12	45	115
	Total	157	96	40	28	68	49	15	57	126

$\alpha_{11(12)} = 4.16$	$\alpha_{11(22)} = 4.89$	$\alpha_{11(32)} = 2.61$
$\alpha_{12(12)} = 3.15$	$\alpha_{12(12)} = 2.27$	$\alpha_{12(32)} = 2.79$

Key: D = Democrat, I = Independent, R = Republican.

In the other submodel, the three-factor interaction term, μ_{ijk}^{ABC}, means that the association between A and B varies with levels of C. As a consequence of the independence of D from the other variables, however, the nature of the interaction is not affected by D.

The situation is most easily seen in the α's. Although the differences among them are not dramatic, they nevertheless change as one moves across levels of partisan attitude. Note, however, that the pattern of α's is the same in both categories of D except for rounding errors.

The interpretation of the three-factor interaction in the three-variable case (Section 5.3.5) applies here as well. Specifically, μ_{ijk}^{ABC} measures the difference between a two-factor interaction, $\mu_{ij(k)}^{AB}$, in the kth subtable and the mean of all such terms across the K subtables *for a given level of D.* Unfortunately, the substantive interpretation of these terms is somewhat awkward: the strength of the relationship between voting and party identification is strongest among individuals who have pro-Democratic or neutral attitudes and weakest among Republicans.

In short, model (5.20) can be decomposed or partitioned into two parts: the first asserts the independence of D from the joint variable

ABC, whereas the second states the presence of a three-factor interaction among A, B, and C. Adopting a notation similar to Goodman's (1970), we represent the model as $[D \otimes ABC] \cap [ABC \neq 0]$.

Notice, incidentally, that this model follows the hierarchy principle: since μ_{ijk}^{ABC} is included, all lower-order relatives are included as well. It would be impermissible, for example, to leave out μ_i^A.

5.4.4 A Model with Four Three-Factor Interactions.

The most complex four-variable model, except for a saturated model, has all possible three-factor interactions, μ_{ijk}^{ABC}, μ_{ijl}^{ABD}, μ_{ikl}^{ACD}, and μ_{jkl}^{BCD}. Following the hierarchy principle, the model also contains all six two-factor interactions, four main effects, and a grand mean. It therefore has 15 sets of parameters, and for even moderate I, J, K, and L, there are large numbers of independent parameters. Most investigators find the interpretation of the higher-order terms extremely difficult. Nevertheless, they often have to be considered.

The three-factor terms have the same meaning as in other models: the association between any two variables depends on the third. The only difference is that, in this model, interaction exists among any set of three variables.

The absence of a four-factor term, μ_{ijkl}^{ABCD}, however, at least indicates that the three-factor interactions are not affected by a fourth variable. Figure 5.1 illustrates the point. In the top panel, the pattern of association between A, B, and C is the same in both levels of D.

We can also describe four-factor interaction by generalizing the familiar odds ratio. Let $\alpha_{ijk(l)}$ denote a measure of association between A, B, and C in the lth category of D:

$$\alpha_{ijk(l)} = \frac{F_{ijkl}F_{IJkl}/F_{Ijkl}F_{iJkl}}{F_{ijKl}F_{IJKl}/F_{IjKl}F_{iJKl}} = \frac{\alpha_{ij(kl)}}{\alpha_{ij(Kl)}},$$

where $\alpha_{ij(kl)}$ is the ij odds ratio at the kth level of C and lth level of D for $i < I$, $j < J$, and $k < K$ (Bhapkar and Koch, 1968a, 1968b). The term $\alpha_{ijk(l)}$ is thus a ratio of odds ratios, the first pertaining to the kth level of C and the other to the Kth (last) level. Both ratios, $\alpha_{ij(kl)}$ and $\alpha_{ij(Kl)}$, are computed within the lth class of D. The model asserts that the $\alpha_{ijk(l)}$, which measure the magnitude of three-factor interactions, are constant across all categories of D,

$$\alpha_{ijk(l)} = \alpha_{ijk*}, \tag{5.22}$$

for $i < I$, $j < J$, $k < K$, and all l.

As heuristic devices, the odds ratios help clarify the meaning of no four-factor interaction. A similar argument can be made for the μ terms. Briefly, consider L three-way $I \times J \times K$ tables and calculate $\mu_{ijk(l)}^{ABC}$ for each $(l = 1, \ldots, L)$ using formula (5.17). Their average is equivalent to μ_{ijk}^{ABC}

FIGURE 5.1. **Intuitive Interpretation of Four-Factor Interaction**

a. No Four-Factor Interaction

D_1

	C_1		C_2		C_3
	B		B		B
A	Strong Relationship	A	Weak Relationship	A	Moderate Relationship

D_2

	C_1		C_2		C_3
	B		B		B
A	Strong Relationship	A	Weak Relationship	A	Moderate Relationship

b. Four-Factor Interaction

D_1

	C_1		C_2		C_3
	B		B		B
A	Strong Relationship	A	Weak Relationship	A	Strong Relationship

D_2

	C_1		C_2		C_3
	B		B		B
A	Weak Relationship	A	Strong Relationship	A	Weak Relationship

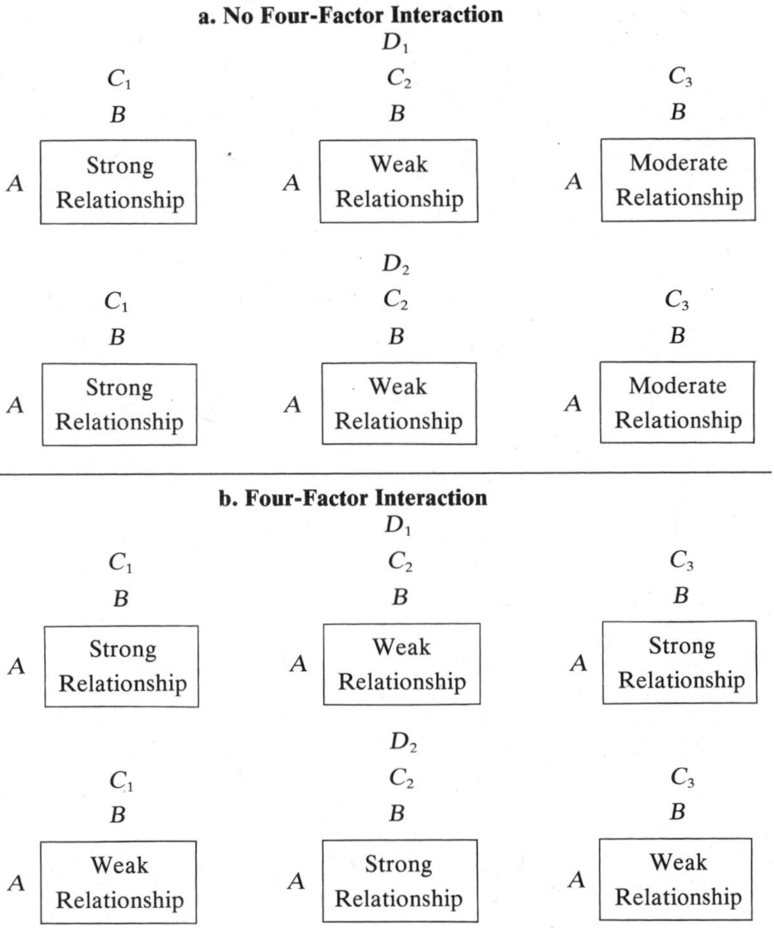

as computed from (5.21) above. If there is no four-factor interaction, the separate $\mu_{ijk(l)}^{ABC}$ equal each other. Consequently, the four-factor interaction is

$$\mu_{ijkl}^{ABCD} = \mu_{ijk}^{ABC} - \mu_{ijk(l)}^{ABC} = 0, \tag{5.23}$$

for all l. In keeping with previous practice, we denote the model $[ABCD = 0]$.

In this as in many other models, it would be wrong to collapse some or all of a variable's categories. Doing so usually changes the μ terms pertaining to the remaining variables. What might be a weak interaction in the full table could become a strong one in the reduced cross-classification. Section 5.6 explains rules for deciding when a variable can safely be collapsed.

5.4.5 Saturated Four-Variable Model.

The saturated four-variable model differs from the previous one only by the inclusion of μ_{ijkl}^{ABCD} terms, the meaning of which should be clear by now. Their presence indicates a lack of constancy in three-variable interactions. Thus, for example, equations (5.22) and (5.23) do not hold. The larger the four-factor terms, the greater the differences among three-factor interactions.

The calculation of μ_{ijkl}^{ABCD} proceeds along the same lines as the computation of other terms:

$$\mu_{ijkl}^{ABCD} = L_{ijkl} - \frac{L_{ijk+}}{L} - \frac{L_{ij+l}}{K} - \frac{L_{i+kl}}{J} - \frac{L_{+jkl}}{I} + \frac{L_{ij++}}{KL} + \frac{L_{i+k+}}{JL} + \frac{L_{i++l}}{JK} + \frac{L_{+jk+}}{IL}$$

$$+ \frac{L_{+j+l}}{IK} + \frac{L_{++kl}}{IJ} - \frac{L_{i+++}}{JKL} - \frac{L_{+j++}}{IKL} - \frac{L_{++k+}}{IJL} - \frac{L_{+++l}}{IJK} + \frac{L_{++++}}{IJKL}.$$

$$(5.24)$$

As in the two- and three-variable cases, the number of included independent parameters equals the number of cells in the cross-classification. A four-way table has $IJKL$ cells, which equals the number of independent main effects, interactions, and grand mean. Roughly speaking, this means that all independent information in the table has been exhausted, leaving none for testing purposes. Furthermore, the structure of the data cannot be simplified, for there is not mutual or conditional independence and each two-variable relationship depends on the remaining variables.

5.4.6 Additional Models for Four or More Variables.

There are various other four-variable models, each having different versions depending on the particular variables included and excluded. They are interpretable within a common framework, however.[12] One simply applies the concepts of equiprobability, mutual and conditional independence, interaction, and the hierarchy principle.

Consider, for instance, a model for an $I \times J \times K \times L$ table containing two three-factor interactions, μ_{ijk}^{ABC} and μ_{ijl}^{ABD}. According to the hierarchy principle, the model also includes five two-factor interactions (that is, μ_{ij}^{AB}, μ_{ik}^{AC}, μ_{il}^{AD}, μ_{jk}^{BC}, μ_{jl}^{BD}), four main effects, and the grand mean. Since μ_{kl}^{CD} is missing, C and D are conditionally independent given the levels of A and B (that is, $[C \otimes D \mid AB]$). The addition of μ_{kl}^{CD} changes the model

---

12. Additional methods for interpreting models are given in Chapter 6.

so that only two three-factor and the four-factor interactions are zero (that is, $[ACD = BCD = ABCD = 0]$).

The same ideas extend to higher-dimensional tables. The only new concepts are r-factor interactions, where r is the number of variables. But these terms are straightforward generalizations of lower-order interactions. For additional explanations of log-linear models and various parameters, see Bishop (1969), Bishop, Fienberg, and Holland (1975), Davis (1974), Fienberg (1970a), Goodman (1970, 1971b, 1972a, 1972b, 1973a, 1975b), Haberman (1974), and Shaffer (1973).

5.5 AN ALTERNATIVE VIEW OF LOG–LINEAR MODELS

Until this point, the "dependent" variable, the logarithm of expected frequencies, has been expressed as a function of various parameters. Attention has been on the interpretation and calculation of these terms while taking for granted the meaningfulness of the dependent variable. Quite often, however, one does not want to explain cell frequencies or probabilities but rather another aspect of the data.

If one variable clearly depends on the others, either temporally or causally, it is possible to rewrite the models to emphasize the dependency. Suppose that one is interested in the rate of voting Democratic among various groups. This rate, called for convenience the voting ratio, is

$$\frac{\text{No. of Individuals Voting Democratic}}{\text{No. of Individuals Voting Republican}}.$$

The goal is to build a model that explicitly explains variation in this ratio. Therefore, instead of looking at the F's alone, one develops models for the ratio of two expected frequencies. Consider a $2 \times J \times K$ population table. The ratio can be stated as the odds of being in the first category of variable A:

$$\Omega_{jk}^{A} = \frac{F_{1jk}}{F_{2jk}}, \tag{5.25}$$

where the subscripts emphasize the dependence of the ratio on the categories of B and C. This expresses the notion, in other words, that the odds of being in A's first category (e.g., the odds of voting Democratic) vary with changes in the level of the other variables.

To obtain a linear model,[13] take logarithms

$$\Phi_{jk}^{A} = \log \Omega_{jk}^{A} = \log\left(\frac{F_{1jk}}{F_{2jk}}\right) = \log(F_{1jk}) - \log(F_{2jk}). \tag{5.26}$$

(This assumes that $F_{ijk} > 0$ for all i, j, k.)

---

13. See the remarks in Section 5.2 on additive versus multiplicative models. As before, one switches from one type to another by taking logarithms and antilogarithms (see Goodman, 1972a, 1972b, 1973a).

Continuing with the example, let Φ_{jk}^{A} be the logarithm of the odds of voting Democratic in the jth category of B (say, party identification) and kth category of C (say, partisan attitude).[14] Although the quantity may be studied from a number of perspectives, it is easy to construct a log–linear model for it. Suppose, for example, we consider a model asserting no three-factor interaction among A, B, and C (i.e., model (5.15)). Letting $L_{1jk} = \log(F_{1jk})$ and $L_{2jk} = \log(F_{2jk})$, we find that

$$\Phi_{jk}^{A} = L_{1jk} - L_{2jk}$$
$$= (\mu + \mu_1^A + \mu_j^B + \mu_k^C + \mu_{1j}^{AB} + \mu_{1k}^{AC} + \mu_{jk}^{BC})$$
$$- (\mu + \mu_2^A + \mu_j^B + \mu_k^C + \mu_{2j}^{AB} + \mu_{2k}^{AC} + \mu_{jk}^{BC}).$$ (5.27)

Most terms cancel, leaving

$$\Phi_{jk}^{A} = (\mu_1^A - \mu_2^A) + (\mu_{1j}^{AB} - \mu_{2j}^{AB}) + (\mu_{1k}^{AC} - \mu_{2k}^{AC}).$$ (5.28)

Recalling that $\sum_i \mu_i^A = 0$, we see that when A has two categories, $\mu_1^A = -\mu_2^A$. Consequently, $(\mu_1^A - \mu_2^A) = 2\mu_1^A$. Denote this by β^A. The other terms can be rewritten in the same manner, leaving

$$\Phi_{jk}^{A} = \beta^A + \beta_j^{AB} + \beta_k^{AC},$$ (5.29)

where

$$\beta_j^{AB} = 2\mu_{1j}^{AB} \qquad \beta_k^{AC} = 2\mu_{1k}^{AC}.$$

Its appearance notwithstanding, expression (5.29) is an alternative but *equivalent* way of viewing the no-three-factor interaction model (5.15). If the no-three-factor interaction model is true for a population table, then the model for Φ_{jk}^{A} will also be true. The difference between them lies mainly in interpretation.

The model calls attention to A's dependence on B and C, but the parameters have essentially the same meaning as in previous sections. The log odds Φ_{jk}^{A} depends on a mean effect, β^A, plus the association with B and C. The model could be generalized to include interaction among all three variables. For example, if the saturated model (5.16) had been used, we would have obtained an additional term, β_{jk}^{ABC}, measuring the impact of the interaction between B and C on the log odds.

In calculating the log odds, one tacitly assumes that the marginal totals of the remaining variables are fixed. For reasons described in Chapter 6, any model should contain parameters corresponding to the variables that are assumed fixed. Here, B and C are fixed, so a model for Φ_{jk}^{A} should be based on a log–linear model containing at least μ_{jk}^{BC}. These terms cancel, of course, but they always underlie the final model.

---

14. One could develop identical expressions for population proportions or probabilities, in which case Φ_{jk}^{A} is often called a logit (see Chapter 7).

Although in principle one can develop similar models for polychotomous variables, the notation becomes awkward. Suppose that B, party identification, depends on the other variables. Since it has three classes, it is first necessary to define appropriate log odds. A possible model for the odds of being a Democrat is

$$\Phi_{ik(D)}^B = \log\left(\frac{F_{i1k}}{F_{i3k}}\right) = \beta_{(D)}^B + \beta_{i(D)}^{AB} + \beta_{k(D)}^{BC}, \tag{5.30}$$

where

$$\beta_{(D)}^B = (\mu_1^B - \mu_3^B) \qquad \beta_{i(D)}^{AB} = (\mu_{i1}^{AB} - \mu_{i3}^{AB}) \qquad \beta_{k(D)}^{BC} = (\mu_{1k}^{BC} - \mu_{3k}^{BC}).$$

The subscript (D) indicates that the quantities pertain to the odds of being Democratic. (Note that the last class of B serves as the base, but any category could serve this purpose.)

In addition, a model for the odds of being independent, $\Phi_{ik(I)}^B$, is required. The final model for B, then, involves vectors:

$$\mathbf{\Phi}_{ik}^B = \mathbf{\beta}^B + \mathbf{\beta}_i^{AB} + \mathbf{\beta}_k^{BC}, \tag{5.31}$$

where $\mathbf{\Phi}_{ik}^B$ is a vector with entries $\Phi_{ik(D)}^B$ and $\Phi_{ik(I)}^B$, $\mathbf{\beta}^B$ is a vector with entries $\beta_{(D)}^B$ and $\beta_{(I)}^B$, and so forth.

One can see that as the categories increase, the number of terms to compute and interpret also increases.

An analogous equation for C is

$$\mathbf{\Phi}_{ij}^C = \mathbf{\beta}^C + \mathbf{\beta}_i^{AC} + \mathbf{\beta}_j^{BC}, \tag{5.32}$$

where, for example, $\mathbf{\Phi}_{ij}^C$ is a vector with entries $\Phi_{ij(D)}^C$ and $\Phi_{ij(N)}^C$.

If the dependent variable has I levels, there will be $I-1$ odds in the vector $\mathbf{\Phi}$ and a correspondingly large number of parameters in the $\mathbf{\beta}$ vectors.

5.5.1 Path Analysis and Diagrams.   A path model for continuous data consists of a group of equations linking variables. "Exogenous" variables, being completely predetermined, do not depend on other variables in the model; "endogenous" variables, on the other hand, depend on both exogenous and other endogenous variables.

Corresponding to the set of equations is a path diagram depicting interrelationships. Unidirectional arrows represent direct casual relationships, with the head of the arrow pointing to the dependent variable. Simple correlations are shown by double-headed arrows. Path coefficients—usually placed next to the arrows—measure "the changes in the dependent variable for a given change in the appropriate independent variable, with all of the remaining variables controlled or held constant" (Namboodiri, Carter, and Blalock, 1975, p. 461). Many social scientists interpret path coefficients as indicators of the relative importance of variables: presumably, the larger the path coefficient, the greater the explanatory power of the independent variables.

A main advantage of path diagrams, however, lies in their heuristic properties. In simple models the correlation between two variables can be decomposed into a sum of various path and correlation coefficients. The decompositions are especially easy to find by reading the path diagrams correctly, unless there are numerous variables and arrows. Examining correlations in terms of their components permits one to explore a model's obvious and nonobvious ramifications.

In a recent series of articles, Goodman (1972b, 1973a, 1973b, 1974a, 1974b) argues that log–linear models can be expressed in a way analogous to path models. A log–linear model is equivalent to a set of equations for the the log odds.[15] Each equation treats a variable as depending in a certain sense on other variables and hence has a corresponding diagram with arrows pointing from the independent to the dependent variable. Goodman enters numerical estimates of the β's next to the arrows, thinking of them as analogous to path coefficients.

Model (5.29), for instance, asserts that the odds of voting Democratic depend on the levels of B and C but that there are no higher-order interactions. Consequently, one could represent the equation by two arrows pointing from B and C to A. Next to each arrow one might write the numerical values of β_j^{AB} and β_k^{AC}. These quantities show the effect on the odds of moving from one level of an independent variable (e.g., party identification) to another.

The diagram could be expanded further by drawing arrows to represent the equations for Φ_{ik}^B and Φ_{ij}^C. The final diagram would contain arrows pointing to and from each variable, suggesting that A, B, and C are both causes and effects. Next to the arrows one would enter values from the appropriate β vectors. The three equations depicted by the arrow diagram are equivalent to (5.15), the no three-factor interaction model, since both assume that μ_{ijk}^{ABC} are zero.

Depending on which basic log-linear model generates the equations for the log odds, the path diagrams may be simple or complex, recursive or nonrecursive. The path analogy works best with dichotomies because the equations, parameters, and consequently diagrams are much simpler. But in principle it is applicable to any set of variables.

5.5.2 Limitations of Path Models.   Goodman makes extensive use of path diagrams to interpret log-linear models. The figures give an overview of a model and often lead to unexpected insights. Nevertheless, the analogy is easily pushed too far.

---

15. They are equivalent if the μ terms assumed to be equal to zero are the same in the log-linear model as in the set of equations for the log odds (Goodman, 1973a).

As just mentioned, it is cumbersome to diagram higher-order interactions or systems for polychotomous variables. Furthermore, with continuous data one can decompose a bivariate correlation in order to measure the portion of the association due to direct and indirect paths. The calculus of path coefficients thus provides a popular tool for investigating relationships. Unfortunately, coefficients in the log-linear version do not have this property and cannot be employed for the same purposes.

Indeed, the interpretation of the two types of parameters differs substantially. Whereas regular path coefficients have a clear meaning, the numerical values of the β's are more difficult to grasp. Certainly they shed light on the magnitude of associations and, in a way, on the relative explanatory importance of variables (assuming that one accepts a statistical index as a measure of importance). But since they cannot be manipulated in the same way as path coefficients, and they normally do not summarize the association in a single number, they seem less useful than path coefficients.

Finally, a model for a single log odds (e.g., the model for Φ_{jk}^{A}) is easily misunderstood. Explaining dependence of one variable on another is fine. But the analysis should not obscure possible relationships among the independent variables. Equation (5.29) ignores important information, namely the interrelationship between B and C. Actually, the model for the log odds of A is based on a model containing μ_{jk}^{BC}. But since these cancel, attention is directed to other aspects of the data.

5.6 THE EFFECTS OF COLLAPSING VARIABLES

Encompassing a wide range of models, log-linear analysis provides social scientists with a powerful and flexible tool for dissecting multidimensional cross-classifications. To many researchers, the method may seem like a godsend, for it appears to put the analysis of categorical data on the same footing as the analysis of interval variables. As a result, researchers may feel free to apply the technique to any kind of table without giving much thought to how the categories arose in the first place.

Unfortunately, the situation is not so simple. A model is defined for a particular population table. But one cannot blithely assume that the *observed* table corresponds to the data as they in fact exist in the population.

For a variety of reasons, researchers prefer to work with as few categories as possible. The temptation to collapse variables by combining adjacent categories is often overwhelming: the frequencies in elementary cells increases, the number of parameters declines, and the graphical display of the data becomes much neater. Instead of analyzing a $5 \times 5 \times 5 \times 5$ table with numerous empty cells, why not combine categories to form a $2 \times 2 \times 2 \times 2$ table? Or, perhaps better still, why not eliminate one variable altogether, leaving a marginal $2 \times 2 \times 2$ table?

The answer, as already intimated, is that conclusions about the inter-relationships may be wrong. What is true in a cross-classification of dichotomies is not necessarily true for the underlying population table, especially if its dimensions differ substantially from the observed array. We have seen examples of how ignoring a variable or combining some of its categories produces a relationship between two other variables when they were not related in the original data (see, for example, Section 5.3.4).

What is needed, then, is a general procedure for determining the "collapsibility" of variables in a given log-linear model. A variable, C, is collapsible with respect to A and B if the terms μ_i^A, μ_j^B, and μ_{ij}^{AB} are the same in the marginal $\{AB\}$ table as they are in the original three-dimensional table. Bishop, Fienberg, and Holland (1975, chap. 2) prove a theorem showing when variables can and cannot be collapsed.[16]

5.6.1 An Algorithm for Determining Collapsibility. Following Bishop, Fienberg, and Holland's theorem, one determines collapsibility by dividing the variables into three mutually exclusive groups:

Group 1. The variable or variables to be collapsed.

Group 2. Variables that are independent of the variable in the first group. "Independent" means that the μ terms linking them are zero.

Group 3. The remaining variables; that is, the variables that are not independent of those in the first group.

The rule for collapsibility is as follows:

The first group of variables is collapsible with respect to the μ terms of the second group, but not with respect to the μ terms involving only those variables in the third group. (The grand mean, μ, will always change when one or more variables is collapsed.)

To illustrate their theorem, consider model (5.14), the model for conditional independence between A and B in an $I \times J \times K$ table. The model includes μ_{ik}^{AC} and μ_{jk}^{BC} plus all main effects and the grand mean.

Let us begin by investigating the consequences of collapsing A. The first group of variables, consisting only of A, is independent of the second group, B, but related to C (via μ_{ik}^{AC}) in the third group. Since the rule states that μ terms involving the second group remain unchanged, μ_{jk}^{BC} and μ_j^B stay the same. But μ_k^C in the reduced $J \times K$ table will differ from the original terms. Therefore, collapsing A changes only the main effects involving C (along with the grand mean) and not the relationship between B and C, which is doubtless of most interest.

---

16. For additional remarks, see Bishop (1971) and Duncan (1976).

Now suppose that C is collapsed instead of A, leaving an $I \times J$ marginal table $\{AB\}$. Although the first group contains C, the second group is empty because C is related (by μ terms) to both A and B. Consequently, the μ terms involving the variables in the third group, A and B, are affected. Specifically, one might now find an AB relationship that does not exist in the full table. Here the problem of collapsing variables is apparent: one can create artificial relationships between A and B. Moreover, even partially collapsing C by, say, combining five categories into two, might produce such a relationship. Thus, the problem cannot be avoided by simply keeping as many variables as possible. One also has to maintain as many categories as is consistent with the underlying true structure of the data.

This algorithm applies, of course, to any log-linear model for any sized table. For instance, in the four-variable model (5.20), one could collapse D. This is valid according to the rule because D is unrelated to A, B, and C (the μ terms linking them are zero) and the third group is thus empty. This result makes sense because inasmuch as D is not connected with any other variable, it should make no difference what is done with it.

Modifying the model by adding μ_{il}^{AD} changes the picture, however. The third group now consists of A. According to the rule, terms involving B and C, such as μ_{ik}^{AC}, μ_{jk}^{BC}, μ_{j}^{B}, and μ_{k}^{C}, are unaffected, but the term involving only A will differ from corresponding term in the original array. Adding both μ_{il}^{AD} and μ_{jl}^{BD} to the model further reduces the number of unaffected parameters. In this case, only C remains independent of D, and terms involving *only* A and B (for example, μ_{ij}^{AB}) change. (See Table 5.3 for additional examples.)

Group 1 is not limited to a single variable. What are the consequences of collapsing C and D in the previous model? Since neither A nor B is unrelated to the composite variable CD, all parameters in the marginal $\{AB\}$ table differ from their counterparts in the full array.

5.6.2 Summary.   Obviously, collapsing or combining categories of variables is justified only under certain circumstances. One should not collapse a variable in a three-way table unless it is independent of at least one of the remaining variables. Models involving four or more variables follow a similar principle.

The essential point is that no one should take the level of measurement for granted. In every instance it is necessary to consider possible distortions introduced by categorizing truly continuous variables and to try to maximize the precision of measurement (see Reynolds, 1976, for several examples). Contrary to common practice, this dictum is especially important in "exploratory studies" where the researcher is not sure which variables are interrelated.

TABLE 5.3. **Examples of the Effects of Collapsing Variables***

a. Model μ, μ^A, μ^B, μ^C, μ^D, μ^{AB}, μ^{AC}, μ^{BC}, μ^{ABC};

Effects of Collapsing Only D

Group	Variables	Terms That Change	Terms That Do Not Change
1	D		
2	A, B, C		μ^A, μ^B, μ^C, μ^{AB}, μ^{AC}, μ^{BC}, μ^{ABC}
3	—	μ	

b. Model μ, μ^A, μ^B, μ^C, μ^D, μ^{AB}, μ^{AC}, μ^{AD}, μ^{BC}, μ^{ABC};

Effects of Collapsing Only D

Group	Variables	Terms That Change	Terms That Do Not Change
1	D		
2	B, C		μ^B, μ^C, μ^{AB}, μ^{AC}, μ^{BC}, μ^{ABC}
3	A	μ, μ^A	

c. Model μ, μ^A, μ^B, μ^C, μ^D, μ^{AB}, μ^{AC}, μ^{AD}, μ^{BC}, μ^{BD}, μ^{ABC};

Effects of Collapsing Only D

Group	Variables	Terms That Change	Terms That Do Not Change
1	D		
2	C		μ^C, μ^{AC}, μ^{BC}, μ^{ABC}
3	A, B	μ, μ^A, μ^B, μ^{AB}	

d. Model μ, μ^A, μ^B, μ^C, μ^D, μ^{AB}, μ^{AC}, μ^{AD}, μ^{BC}, μ^{BD}, μ^{ABC};

Effects of Collapsing C and D

Group	Variables	Terms That Change	Terms That Do Not Change
1	C, D		
2	—		
3	A, B	μ, μ^A, μ^B, μ^{AB}	

* Subscripts have been omitted for μ's for clarity.

It is equally important to think about what variables might have been left out of the analysis, for these omitted variables are in a sense collapsed. In looking only at A and B, one tacitly assumes that, say, C is unrelated to at least one of them. Otherwise, observed relationships could be spurious. (This, incidentally, applies to all multivariate procedures, not just log-linear analysis). At any rate, Bishop, Fienberg, and Holland's theorem warns us against the pitfalls of mechanically applying log-linear models to any cross-classification we happen to run across.[17]

---

17. For additional comments, see Reynolds (1976).

5.7 A NOTE ON THE CALCULATION OF μ TERMS

The calculation of μ parameters generalizes from the previously stated principles. For completeness a method is presented for finding μ terms in any size table. In a sense, the material presented here may be superfluous, since a social scientist will normally rely on computer programs for the analysis of large cross-classifications and would not compute parameters by hand. Nonetheless, the computations may offer additional insights into a model's meaning.

5.7.1 Saturated Models.

As before, let L's stand for the logarithms of expected frequencies, F's, and assume that all F's are greater than zero. A bar notation, $\bar{L}$, represents means of the logged frequencies. In a five-dimensional $I \times J \times K \times L \times M$ table, for example,

$$\bar{L}_i = \frac{\sum\limits_{jklm} L_{ijklm}}{JKLM} \qquad \bar{L}_{ij} = \frac{\sum\limits_{klm} L_{ijklm}}{KLM} \qquad \bar{L}_{ijm} = \frac{\sum\limits_{kl} L_{ijklm}}{KL}.$$

(Subscripts indicate the relevant variables.[18])

The grand mean in a five-dimensional table is

$$\mu = \bar{L}_{ijklm} = \frac{\sum\limits_{ijklm} L_{ijklm}}{IJKLM}.$$

In a five-dimensional table, the calculation of main and interaction effects follows the pattern suggested in previous sections. For instance;

$$\mu_i^A = \bar{L}_i - \mu,$$
$$\mu_{ij}^{AB} = \bar{L}_{ij} - \bar{L}_i - \bar{L}_j + \mu,$$
$$\mu_{ijk}^{ABC} = \bar{L}_{ijk} - \bar{L}_{ij} - \bar{L}_{ik} - \bar{L}_{jk} + \bar{L}_i + \bar{L}_j + \bar{L}_k - \mu,$$
$$\begin{aligned}\mu_{ijkl}^{ABCD} = \bar{L}_{ijkl} &- \bar{L}_{ijk} - \bar{L}_{ijl} - \bar{L}_{ikl} - \bar{L}_{jkl} \\ &+ \bar{L}_{ij} + \bar{L}_{ik} + \bar{L}_{il} + \bar{L}_{jk} + \bar{L}_{jl} + \bar{L}_{kl} \\ &- \bar{L}_i - \bar{L}_j - \bar{L}_k - \bar{L}_l + \mu.\end{aligned}$$

There is obviously a pattern here. To find an r-factor interaction, let W be a set of r letters. (For example, if we want a three-factor interaction, μ_{jkm}^{BCE}, in a five-dimensional table, then $r = 3$ and W is the set $\{BCE\}$.) The r-factor interaction, μ^W, in a table of dimension q ($r \le q$) has the general form:

$$\mu^W = (r\text{-variable mean}) - \sum[(r-1)-\text{variable means}]$$
$$+\sum[(r-2)-\text{variable means})] - \cdots \pm \mu. \tag{5.33}$$

---

18. Note that this notation differs slightly from the previous notation. As an example, $\bar{L}_i$ refers to the average of the logarithms in the ith row of the table whereas in the previous sections L_{i++++} denoted the sum of the logarithms.

The term "$\sum[(r-1)-\text{variable means}]$" refers to the sum of the means of the logged frequencies of all possible combinations of $r-1$ variables drawn from the set W. (If $W=\{BCE\}$, then for $r-1=2$, one takes the average logged frequencies for all possible pairs, that is, $\bar{L}_{jk}$, $\bar{L}_{jm}$, and $\bar{L}_{km}$.) The plus and minus signs alternate so that if r is even, the last term is $+\mu$; if r is odd, it is $-\mu$. Putting these ideas together, the term μ_{jkm}^{BCE} is

$$\mu_{jkm}^{BCE} = \bar{L}_{jkm} - \bar{L}_{jk} - \bar{L}_{jm} - \bar{L}_{km} + \bar{L}_j + \bar{L}_k + \bar{L}_m - \mu.$$

It is easy to verify that previous equations for μ terms are all particular applications of expression (5.33).

So far these parameters have been defined solely for population tables. For *saturated* models one obtains their estimates, $\hat{\mu}$, by simply substituting observed frequencies, f, for expected frequencies. Otherwise, the computational procedures are identical.

Goodman (1970) recommends adding $\frac{1}{2}$ to each frequency in the observed table, presumably to eliminate sampling zeroes. In large tables one almost always finds at least a few empty cells. Theoretically these should disappear with a large enough sample size, since it is assumed that all F's are positive. (The tenability of this assumption is an open question in many cases.) Nevertheless, logarithms and hence parameters cannot be calculated if zeroes are present, and Goodman's procedure or some other device (see Chapter 6) is normally required.

5.7.2 Calculating μ Terms in Unsaturated Models.   To find μ terms in unsaturated models, one first calculates estimated expected frequencies under a particular model (see Chapter 6). The estimated frequencies, not the observed ones, are then substituted in the formulas.

Here, too, zeroes present problems. One of the advantages of the estimation procedures to be described is that it generally produces nonzero estimates even for cells having no observations. This method breaks down, however, if the observed zeroes are distributed in certain ways. In these instances, one must adjust the data in some manner to remove the zeroes. An easy but mindless method is to replace each zero with a very small number, say 1 divided by the total number of cells in the table. Other, more sophisticated solutions are considered later.

5.7.3 Variances of μ Terms.   As with all statistics, it is frequently helpful to know the sampling distribution and variance of the parameters. Dividing an estimated parameter by its standard deviation produces a "standardized" μ term. These parameters have several uses. When calculated for saturated models they serve as guides to unsaturated models that might fit the data (see Chapter 6). They are also used to rank the magnitudes of interactions.

Except for small tables, however, the calculation of variances involves several difficulties. Their estimation in saturated models is straightforward, but the necessary formulas are too cumbersome to present here (Goodman, 1973c). Besides, widely available computer programs compute estimated variances automatically. Variances in unsaturated models have only recently been worked out and involve considerably more complex concepts. For this reason, the topic is not pursued further.

6 ESTIMATING AND PARTITIONING LOG-LINEAR MODELS

6.1 INTRODUCTION

As in any statistical procedure, the initial step in log-linear analysis entails hypothesizing a model. The model, a tentative statement about how variables are interrelated, raises the question: what would a set of data look like if it were true? Or, more precisely, what cell frequencies could one reasonably expect to find for a sample of size n drawn in a particular way? With these estimated frequencies, one can test the model's fit to the observed data.

The familiar chi square test illustrates these ideas. It is in effect a test of the independence model in an $I \times J$ table. Expected frequencies, estimated under the assumption of statistical independence, are compared to the observed frequencies with either the goodness-of-fit or likelihood-ratio chi square statistic (Chapter 1).

Actually, the estimated values obtained in the chi square test are special cases of a general estimating procedure, *maximum likelihood estimation*. Even though its intricacies lie beyond the scope of this book, maximum likelihood estimation has several important characteristics worth noting.[1]

6.1.1 Maximum Likelihood Estimation of Log-Linear Models.
Maximum likelihood estimation has a significant characteristic: all of the information necessary for computing expected frequencies

---

1. For the definition of maximum likelihood estimation, see Hoel (1962) or Freund (1962).

under a hierarchical model is contained in the marginal totals corresponding to the model's μ parameters. The two-variable independence model, for example, contains just the main effects μ_i^A and μ_j^B (plus a grand mean). Corresponding to these terms are the marginal tables $\{A\}$ and $\{B\}$ with entries f_{i+} and f_{+j}, respectively. Using only these marginal totals, often called *configurations*, one can find unique estimates of the expected frequencies. Marginal totals are thus "sufficient statistics" for estimating a hierarchical model's expected frequencies.

As another example, suppose that the model under investigation is

$$L_{ijk} = \mu + \mu_i^A + \mu_j^B + \mu_k^C + \mu_{ij}^{AB} + \mu_{ik}^{AC} \tag{6.1}$$

Estimated frequencies for this model are

$$\hat{F}_{ijk} = \frac{f_{ij+}f_{i+k}}{f_{i++}}, \tag{6.2}$$

where $\hat{F}_{ijk}$ denotes the estimated expected frequency in the ijkth cell. The two terms in the numerator, which are entries from marginal tables $\{AB\}$ and $\{AC\}$ (see Section 1.2), correspond to the parameters μ_{ij}^{AB} and μ_{ik}^{AC}. These marginals constitute the set of sufficient statistics for model (6.1).

A further property of the maximum likelihood procedure is that the sufficient marginal totals constrain the estimates. As noted in Chapter 1, the marginal totals of the expected frequencies equal the marginal totals of the observed frequencies. This principle generally holds in log-linear analysis: *estimated expected frequencies for a log-linear model fit the set of sufficient marginal tables.*[2]

For instance, the estimates in formula (6.2) fit—that is, sum to—the marginal tables $\{AB\}$ and $\{AC\}$. In other words,

$$\sum_k \hat{F}_{ijk} = \sum_k f_{ijk} = f_{ij+} \qquad \sum_j \hat{F}_{ijk} = \sum_j f_{ijk} = f_{i+k}.$$

However, the estimates $\hat{F}_{ijk}$ do not sum to the $\{BC\}$ marginal table because μ_{jk}^{BC} is not part of the model and therefore $\{BC\}$ is not one of the sufficient statistics.

Since only hierarchical models are considered, the estimates also fit marginal totals corresponding to implied parameters. The presence of μ_{ij}^{AB} and μ_{ik}^{AC} implies the presence of main effects for A, B, and C. Therefore, the estimated frequencies, $\hat{F}_{ijk}$, also fit marginal tables $\{A\}$, $\{B\}$, $\{C\}$. For example,

$$\sum_{jk} \hat{F}_{ijk} = \sum_{jk} f_{ijk} = f_{i++}.$$

As a consequence of this principle, log-linear models are described either by their μ terms or by the *set of fitted marginals*. It is simplest, in

---

2. For a full discussion, see Birch (1963), Goodman (1970), and especially Bishop, Fienberg, and Holland (1975).

fact, to use only the *sufficient* or *minimal set of fitted marginals*. In this way, $\{AB\}$ and $\{AC\}$, which imply $\{A\}$, $\{B\}$, and $\{C\}$, succinctly define model (6.1). Using marginal totals instead of an equation obviously simplifies the notation, but the two forms, it should be emphasized, mean the same thing.

Besides the uniqueness of the estimates obtained from sufficient configurations, maximum likelihood estimation has two other practical advantages.[3] Estimates are valid for samples drawn from multinomial or product-multinomial distributions (Section 1.2) where either n or certain marginal totals are fixed.

Another advantage is that the procedure often yields nonzero estimates even for cells with observed zeroes. Even though one assumes that F, (the population expected frequency, is greater than zero) for all cells in the table, sampling zeroes inevitably arise, even in moderate-sized tables. There is no problem if estimated frequencies, $\hat{F}$, are all greater than zero, as they usually are. Of course, there may be so many empty cells or they may be distributed in such a way that parameters cannot be estimated. The problem of sampling zeroes is discussed further in Section 6.5.

6.1.2 Direct versus Indirect Estimates. Formulas provide explicit directions for estimating frequencies. Formula (6.2), for example, shows how to estimate the frequency for the first cell: multiply f_{11+} and f_{1+1} and divide by f_{1++} to obtain $\hat{F}_{111}$. (Each quantity comes from an appropriate marginal table.) The difficulty lies in deriving a valid formula for various log-linear models.

Unfortunately, this is not the only difficulty. For some models, no formulas exist. In this case, estimated expected frequencies have to be found by a procedure called *iteration*. Consider the model of no three-factor interaction in an $I \times J \times K$ table. There is no explicit formula for obtaining expected frequencies under this model. Instead, they are computed by iteration. Beginning with trial values, one successively approximates the estimates until they converge within a predetermined degree of accuracy to the required marginal configurations.

The upshot, then, is that log-linear models fall into two groups: those having estimates based on explicit formulas and those for which no such formulas exist. Estimates in the first group are called *direct* or *closed-formed*; estimates in the second group are called, naturally enough, *indirect or open-formed*.

---

3. Although of less immediate concern to practitioners, maximum likelihood statistics have highly desirable statistical properties and in this respect at least equal if not surpass alternative estimating schemes. Bishop, Fienberg, and Holland (1975), Goodman (1971a, 1972a), and Koch and Reinfurt (1970) discuss the relative merits of maximum likelihood estimation and its chief competitor, weighted least squares (see Chapter 7).

6.1.3 How to Tell if Explicit Formulas for Expected Frequencies Exist. Maximum likelihood estimates of expected frequencies are found for every hierarchical model from the sufficient configurations. In each case, one might examine the marginal tables, algebraically manipulate them, and see whether or not direct estimates exist. Or, for simpler models, rules of elementary probability are applicable. Model (6.1) asserts that B and C are conditionally independent, given A. At each level of A, therefore, one finds the expected frequencies in exactly the same way as in the independence model for two variables. Hence, formula (6.2) seems quite natural.

For other models, however, the form of the estimates is not so obvious. It is easier to rely on a general scheme described by Bishop, Fienberg, and Holland (1975) for determining the existence of direct or closed-formed estimates.[4]

Using letters to denote variables, first list the minimal set of marginal configurations. In model (6.1) this set is $\{AB\}$ and $\{AC\}$. Then, if possible, carry out each of these steps:

1. Relabel any variables that always appear together as a single variable. (For example, in the four-variable model $\{ABC\}\{ABD\}$ $\{CD\}$, variables A and B always appear together, so write them as A', leaving $\{A'C\}\{A'D\}$ and $\{CD\}$.)
2. Remove any variables that appear in only one configuration. (In $\{AB\}\{AC\}$, both B and C appear only once, so they should be deleted, leaving $\{A\}$ and $\{A\}$.)
3. Remove a variable that appears in every configuration. (In model (6.1), A appears in each set of minimal marginals, so it should be removed.)
4. Remove redundant configurations. (The hierarchy principle says, for instance, that if marginal table $\{AB\}$ is fitted, then marginal table $\{A\}$ will also be fitted. Thus in the set of marginals, $\{AB\}$ and $\{A\}$, $\{A\}$ is redundant.)
5. Repeat Steps 1 through 4 until no variables remain, in which case an explicit formula exists, or until no further steps are possible, in which case iteration is required.

Actually, Bishop, Fienberg, and Holland (1975) show that direct estimates exist whenever the number of configurations can be reduced to two. Thus, model (6.1) with two minimal marginals has a closed-form expression for the expected frequencies.

Perhaps a few additional examples will illustrate the algorithm. Let $L_{ijk} = \mu + \mu_i^A + \mu_j^B + \mu_k^C + \mu_{ij}^{AB}$. The minimal marginals are $\{AB\}\{C\}$. At Step 1, relabel $\{AB\}$ as $\{A'\}$ since A and B always appear together, and

---

4. Also see Goodman (1971b) and Bishop (1969).

at Step 2 eliminate both $\{A'\}$ and $\{C\}$. Consequently, a formula for the model exists.

Now consider the model of no three-factor interaction in an $I \times J \times K$ table with minimal marginals $\{AB\}\{AC\}$ and $\{BC\}$. None of the steps can be taken, so direct estimates are not available.

Moving to four-variable models, the model containing all pairwise interactions, but no higher-order ones, has minimal configurations: $\{AB\}$, $\{AC\}$, $\{AD\}$, $\{BC\}$, $\{BD\}$, and $\{CD\}$. Since none of the steps can be taken, direct estimates do not exist. This result holds in general; explicit formulas do not exist if all pairwise interactions are present (Bishop, Fienberg, and Holland, 1975, pp. 79–82).

For a model with minimal marginals $\{ABC\}\{ABD\}$ and $\{CD\}$, Step 1 leaves $\{A'C\}$, $\{A'D\}$, and $\{CD\}$, but as no other steps are possible, iteration is required. (This result is expected because on the basis of the hierarchy principle one sees that once implied terms are considered the model includes every pairwise interaction.)

Finally, a five-variable model: $\{ABC\}\{BCD\}\{CDE\}$. Step 2 eliminates both A and E, leaving $\{BC\}\{BCD\}$ and $\{CD\}$. As it is common to all three configurations, C is dropped at Step 3 and the remaining variables, B and D, are removed at Step 4 and the reapplication of Step 2; therefore, this is a direct model having an explicit formula for the estimated expected frequencies.

6.2 FORMULAS FOR CALCULATING EXPECTED FREQUENCIES

Determining the existence of direct estimates for a model is only half the work. One needs to know the formulas themselves. Estimated expected frequencies differ from model to model since the sufficient configurations vary. It might be possible to list each formula separately, but as the number of variables increases, so does the number of possible models. It would take pages and pages to describe all the possible formulas. It is therefore preferable to have a general method for finding them. Another, more important reason for not listing specific formulas is that the general procedure frequently yields additional insights into a model. In particular, many models can be *partitioned* into submodels. Besides improving one's understanding of them, partitioning also shows more precisely why a model does not fit.

6.2.1 Notation.   Some more notation is needed at this point. As always, letters represent variables. The minimal marginal tables used to describe a model, therefore, consist of sets of letters. Suppose that there are T such sets, denoted $Y_1, Y_2, \ldots, Y_T$. In model (6.1), for example, $Y_1 = \{AB\}$ and $Y_2 = \{AC\}$, where $T = 2$.

In addition, capital letters, usually those at the end of the alphabet, represent different sets of letters. Z, for instance, stands for all of the variables. In a four-dimensional table, $Z = (ABCD)$; in five dimensions, $Z = (ABCDE)$. Similarly, U denotes variables that are not in *any* of the sufficient configurations. In other words, U consists of those variables that are not represented in any μ terms. In model (6.1), U is empty, but in

$$L_{ijk} = \mu + \mu_i^A + \mu_j^B \tag{6.3}$$

U consists of C, since in this three-variable model C is not included in any of the minimal set of marginal tables. Other letters denoting sets of variables are introduced as required (see Table 6.1).

6.2.2 Goodman's Algorithm for Excluded Variables. Goodman (1971b) gives a very helpful procedure for deriving explicit formulas for estimated expected frequencies. We first deal with variables in U, those that are not in any of the minimal configurations. A model excluding one or more variables asserts that the classes of the variable or variables are equally probable. The parameters of such models pertain to a reduced table since the excluded variables can, in a sense, be collapsed. Consequently, the calculation of the expected frequencies is split into two parts. First, the frequencies are computed under the model as it applies to the reduced table; then these frequencies are divided by the total number of classes pertaining to the excluded variables in order to obtain estimates for the full table.

Model (6.3) above asserts that A and B are independent (that is, $[A \otimes B]$) *and* that the classes of C are conditionally equiprobable (that is, $[C = \nabla | AB]$, where ∇ denotes equiprobability). Therefore, one first calculates the expected frequencies under the hypothesis of independence in the marginal $\{AB\}$ table, denoting them $\hat{F}_{ij+}$, and divides these estimates by the number of categories in C to obtain the estimated expected frequencies, $\hat{F}_{ijk}$, under the full model:[5]

$$\hat{F}_{ijk} = \frac{\hat{F}_{ij+}}{K}.$$

To generalize, let Z represent all of the variables in the complete table; let U represent the variables appearing in none of the Y_t for $t = 1, \ldots, T$; and let U^- be the complement of U, that is, all of the variables that are included in at least one Y_t. (In the previous example, $Z = (ABC)$, $U = (C)$, and $U^- = (AB)$.) Let g designate the product of the number of categories of the variables in U. If U is empty, then $g = 1$. (For model (6.3), $g = K$.) Finally, let $\hat{F}^-$ represent the estimated expected

---

5. It is shown later how the statistic used to test the model is divisible into two parts—one for testing the independence of A and B in the marginal $\{AB\}$ table and the second for testing the conditional equiprobability of C in the full table.

frequencies under the model as it is applied to the reduced table involving the variables in U^-.

Then the formula

$$\hat{F}^Z = \frac{\hat{F}^-}{g}, \tag{6.4}$$

gives the estimated expected frequencies in the full table, where $\hat{F}^Z$ denotes these frequencies. Of course, the formula for $\hat{F}^-$ is still undefined—a problem soon rectified—but once it is availabe, one has the $\hat{F}$'s for the full table. In the previous case, $\hat{F}^z = \hat{F}_{ijk}^{ABC}$, which was denoted $\hat{F}_{ijk}$ for simplicity, and $\hat{F}^- = \hat{F}_{ij+}^{AB}$, which also for simplicity was denoted $\hat{F}_{ij+}$.

Example: Consider a model for a four-dimensional table (that is, $Z = (ABCD)$) with minimal marginal configuration $\{AB\}$.[6] This model asserts that the classes of C and D are conditionally equally probable (given the levels of A and B) *and* that A and B are related in the two-way $\{AB\}$ marginal table. In this situation, $U = (CD)$, $U^- = (AB)$, and $g = KL$. Thus

$$\hat{F}_{ijkl} = \frac{\hat{F}_{ij++}^-}{KL} = \frac{f_{ij++}}{KL}.$$

The last equality holds because the model for the variables in U^- is the saturated model and expected frequencies for a saturated model always equal observed values.

Formula (6.4) should be understandable. After all, if the categories of a variable are equally probable, one would divide the expected frequencies of the remaining variables by its number of classes. As noted in Chapter 5, however, models of this sort are not likely to concern social scientists except under special circumstances.

6.2.3 Goodman's Algorithm for Included Variables. Having eliminated variables that do not appear in any of the Y_t's (that is, the set of minimal marginals), one then estimates the expected frequencies under the model for the variables in U^-. (Note that if U is empty, $U^- = Z$, the full set of variables, and $g = 1$. Formula (6.4) then reduces to a tautology.) Although the notation may be confusing at first, the algorithm for included variables is straightforward.

Let U_s be letters of variables that are in a configuration, Y_s, but are not in any other Y_t; let U_s' be the letters representing variables belonging in Z but not in U_s. (Therefore, U_s plus U_s' equals the entire set of letters, Z.) In model (6.1), for example, with minimum configurations $Y_1 = \{AB\}$ and $Y_2 = \{AC\}$, let $U_s = (C)$ and $U_s' = (AB)$. (Conversely, one could let

---

6. Remember that this notation is equivalent to the model $L_{ijkl} = \mu + \mu_i^A + \mu_j^B + \mu_{ij}^{AB}$.

$U_s = (B)$ and $U'_s = (AC)$; the choice is immaterial, since the same formula emerges.) Further, let U_s^* be the letters in Y_s that are not in U_s. (In the example, where $Y_s = \{AC\}$ and $U_s = (C)$, let $U_s^* = (A)$.) Table 6.1 summarizes these sets of letters.

TABLE 6.1. **Sets of Letters Used in Calculating Estimated Expected Frequencies**

Set	Contains Letters Representing
Z	Variables in full table
U	Variables not included in any of minimal marginals
U^-	Variables that are included in at least one set of minimal marginals
U_s	Variables in a given Y_s that are not included in any other Y_t for all $t \neq s$
U'_s	Variables in Z that are not in U_s
U_s^*	Variables in Y_s that are not in U_s

Source: Goodman (1971b).

Corresponding to these sets are expected and observed marginal frequencies. The symbol f^s denotes entries from the marginal table pertaining to the variables represented by the letters in Y_s; f^* denotes entries from the marginal table pertaining to the variables represented by the letters in U_s^* (if U_s^* is empty, f^* equals n); and $\hat{F}'$ denotes estimated expected frequencies under the model in the table consisting of the variables in U'_s. (Note, incidentally, that f^s and f^* do not mean powers of f.) In essence, one modifies a model by removing the variables in U_s. This leaves U'_s, and the variables in this set constitute a reduced or marginal table. $\hat{F}'$ are expected frequencies for this reduced table. In the example, the removal of C changes model (6.1) with configurations $\{AB\}$ and $\{AC\}$ to a new model for a two-way table with configuration $\{AB\}$. The $\hat{F}'$ pertain to this new model: they are the estimated expected frequencies under the assumption that the new, modified model is true.

The general formula for estimated frequencies under any model having closed-form or direct estimates is

$$\hat{F}^Z = \frac{\hat{F}' f^s}{f^*}, \tag{6.5}$$

where $\hat{F}^Z$ stands for the estimated values in the full table. The formula is best understood with the help of examples.

6.2.4 Examples. Beginning with the by-now familiar three-variable model (6.1) with minimal marginals $\{AB\}$ and $\{AC\}$, let, as before, $Z = (ABC)$, $Y_s = \{AC\}$, $U_s = (C)$, $U'_s = (AB)$, and $U_s^* = (A)$. Therefore, f^s

represents f_{i+k}, the entries from the marginal $\{AC\}$ table; f^* represents f_{i++}, the entries from the marginal table $\{A\}$, and $\hat{F}'$ represents the estimated frequencies under the hypothesis that the model pertaining to the table consisting of variables in U'_s (that is, the A and B) is true. With C removed from the configurations, this modified model is $\{AB\}\{A\}$, which, by the hierarchy principle, is identical to $\{AB\}$. Since the model $\{AB\}$ is the saturated model for the two-way table, $\hat{F}'$ equals f_{ij+}, the observed values in the marginal $\{AB\}$ table. (In a saturated model, expected and observed values always equal each other.) The formula for finding estimated frequencies under model (6.1) is thus

$$\hat{F}_{ijk} = \frac{f_{ij+}f_{i+k}}{f_{i++}},$$

which agrees with equation (6.2), as it should. As an example of the computations, consider the data in Table 4.1. After forming the marginal tables $\{AB\}$, $\{AC\}$, and $\{A\}$, one can find $\hat{F}_{ijk}$. For example, $\hat{F}_{111}$ is

$$\hat{F}_{111} = \frac{(1103)(772)}{1527} = 557.640,$$

where, for example, 1103 equals f_{11+} in the marginal $\{AB\}$ table.

Now for a four-variable model: $\{ABC\}$, $\{CD\}$. For convenience let $Y_s = \{CD\}$, $U_s = (D)$ (that is, D appears in Y_s but not in the other configuration), $U'_s = (ABC)$, and $U^*_s = (C)$. Here, f^s represents the entries, f_{++kl} from the $\{CD\}$ marginal table; f^* represents the entries f_{++k+} from the $\{C\}$ marginal table, and $\hat{F}'$ corresponds to the estimated expected frequencies in the marginal $\{ABC\}$ table. Since D has been eliminated, the model for this table is now $\{ABC\}\{C\}$, which is equivalent to $\{ABC\}$. The model $\{ABC\}$ is, of course, saturated for the three-way table, so $\hat{F}' = f_{ijk+}$. Applying formula (6.5), we find:

$$\hat{F}_{ijkl} = \frac{f_{ijk+}f_{++kl}}{f_{++k+}}.$$

Formula (6.5) may be applied successively. Consider the model of mutual independence in a three-way table: $\{A\}$, $\{B\}$, and $\{C\}$. The estimates are found in two steps. Start by letting $U_s = (C)$. Then, $Y_s = \{C\}$ and U^*_s is empty. Since U^*_s is empty, $f^* = n$, the sample size. Also, $f^s = f_{++k}$, entries from the marginal $\{C\}$ table. At this point U'_s is (AB), and the modified model with C removed is $\{A\}$ and $\{B\}$, which states that A and B are independent in the two-way table. Let $\hat{F}' = \hat{F}_{ij+}$ be the expected frequencies under the modified model as it applies to the $\{AB\}$ marginal table. Then the estimates at the first step are

$$\hat{F}_{ijk} = \frac{\hat{F}_{ij+}f_{++k}}{n}. \tag{6.6a}$$

To obtain the necessary formula for $\hat{F}_{ij+}$, simply reapply (6.5). The reduced model is $\{A\}$ and $\{B\}$. Letting $U_s = (B)$, the other sets are $U'_s = (A)$; U_s^* is empty. The corresponding frequencies are $f^s = f_{+j+}$ and $f^* = n$, since U_s^* is empty. The model has been further modified by the elimination of B. Consequently, $\hat{F}'$ is the expected frequency in the one-way table $\{A\}$ under the model $\{A\}$; obviously, $\hat{F}'$ now equals f_{i++}, the observed frequency. Thus $f_{i++}f_{+j+}/n$ replaces $\hat{F}_{ij+}$ in the preceding expression, leaving

$$\hat{F}_{ijk} = \frac{f_{i++}f_{+j+}f_{++k}}{n^2}. \tag{6.6b}$$

This illustrates an important aspect of Goodman's step-by-step procedure. The calculation of expected frequencies often leads to a partition of the model into separately testable components. Mutual independence, for instance, can be broken down into a component, belonging to the three-way table, that asserts that C is independent of the joint variable AB (see (6.6a)) and a component that asserts that A and B are independent in the two-way $\{AB\}$ table. The failure of a model to fit the data may be attributable to one submodel or both submodels.[7]

In conclusion, a five-variable model, $\{AB\}$, $\{AC\}$, and $\{CE\}$, illustrates both formulas (6.4) and (6.5). The model asserts that classes of D are equiprobable, at least given the levels of the other variables. (This assertion is evident from the absence of D in any of the minimal marginals.) Letting $g = L$, the number of classes of, D equation (6.4) gives

$$\hat{F}_{ijklm} = \frac{\hat{F}_{ijk+m}^-}{L},$$

where $\hat{F}_{ijk+m}$ denotes estimated frequencies under the model (that is, $\{AB\}, \{AC\}, \{CE\}$) applied to the four-way $I \times J \times K \times M$ table. Applying the step-by-step method, let $U_s = (E)$, as it belongs to only one set of minimal marginals. The other sets are $Y_s = \{CE\}$, $U'_s = (ABC)$, and $U_s^* = (C)$. These sets lead to an expression for $\hat{F}_{ijk+m}^-$ that when put in the preceding formula gives

$$\hat{F}_{ijklm} = \frac{\hat{F}'_{ijk++}f_{++k+m}}{f_{++k++}L},$$

where $\hat{F}'_{ijk++}$ denotes the estimated frequencies under the model $\{AB\}\{AC\}$—note that E has been removed in the previous step—for the $\{ABC\}$ marginal table. At the next step let $U_s = (C)$, $Y_s = \{AC\}$, $U'_s = (AB)$, and $U_s^* = (A)$. The estimates now become

$$\hat{F}_{ijklm} = \frac{\hat{F}'_{ij+++}f_{i+k++}f_{++k+m}}{f_{i++++}f_{++k++}L}.$$

---

7. Partitioning is discussed in greater detail in Section 6.6.

Finally, since the model has been reduced to $\{AB\}$ for the two-way table, $\hat{F}'_{ij+++}$ in the above expression is replaced by f_{ij+++}.

6.2.5 Summary of Goodman's Method for Obtaining Direct Estimates.

The previous expression, along with all of the others, follows a pattern. When direct estimates exist, they are functions of the marginal tables corresponding to the μ terms in the model. The numerator of these expressions is always the product of entries from each sufficient configuration (Bishop, 1971, p. 554). The denominator contains entries from common configurations (raised to an appropriate power), n (again raised to an appropriate power), and, occasionally, a term (g) for variables that have been omitted.

One can check his computations by noting if the expression for the estimates has this general form and by adding the estimates to make sure they sum to the appropriate marginal totals.

6.3 ESTIMATION BY ITERATION

The hypothesis of no three-factor interaction in a three-dimensional table cannot be described in terms of conditional independence or conditional equiprobability (Goodman, 1970). Furthermore, its estimated expected frequencies cannot be determined from an explicit formula. Required, instead, is an "iterative proportional fitting" procedure. But in other respects estimation obeys the same principles as when direct formulas exist.

In particular, the statistics used in estimation are the marginal tables corresponding to the model's parameters. Under the no three-factor interaction model, the estimates are functions of the marginal tables $\{AB\}$, $\{AC\}$, and $\{BC\}$ with entries f_{ij+}, f_{i+k}, and f_{+jk}, respectively. In addition, estimates derived from iteration "fit" these marginals:

$$\sum_k \hat{F}_{ijk} = \hat{F}_{ij+} = f_{ij+}, \tag{6.7a}$$

$$\sum_j \hat{F}_{ijk} = \hat{F}_{i+k} = f_{i+k}, \tag{6.7b}$$

$$\sum_i \hat{F}_{ijk} = \hat{F}_{+jk} = f_{+jk}. \tag{6.7c}$$

The iterative procedure, presented without much comment or justification, involves more computation than thought and consequently is not especially instructive. To simplify matters, we begin with the three-variable case. Once the basic ideas are mastered, it is easy to handle models with more variables.

6.3.1 Iterative Proportional Fitting for Three Variables. Estimated frequencies have to satisfy the constraints imposed by the previous equations. Starting with estimates that fit only the {AB} entries, one adjusts these estimates so that they fit the second set of marginals, {AC}. Since the third set, {BC}, is still not satisfied, they must be further adjusted. But in so doing their agreement with the previous sets (that is, {AB} and {AC}) is lost. Hence, it is necessary to begin a new cycle. At each step (s) of a cycle, the estimated frequencies are made to fit one set of marginals, although they do not fit the other two.

The adjustment procedure has a fortunate property, however: as the cycles increase, the estimates come closer and closer to satisfying simultaneously all sets of constraints. In the rth cycle, for instance, the difference between $\hat{F}_{11+}$ and f_{11+} may be less than 5; in the $(r+1)$th cycle, the difference may be less than 1. Iteration is continued until the estimates obtained at the end of one cycle do not differ from the estimates obtained at the previous cycle by more than δ, where δ is a small number, usually .01. Convergence is quite rapid; it seldom takes more than 10 cycles. At the end, marginal totals obtained from estimated frequencies agree quite closely with the observed marginals.

In an $I \times J \times K$ table with variables A, B, and C, the formulas for carrying out the iterations are as follows:

$$\hat{F}_{ijk}^{s+1} = \frac{\hat{F}_{ijk}^s f_{ij+}^{AB}}{\hat{F}_{ij+}^s}, \tag{6.8a}$$

$$\hat{F}_{ijk}^{s+2} = \frac{\hat{F}_{ijk}^{s+1} \cdot f_{i+k}^{AC}}{\hat{F}_{i+k}^{s+1}}, \tag{6.8b}$$

$$\hat{F}_{ijk}^{s+3} = \frac{\hat{F}_{ijk}^{s+2} f_{+jk}^{BC}}{\hat{F}_{+jk}^{s+2}}, \tag{6.8c}$$

where, for example, $\hat{F}_{ijk}^s$ is the estimated frequency obtained at Step s; and $\hat{F}_{ij+}^s$ is an entry from an {AB} marginal table formed by adding estimates obtained at Step s. The other quantities have similar meanings. (The f's are clearly entries from observed marginal tables.) Iteration must begin somewhere, so at the initial step ($s = 0$), let $\hat{F}_{ijk}^0 = 1$ for all i, j, and k.[8]

In essence, one adjusts estimates obtained at one step, $\hat{F}_{ijk}^s$, by a fraction, such as $f_{ij+}^{AB}/\hat{F}_{ij+}^s$. As the estimates come closer to the desired marginals, these fractions approach 1, and the discrepancies between the $\hat{F}$'s at adjacent cycles become smaller and smaller.

A numerical example may be helpful at this point. Table 6.2 contains data on gubernatorial voting in Georgia as well as necessary marginal

---

8. For a discussion of alternative starting values, see Bishop, Fienberg, and Holland (1975, pp. 92–95).

TABLE 6.2. **Vote for Governor by Birthplace by Education**

a. Full Table

		C: Education			
		Low		High	
		B: Birthplace		B: Birthplace	
		Rural	Urban	Rural	Urban
A: Vote	Calloway	17	16	44	45
	Maddox	28	8	9	9
	Total	45	24	53	54

b. Marginal Tables

{AB}				{AC}			
		B: Birthplace				C: Education	
		Rural	Urban			Low	High
A: Vote	Calloway	61	61	A: Vote	Calloway	33	89
	Maddox	37	17		Maddox	36	18
	Total	98	78		Total	69	107

{BC}			
		C: Education	
		Low	High
B: Birthplace	Rural	45	53
	Urban	24	54
	Total	69	107

Note: Entries are frequencies.   *Source:* Orum and McCranie (1970).

tables (Orum and McCranie, 1970). Table 6.3 shows the iterative calculations used to find estimated frequencies under the model of no three-factor interaction.

For example, starting with $\hat{F}^0_{ijk} = 1$, the estimate of F_{111} at the next step is

$$\hat{F}^1_{111} = \frac{\hat{F}^0_{111} f^{AB}_{11+}}{\hat{F}^0_{11+}} = \frac{(1)(61)}{2} = 30.5.$$

The 2 in the denominator is found by adding $\hat{F}^0_{111}$ and $\hat{F}^0_{112}$. Notice also that at the end of this step

$$\hat{F}^1_{111} + \hat{F}^1_{112} = f^{AB}_{11+} = 61,$$

as required. But other marginals—{BC}, for example—do not fit.

TABLE 6.3. **Iterative Calculations for Data in Table 6.2**

Cell			0	Cycle 1			Step 4	Cycle 2		...	...	Step 15	Observed
i	*j*	*k*		Step 1	Step 2	Step 3		Step 5	Step 6				
1	1	1	1	30.50	16.50	18.03	18.48	21.86	21.21	...	...	19.16	17
2	1	1	1	18.50	24.67	26.96	25.94	24.52	23.79	...	...	25.84	28
1	2	1	1	30.50	16.50	8.75	9.42	11.14	11.82	...	...	13.84	16
2	2	1	1	8.50	11.33	15.25	12.14	11.48	12.18	...	...	10.16	8
1	1	2	1	30.50	44.50	41.50	42.52	40.22	40.43	...	...	41.84	44
2	1	2	1	18.50	12.33	11.50	11.06	12.51	12.57	...	...	11.16	9
1	2	2	1	30.50	44.50	47.90	51.58	48.78	48.54	...	...	47.16	45
2	2	2	1	8.50	5.67	6.50	4.86	5.49	5.46	...	...	6.84	9

Note: Calculations were carried out to more decimals than indicated.

On the next step,

$$\hat{F}^2_{111} = \frac{\hat{F}^1_{111} f^{AC}_{1+1}}{\hat{F}^1_{1+1}} = \frac{(30.5)(33)}{61} = 16.50,$$

where again the denominator is found from the marginal table belonging to the estimated frequencies, $\hat{F}_{i+k}$, obtained at the previous step (that is, $\hat{F}^1_{111} + \hat{F}^1_{121} = 30.5 + 30.5 = 61$).

At the end of the first cycle,

$$\hat{F}^3_{111} = \frac{\hat{F}^2_{111} f^{BC}_{+11}}{\hat{F}^2_{+11}} = \frac{(16.50)(45)}{41.17} = 18.03.$$

Now $\{BC\}$ has been fitted (for example, $\hat{F}^3_{111} + \hat{F}^3_{211} = 18.03 + 26.96 = 45$), but the other marginals no longer match (for example, $\hat{F}^3_{111} + \hat{F}^3_{121} = 18.03 + 8.75 = 26.78$ when it should equal 33).

Having carried the computations through fifteen steps (five complete cycles), the largest deviation between the F's is less than .01 (see Table 6.3).[9] (In other words, the frequencies obtained at the end of the fourth cycle do not differ from the frequencies reached at the end of the fifth cycle by more than .01.) The expected values closely approximate the observed frequencies—compare the last two columns—suggesting the adequacy of the model for these data.

6.3.2 Iterative Proportional Fitting in General. The iterative procedure generalizes quite readily. As before, let $Y_1, Y_2, \ldots, Y_T$ represent the variables in the set of minimal marginal configurations. (In the previous example, $Y_1 = \{AB\}$, $Y_2 = \{AC\}$, and $Y_3 = \{BC\}$.) Entries from the tth observed marginal tables can be denoted f^t. (In the general formula presented below, subscripts are omitted.) Let $\hat{F}^{Y_t}_s$ denote entries from the marginal table corresponding to Y_t but calculated from the set of estimated expected frequencies at Step s, and let $\hat{F}^Z$ stand for the estimated frequencies in the full table. (Recall that Z means the set of letters representing all the variables in the table.) Note that this notation differs slightly from that used in previous sections. With the new notation, the formula for iterative proportional filling is

$$\hat{F}^Z_{s+1} = \frac{\hat{F}^Z_s f^{Y_t}}{\hat{F}^{Y_t}_s}. \tag{6.9}$$

Setting $\hat{F}^Z_0 = 1$ for every cell at the initial step,[10] the iterations are

---

9. There are other stopping rules. For these alternatives, see Bishop, Fienberg, and Holland (1975, pp. 95–97).

10. Actually, any starting values—not just 1's—are acceptable, as long as they do not reflect any interactions not present in the model. In most applications, however, the advantages of other values will be minimal. See Bishop, Fienberg, and Holland (1975).

continued until the discrepancies between the $\hat{F}^Z$'s from one cycle to the next are all less than δ, which is usually .01. If there are T sufficient configurations, each cycle has T steps (not counting the initial step), one for each configuration.

The four-way variable model $\{ABC\}$, $\{ABD\}$, $\{ACD\}$, and $\{BCD\}$ requires iteration. The specific applications of equation (6.9) are

$$\hat{F}_{s+1}^{ABCD} = \frac{\hat{F}_s^{ABCD} f^{ABC}}{\hat{F}_s^{ABC}},$$

$$\hat{F}_{s+2}^{ABCD} = \frac{\hat{F}_{s+1}^{ABCD} f^{ABD}}{\hat{F}_{s+1}^{ABD}},$$

$$\hat{F}_{s+3}^{ABCD} = \frac{\hat{F}_{s+2}^{ABCD} f^{ACD}}{\hat{F}_{s+2}^{ACD}},$$

$$\hat{F}_{s+4}^{ABCD} = \frac{\hat{F}_{s+3}^{ABCD} f^{BCD}}{\hat{F}_{s+3}^{BCD}}.$$

Although the subscripts have been dropped, the meaning of the $\hat{F}$'s can be inferred from the superscripts. In the first equation, for instance, $\hat{F}_s^{ABC}$ really means $\hat{F}_{ijk+}$, an entry from the marginal table formed by adding appropriate $\hat{F}$'s at the sth step. The computations exactly parallel those in the three-variable cases.

One should understand that formula (6.9) is completely general. It gives maximum likelihood estimates for any model, even those having direct estimates. When direct estimates exist, the iterations converge at the end of the first cycle[11] and the estimates are identical to those obtained from the formula. Normally, however, it is easier to use an explicit formula, unless a computer program is available. Computer programs always follow the iteration algorithm since the calculations for it are trivial.

Zeroes often appear in the observed cross-classification, but their presence does not invalidate the method. On the contrary, the iterative technique often yields positive estimates for every elementary cell. Occasionally the distribution of observed zeroes may cause one or more of the sufficient configurations to have a zero entry. Then, the empty cells summing to the empty configurations will have zero estimates (Bishop, Fienberg, and Holland, 1975, p. 90). One can still test the model—after making appropriate adjustments in the degrees of freedom—but will be unable to estimate parameters.

---

11. This is true for models with less than seven variables; with seven or more variables additional cycles may be needed, but the algorithm always gives the correct maximum likelihood estimates (Goodman, 1971b).

6.3.3 Iteration for Incomplete Tables. As mentioned in Chapter 1, interest often centers on incomplete tables. Certain cells in an incomplete table are usually considered zero because the investigator wishes to test for independence in the remaining cells. The test for quasi-independence, like any chi square test, requires estimated expected frequencies under a model. In some situations, the estimates are obtainable from an explicit formula; in other cases, however, iteration is necessary.

In general, one can adapt formula (6.9) to find estimated frequencies under quasi-independence by setting the starting values to zero for deleted cells and 1 for the included cells. There are then just two marginal constraints, $\{A\}$ and $\{B\}$, and each cycle has only two steps. Otherwise, the principles are exactly the same as estimating frequencies in complete tables.

In Table 1.4 (Section 1.5) where interest was in the off-diagonal cells, the estimates were obtained by letting $\hat{F}_0^{AB} = 1$ for all cells where $i \neq j$ and $\hat{F}_0^{AB} = 0$ for cells where $i = j$.

The algorithm can be used for finding estimates for incomplete multidimensional tables, but there are several technical subtleties not discussed here. For details see Bishop, Fienberg, and Holland (1975); Fienberg (1969, 1970b, 1972); Mantel (1970); Bishop and Fienberg (1969); and Goodman (1968).

6.4 TEST STATISTICS

An investigator first proposes a model and then estimates frequencies under the assumption that the model is true. At the next step, quite logically, he compares the expected and observed frequencies. If the fit is good, he retains and possibly refines the model; if the fit is bad, he abandons the model in favor of a new one.

The question naturally arises: what is a good fit? One could, of course, compare the observed and expected values on a cell-by-cell basis. Although this analysis often leads to interesting insights, it is still desirable to have an overall index, a single summary statistic for assessing the degree of fit.

Either the usual goodness-of-fit (GFX^2) or the likelihood-ratio (LRX^2) chi square is suitable.[12] Under the hypothesis that a log-linear model is true, both have approximately chi square distributions with v degrees of freedom, where v depends on the number of independent parameters in the model (see below). Large values of GFX^2 or LRX^2 (for a given v) indicate a poor fit to the data and, conversely, small ones suggest a good fit.

---

12. See Section 1.2 for the formulas for these statistics. $\hat{F}^Z$, calculated under a particular model, replaces $\hat{F}_{ij}$ in the formulas.

Since the chi square statistics approximate the theoretical chi square distribution, the investigator must be satisfied that the approximation is reasonable. Assuming a multinomial or product-multinomial distribution, the approximation is generally satisfactory if the sample size is sufficiently large. Unfortunately, "sufficiently large" is not easy to define. A rule of thumb for most applications is that if the sample size divided by the number of cells in the tables exceeds 5, the test statistics should be accurate. Like any generalization, however, there are exceptions—particularly if the observations are bunched into a few cells.

The goodness-of-fit chi square is asymptotically equivalent to the likelihood-ratio statistic in the sense that, given a large sample, one will reach the same conclusion whichever statistic he uses. But the LRX^2 has the advantage that it can be partitioned into additive components, each providing an independent test of a submodel (see Section 6.6).

The calculation of a summary statistic, such as GFX^2 or LRX^2, is only a step in assessing goodness of fit. The fit in each cell should also be assessed. The pattern of deviations between observed and expected values sometimes suggests alternative models. (The comments in Section 1.3 apply here.) Similarly, the magnitudes of the parameter estimates may add insights. Finally, once a model has been accepted, it can sometimes be refined further. Finding a nonsignificant chi square, therefore, is not necessarily the last step in the analysis.

Perhaps the simplest way to compute degrees of freedom for a model is to count the number of excluded *independent* parameters. The model of independence in an $I \times J$ table assumes the absence of μ_{ij}^{AB}. This, of course, means that $(I-1)(J-1)$ independent parameters have been excluded, and that number, $(I-1)(J-1)$, is consequently the number of degrees of freedom. Or consider the hypothesis of no three-factor interaction in an $I \times J \times K$ table. The degrees of freedom equals $(I-1)(J-1)(K-1)$, since these many independent parameters have been excluded.

An alternative but equivalent method of determining degrees of freedom is to subtract the number of included independent parameters from the total number of cells. The number of cells in a two-way table is IJ. The independence model contains $I-1$ independent parameters for μ_i^A plus $J-1$ independent parameters for μ_j^B plus one more for the grand mean. That total, subtracted from IJ, is $(I-1)(J-1)$, as expected.

6.5 THE PROBLEM OF SAMPLING ZEROES

Log-linear analysis rests partly on the assumption that all P's or F's in the population cross-classification are greater than zero. Although any table may contain a few empty cells, these zeroes should theoretically disappear by increasing the sample size.

Unfortunately, there are practical limits on sample sizes. And as the number of categories for each variable increases, it becomes difficult to fill every cell, particularly if the variables are highly interrelated. In the analysis of most attitude surveys, even ones having a large number of cases, an analyst almost always encounters sampling zeroes.

One way to avoid them is to collapse the data. Combining categories to form dichotomies or trichotomies eliminates the empty cells, but as argued in Section 5.6, collapsing variables usually raises more problems than it solves. Unless the investigator knows for sure that collapsing variables is not going to affect the results, he should seek some other solution.

Another approach is to "smooth" the data. Smoothing data involves adjusting the observed frequencies to make them amenable for other purposes. The main purpose in the present context is the elimination of sampling zeroes.

6.5.1 Estimating Parameters in Saturated Models.   In order to calculate μ terms, each frequency must be positive. Otherwise it is impossible to take logarithms. For this reason, the table of observed frequencies cannot contain zeroes.

Several rather *ad hoc* procedures have been proposed. Goodman, for example, recommends adding $\frac{1}{2}$ to each elementary cell before analyzing saturated models. Others suggest replacing each sampling zero by $1/R$, where R is the total number of cells in the table. Both methods ensure that all cells are positive, although expediency aside, the statistical justification for these common practices is still debated among statisticians.

Fienberg and Holland (1973) propose a general method for smoothing tables. Their technique, unlike the *ad hoc* methods, does not treat each sampling zero in the same way. They also find that their method is often superior to adding $\frac{1}{2}$ to every observed frequency. We do not pursue Fienberg and Holland's methods because the practical gains may not always outweigh the simplicity of the *ad hoc* approaches, at least for many problems commonly encountered in the social sciences. Furthermore, even this method has its critics. If, on the other hand, one requires precise estimates of the parameters in a saturated model, he should certainly study the topic in greater detail. For most investigators, however, who can be satisfied with rough estimates, adding $\frac{1}{2}$ to every frequency or changing zeroes to $1/R$ should generally be satisfactory, especially if the number of empty cells is not large.

6.5.2 Testing Unsaturated Models.   Sampling zeroes are more bothersome in unsaturated models.[13] The maximum likelihood estimation procedures normally eliminate zeroes even when the observed table contains several empty cells. Unfortunately, zeroes are sometimes distributed in such a way that they persist in a few marginal tables. Below is a $2 \times 3 \times 2$ table with zeroes in cells $(1, 1, 1)$ and $(1, 1, 2)$.

$$
\begin{array}{ccc\quad ccc}
0 & 5 & 1 & 0 & 10 & 2 \\
4 & 2 & 8 & 1 & 4 & 16
\end{array}
$$

Letting A, B, and C represent the row, column, and layer variables, respectively, the marginal table $\{AB\}$ has a zero in its first cell (that is, $f_{11+} = 0$). Any estimated frequencies based on this cell will be zero. Under the model $\{AB\}\{C\}$, for example, estimated frequencies are

$$
\hat{F}_{ijk} = \frac{f_{ij+}f_{++k}}{n}.
$$

The estimate of $\hat{F}_{111}$ is zero, since

$$
\hat{F}_{111} = \frac{(0)(20)}{53} = 0.
$$

Zero estimates cause problems in two ways. First, although the chi square statistics are still appropriate, the degrees of freedom have to be adjusted. Second, μ terms cannot be estimated without removing the zeroes.

The adjustment of degrees of freedom is occasionally straightforward. Bishop, Fienberg, and Holland (1975, pp. 115–116) provide a routine for obtaining the correct number:

1. Compute the degrees of freedom, v, in the normal manner by counting independent parameters excluded from the model or by subtracting the number of independent parameters included from the total number of cells.
2. Count the number of cells with zero estimates, Z_e.
3. Count the number of parameters that cannot be estimated, due to zeroes in the corresponding marginal configurations, Z_p.
4. The adjusted degrees of freedom, v', is then

$$
v' = v - Z_e + Z_p. \tag{6.10}
$$

The previous three-way table consisted of $2 \times 3 \times 2 = 12$ elementary cells. Under the model $\{AB\}\{C\}$, two cells, $(1, 1, 1)$ and $(1, 1, 2)$, have zero estimates. Furthermore, $\{AB\}$ contains one zero, thereby reducing the number of parameters in the set μ_{ij}^{AB} by 1. Since v was originally 5, the adjusted degrees of freedom is

$$
v' = 5 - 2 + 1 = 4.
$$

---

13. See Fienberg and Holland (1973) and Bishop, Fienberg, and Holland (1975, chap. 12) for a thorough discussion of this topic.

For some observed values of chi square, the change in degrees of freedom might affect the decision to accept or reject a model. This possibility is particularly strong in large tables having many empty cells, and where the drop in degrees of freedom may be as great as 10 or 15.

The algorithm for adjusting the degrees of freedom is sometimes tricky. Sampling zeroes may be distributed in such a way that several marginal tables, not just those in the minimal set, have zeroes. Suppose as an illustration that the first columns in both of the previous subtables are empty. Then the $\{AB\}$ marginal table is

$$0 \quad 15 \quad 3$$
$$0 \quad 6 \quad 24$$

Furthermore, $\{B\}$ also contains a zero:

$$0 \quad 21 \quad 27$$

Consequently, the zeroes in $\{AB\}$ satisfy the constraint that μ_{11}^{AB} and μ_{21}^{AB} must sum to zero. Therefore, the loss of independent parameters is not 2, but 1.

In such cases, the algorithm has to be generalized. First, as before, determine the total number of elementary cells with zero estimates, Z_e. Next, examine each minimal marginal and their lower-order relatives. (The configuration $\{B\}$ is a lower-order relative of $\{AB\}$.) The arrangement of zeroes in some marginals may be such that they carry over to lower-order tables. If so, these zeroes satisfy some of the constraints on μ terms and the loss of independent parameters is less than the number of zeroes. If, on the other hand, zeroes do not persist, then the loss of independent terms equals the number of zeroes.

In this example, where the first column of each table is empty and the model is $\{AB\}\{C\}$, four cells have zero estimates ($Z_e = 4$). There are two zeroes in $\{AB\}$, but only one independent parameter is lost ($Z_p = 1$) because of the zero in $\{B\}$. There are no empty cells in $\{C\}$. The adjusted degrees of freedom is thus

$$v' = 5 - 4 + 1 = 2.$$

Once more, the importance of adjusting the degrees of freedom is apparent. The difference between the adjusted and unadjusted values may be large enough to influence one's conclusions about the tenability of a model.

6.5.3 Estimating Parameters in Unsaturated Models. If zero estimates turn up in an unsaturated model, parameters cannot be estimated. After testing and accepting the model, one might resort to one of the procedures mentioned previously, namely adding a number to some or all of the estimates to make them positive. Or, preferably, one can obtain smoothed estimates using Fienberg and Holland's procedure. The choice depends on the investigator's goals and needs, including the desired level of precision. Many social scientists who use log-linear analysis to explore the structrue of their data may be willing to forego estimation altogether if sampling zeroes persist.

Although sampling zeroes are handled in several ways, none of the solutions is completely satisfactory. In addition, small but nonzero estimated frequencies can also pose problems. The chi square statistics are only approximations; it is not known how small the sample has to be before the approximation becomes too crude to be useful. In view of these considerations, significance tests based on tables with numerous sampling zeroes or small frequencies should be interpreted cautiously.

6.6 PARTITIONING MODELS

A social scientist rarely stops with the test of a single model. If it does not fit the data, he quite naturally wants to know why. If, on the other hand, it does fit, he frequently tries to refine or simplify it. In either case, he requires a thorough understanding of the model and its ramifications.

Most log-linear models implicitly make several claims about the structure of the data. There are, in other words, two or more subhypotheses or submodels contained within many models. Each submodel often has substantive interest of its own. Moreover, the poor fit of the parent model is sometimes traceable to one of its constituents. For these reasons, it is helpful to dissect models.

Fortunately, the likelihood-ratio chi square statistic lends itself to these purposes. Under the right circumstances, the LRX^2 is divisible into two (or more) additive components. Each pertains to a specific submodel, with the component tests and their degrees of freedom summing to the total likelihood-ratio chi square and its degrees of freedom.

Suppose that M stands for a hierarchical log-linear model for an m-dimensional table. Suppose further that M_a and M_b are two submodels, a concept to be explained shortly. Then, assuming that the models are properly specified and given a large enough sample, the test for M can be divided or partitioned into two additive components,

$$LRX^2(M) = LRX^2(M_a) + LRX^2(M_b),\qquad (6.11)$$

where the $LRX^2(M)$'s are likelihood-ratio chi square statistics for the various models. The degrees of freedom for each component sum to the degrees of freedom for M. Since M_a and M_b are log-linear models, they too may be partitioned, leading to an even finer analysis of M.

The model M states that both components are true. If M does not fit the data, the trouble might lie with M_a or M_b or both. The converse does not hold, however: whereas M_a and M_b may fit the data, M does not necessarily have to be true.

One of the submodels frequently involves a reduced table. If M is a model about an m-way table, either M_a or M_b may be a model about an $(m-1)$-way table. By successively partitioning, one can isolate increasingly smaller sets of variables. Each submodel has its own interpretation. Breaking down M in this manner thus leads to a clear understanding of the model's meaning and the reasons for its success or failure in explaining a set of data.

6.6.1 Nested Models. Consider two log-linear models, M_1 and M_2, with M_2 consisting entirely of a subset of the terms in M_1. Suppose that M_1 is $\{AB\}\{AC\}\{BC\}$ and M_2 is $\{AB\}\{AC\}$. The parameters of M_2 constitute a subset of M_1's parameters. When the parameters of one model are a subset of the parameters of another, the models are *nested*. Thus, in the example, M_2 is nested within M_1.

The test for M_2, which has fewer terms than M_1, can be broken into two parts: a test for M_1 and a test of M_2 applied to the estimated expected frequencies under M_1. Treating the estimated values obtained under M_1 as though they were observed frequencies, one simply tests M_2.

It can be shown that

$$LRX^2(M_2) = LRX^2(M_2 \mid M_1) + LRX^2(M_1). \tag{6.12}$$

The test for M_2 can therefore be split into two parts. The first component, $LRX^2(M_2 \mid M_1)$, is a conditional test of M_2 given M_1. In essence, the expected frequencies obtained under M_1 serve as the observed frequencies. This part indicates how much the $\hat{F}$'s of M_2 differ from the $\hat{F}$'s of M_1. If the differences are small, then the additional μ terms in M_1 do not contribute very much. But if the deviations are large, the extra parameters are important. Since $LRX^2(M_2 \mid M_1)$ is a chi square statistic, it tests the statistical significance of the terms included in M_1 but not in M_2.

The other component, $LRX^2(M_1)$ simply tests the fit of M_1 to the data. Consequently, M_2 asserts that both $(M_2 \mid M_1)$ and (M_1) are true. If one finds that M_2 does not fit, he can partition it to locate the source of the lack of fit. On the other hand, assuming that M_1 is true, $(M_2 \mid M_1)$ will be true only if M_2 is also true.

The degrees of freedom for each component sum to the degrees of freedom for M_2. By making the usual calculations for M_1 and M_2, both $LRX^2(M_2 \mid M_1)$ and its associated degrees of freedom are found by subtraction.

As an example, return to Orum and McCranie's data on gubernatorial voting in Georgia (Table 6.2), in which A represents vote, B represents birthplace, and C represents level of education. One model of interest, M_1, states that there is no three-factor interaction among the variables.

The LRX^2 for this model is 2.52 with 1 degree of freedom. Although this model conforms to the data, an investigator might suspect or hope that a simpler one would fit just as well. Suppose, for instance, that he believed that education and voting were conditionally independent; that is, he proposes M_2: $\{AB\}\{BC\}$. The difference between M_1 and M_2 lies in μ_{ik}^{AC}, which measures the partial association between A and C, assuming that M_1 holds. The LRX^2 for M_2 is 24.54 with 2 degrees of freedom, indicating that it is not very plausible for these data. It can be partitioned, however, to see where it breaks down and to assess the impact of μ_{ik}^{AC}.

Substituting 24.54 and 2.52 into equation (6.13), one finds by subtraction that $LRX^2(M_2 \mid M_1)$ equals 22.02 with 1 degree of freedom. The results are summarized in an analysis-of-variance-type table:

Model	Component Due to:	LRX^2	df
M_1	Three-factor interaction	2.52	1
$M_2 \mid M_1$	Partial association between A and C	22.02	1
M_2	Conditional association of A and C given B	24.54	2

In short, M_2 tests the hypothesis that voting and education are conditionally independent due to place of birth. Most of the lack of fit is attributable to the partial association between voting and education and very little to the three-factor interaction. These findings suggest that μ_{ik}^{AC} must be retained in the model.

Continuing the analysis, one can determine the significance or contribution of μ_{jk}^{BC} by defining M_2 as $\{AB\}$ and $\{AC\}$ while letting M_1 stay $\{AB\}$, $\{AC\}$, and $\{BC\}$. The LRX^2 for M_2 is 4.22 with 2 degrees of freedom and, by subtraction, $LRX^2(M_2 \mid M_1)$ is 1.70 with 1 degree of freedom. Inasmuch as the partial association between education and place of birth makes an insignificant contribution, an adequate model is $\{AB\}$ and $\{AC\}$.

Thus, in addition to the substantive insights partitioning affords, it provides a natural way to test the significance of one or more sets of μ terms. Furthermore, differences between nested models may provide a rough measure of the magnitude of a set of parameters such as μ_{ik}^{AC}.

A possible problem comes when the significance or magnitude of a set of parameters can be determined from more than one comparison. In a four-way table with variables A, B, C, and D, suppose that we have M_1: $\{ABC\}$, $\{DC\}$ and M_2: $\{ABC\}$, $\{D\}$. Comparing these models tests the significance of the μ_{kl}^{CD}'s. But so does the comparison of M_1' and M_2' where M_1' is $\{AB\}\{AC\}\{BC\}\{DC\}$ and M_2' is $\{AB\}\{AC\}\{BC\}\{D\}$. Obviously, other comparisons are possible. Although they often lead to the same conclusions, it is advisable to take as M_2 the best-fitting model (see Bishop, Fienberg, and Holland, 1975).

6.6.2 Tests on Marginal Tables. As an aside, it is worth knowing when marginal tables can provide tests of μ terms. It is usually misleading to analyze marginal tables by themselves (see Section 5.6). Under certain circumstances, however, they permit an assessment of the significance and magnitude of various terms.

Consider two models, M_1 and M_2, both of which have direct or closed-formed estimates, and which differ only by a single set of μ terms. In this situation one may test the parameters either by comparing the two models as a whole or by analyzing the marginal table corresponding to the μ terms in question.

Using Orum and McCranie's data as an example, suppose that M_1 is $\{AB\}\{AC\}$ and M_2 is $\{AC\}\{B\}$. Since $LRX^2(M_2) = 9.53$ and $LRX^2(M_1) = 4.22$, $LRX^2(M_2 \mid M_1)$, the test of the partial association between A and B, is 5.31 with a single degree of freedom. Here partitioning was used to test μ_{ij}^{AB}. But since both M_1 and M_2 have direct estimates, this same test can be carried out on the marginal $\{AB\}$ table, which is

	B: Birthplace	
A: Vote	61	61
	37	17
	98	78

A test for the significance of μ_{ij}^{AB} is equivalent to a test for the independence of A and B in this table. Therefore, after computing estimated expected frequencies in the usual way, we find that LRX^2 equals 5.31 with 1 degree of freedom. This figure agrees with that formed by partitioning. The agreement should not surprise us in view of the previous comments on collapsing (Section 5.6). In a three-dimensional table, a variable (here C) can be collapsed without disturbing the μ terms involving the other variables (here A and B) if and only if the variable to be collapsed is independent of at least one of the remaining variables (which is the case, since $\mu_{jk}^{BC} = 0$).

Briefly, when two *direct* models differ only by a single set of μ terms, the significance of the terms can be tested either by partitioning or by examining the corresponding marginal table. The analysis of marginal tables occasionally saves labor, but the principle does not always hold for models without direct estimates.[14]

---

14. See Bishop, Fienberg, and Holland (1975, pp. 129–30) and Goodman (1970, pp. 250–52) for a more thorough discussion of the analysis of marginal tables.

6.6.3 A General Method of Partitioning. Goodman's step-by-step method for deriving estimated frequencies leads to the partitioning of direct and a few indirect models. Before explaining the procedure, it might be useful to review the notation.

In an m-dimensional table, let Z denote the full set of letters corresponding to the variables. The set of T minimal marginals is represented by $Y_1, Y_2, \ldots, Y_T$. U_s stands for the letters associated with the variables in Y_s that are not in any other Y_t, for all $t \neq s$. Very often Y_s contains additional letters that are members of other minimal marginals; these letters are denoted U_s^*. Otherwise, U_s^* is empty. Further, let U_s' denote the letters that belong to Z but are not in U_s.

Corresponding to these sets of letters are observed and expected frequencies. Let f^s represent entries from the marginal table based on the variables in Y_s; similarly, let f^* be entries from the marginal table based on the variables in U_s^*. (If U_s^* is empty, then $f^* = n$.) Naturally, f' denotes the entries from the observed marginal table corresponding to the variables in U_s'. Capital $\hat{F}$'s stand for estimated frequencies under various models.

To further refresh the understanding of these sets, consider a four-way table with variables A, B, C, and D. Suppose, in addition, that the model in question is M: $\{AB\}\{AC\}\{CD\}$. Thus, $Z = (ABCD)$ and $Y_1 = \{AB\}$, $Y_2 = \{AC\}$, and $Y_3 = \{CD\}$. At the first step, let $Y_s = \{CD\}$ and $U_s = (D)$ so that $U_s^* = (C)$ and $U_s' = (ABC)$. The corresponding observed and expected frequencies are $f^s = f_{++kl}$; $f^* = f_{++k+}$; $\hat{F}^Z = \hat{F}_{ijkl}$, and $\hat{F}' = \hat{F}_{ijk+}$. (The last F represents the expected frequencies in the $\{ABC\}$ table under the hypothesis $\{AB\}\{AC\}$. This hypothesis arises because D has been removed at the first step.) Putting these quantities in formula (6.5) gives

$$\hat{F}_{ijkl} = \frac{\hat{F}'_{ijk+}f_{++kl}}{f_{++k+}}. \tag{6.13}$$

Estimates of $\hat{F}'_{ijk+}$ are found by reapplying the algorithm. Hence, at the second step, the model is $\{AB\}\{AC\}$. Now let $Y_s = \{AC\}$, $U_s = (C)$, $U_s^* = (A)$, and $U_s' = (AB)$. A full expression for the estimated frequencies is

$$\hat{F}_{ijkl} = \frac{f_{ij++}f_{i+k+}f_{++kl}}{f_{i+++}f_{++k+}}. \tag{6.14}$$

Note that $\hat{F}' = \hat{F}_{ij++} = f_{ij++}$ because after the removal of C the model is $\{AB\}$ and the estimated frequencies under this (saturated) model are simply the observed frequencies.

With this notation in mind, let us examine the general method of partitioning.

The likelihood-ratio statistic for testing a model M with estimated expected frequencies $\hat{F}^Z$ is

$$LRX^2(M) = 2 \sum F^Z \log\left(\frac{f^Z}{\hat{F}^Z}\right), \tag{6.15}$$

where f^Z denotes observed frequencies and $\hat{F}^Z$ is given by formula (6.5). After algebraic manipulation, this statistic can be divided into two asymptotically independent components,

$$LRX^2(M) = 2 \sum f^Z \log\left(\frac{f^Z}{\hat{\hat{F}}^Z}\right) + 2 \sum f' \log\left(\frac{f'}{\hat{F}'}\right), \tag{6.16}$$

where f' and $\hat{F}'$ are observed and expected frequencies in a marginal table composed of the variables in U_s'. (The $\hat{F}'$ are estimates under a modification of M obtained by removing the variables in U_s.) Furthermore, $\hat{\hat{F}}^Z$ is given by

$$\hat{\hat{F}}^Z = \frac{f'f^s}{f^*}, \tag{6.17}$$

where f', f^s, and f^* denote entries from marginal tables composed of variables in U_s', Y_s, and U_s^*, respectively.

The first component of (6.16) pertains to a model or hypothesis about the full table: it asserts that the variables in U_s are independent (if U_s^* is empty) or are conditionally independent (if U_s^* is not empty) of variables in U_s'. If conditional independence holds, the variables in U_s are independent of those in U_s'', given the variables in U_s^*, where U_s'' is the set of letters U_s' minus those in U_s^*. Using the symbols introduced in Chapter 5, conditional independence is represented as

$$[U_s'' \otimes U_s \mid U_s^*]. \tag{6.18a}$$

When U_s^* is empty, there is no conditioning variable and the submodel reduces to

$$[U_s' \otimes U_s]. \tag{6.18b}$$

At the first step of the previous example, where $U_s = (D)$, $U_s' = (ABC)$, and $U_s^* = (C)$, $U_s'' = (AB)$ and the submodel is

$$[AB \otimes D \mid C]$$

which means that the joint variable, AB, is independent of D, given the level of C.

The second component (i.e., the second part of (6.16)) is the chi square statistic for testing a submodel in the marginal table consisting of the variables in U_s'. In this reduced table the observed frequencies are f', whereas the expected values, $\hat{F}'$, are derived under a modification of the original model, the modification being that the variables in U_s are "removed" from the set of minimal marginal tables.

To help understand the method, let us complete the previous example. The basic four-variable model is $\{AB\}\{AC\}\{CD\}$. The likelihood-ratio chi square for testing this model is divided into two parts. Consider the component belonging to the full table (the first part of equation (6.16)). Using (6.17), the estimated frequencies are

$$\hat{\hat{F}}^{Z} = \hat{\hat{F}}_{ijkl} = \frac{f_{ijk+} f_{++kl}}{f_{++k+}}, \tag{6.19}$$

which when substituted into the chi square formula tests the hypothesis that the joint variable AB is conditionally independent of D, given C (That is, $[AB \otimes D \mid C]$). Incidentally, this submodel itself can be further partitioned. To see how, note that the submodel indicated by $[AB \otimes D \mid C]$ is equivalent to the model $\{ABC\}\{CD\}$. This four-variable model can, in turn, be partitioned, using exactly the same techniques, into two parts—one asserting $[A \otimes D \mid BC]$ and the other asserting $[B \otimes D \mid C]$. The reader can verify this for himself by making the appropriate definitions of U_s, U'_s, and U^*_s.

The second component dealing with the reduced table tests the model $\{AB\}\{AC\}$ with expected frequencies given by $\hat{F}'_{ijk+}$. But this model, too, can be partitioned. The first component involves the three-way table $\{ABC\}$ and the second involves the two-way table $\{AB\}$. To carry out this partitioning we begin from scratch: let $U_s = (C)$, $U'_s = (AB)$, and $U^*_s = (A)$. The estimated frequencies from the first component are given by (6.17):

$$\hat{\hat{F}}_{ijk+} = \frac{f_{ij++} f_{i+j+}}{f_{i+++}},$$

and from (6.18a) the interpretation of this model is

$$[B \otimes C \mid A]$$

that is, B is independent of C given A.

The last component concerns the two-way table $\{AB\}$. Since the model is now $\{AB\}$, the expected frequencies under it, $\hat{F}'_{ij++}$, match the observed frequencies and the chi square statistic is therefore zero.

In summary, the test of the model M: $\{AB\}\{AC\}\{CD\}$ is divided into three components, one of which happens to be zero. A short way of expressing the partition is

$$LRX^{2}(M) = LRX^{2}(B \otimes C \mid A) + LRX^{2}(AB \otimes D \mid C).$$

The last component, as pointed out above can also be partitioned into $[A \otimes D \mid BC]$ and $[B \otimes D \mid C]$. Thus, the test for the total model breaks down into

$$LRX^{2}(M) = LRX^{2}(B \otimes C \mid A) + LRX^{2}(B \otimes D \mid C) + LRX^{2}(A \otimes D \mid BC).$$

According to the model, M, all three conditions are true. If it fails to hold, the partitioning may pinpoint the source of the failure. It is possible, for example, that most of the overall chi square is attributable to one component—the first, for example. Having this information helps one find a more suitable model.

At this stage it might be helpful to consider a concrete example. Table 6.4 contains data from Cowart's 1973 study of nonpresidential voting. The variables are A, vote for U.S. senator; B, incumbent's party affiliation; C, respondent's partisan attitude; and D, respondent's party affiliation. Inasmuch as the influence of party identification and partisan attitudes on voting is well known, any model ought to contain at least μ_{ik}^{AC} and μ_{il}^{AD}. It also seems likely that attitudes and party are related, but

TABLE 6.4.   **Relationship between Voting, Incumbent's Party, Partisan Attitude, and Party Identification**

D: Party	C: Attitude	B: Incumbency	A: Vote D	A: Vote R
D	D	D	288	25
D	D	No	139	18
D	D	R	193	37
D	N	D	185	18
D	N	No	83	15
D	N	R	99	31
D	R	D	49	20
D	R	No	29	14
D	R	R	38	29
I	D	D	48	13
I	D	No	14	6
I	D	R	27	21
I	N	D	81	51
I	N	No	20	29
I	N	R	50	70
I	R	D	30	51
I	R	No	18	39
I	R	R	21	63
R	D	D	7	19
R	D	No	2	8
R	D	R	4	28
R	N	D	20	63
R	N	No	13	49
R	N	R	19	88
R	R	D	23	155
R	R	No	13	129
R	R	R	14	227

Key: D = Democrat, I = Independent, R = Republican, N = neutral, No = no incumbent.
Source: Cowart (1973, table 2).

quite possible that incumbency is unrelated to any other variable. Since at this point there is no reason to expect higher-order interactions, a good starting model is

$$L_{ijkl} = \mu + \mu_i^A + \mu_j^B + \mu_k^C + \mu_l^D + \mu_{ik}^{AC} + \mu_{il}^{AD} + \mu_{kl}^{CD},$$

which has minimal marginal configurations $\{AC\}$, $\{AD\}$, $\{CD\}$, and $\{B\}$. The likelihood-ratio statistic turns out to be $LRX^2 = 121.53$ with 38 degrees for freedom.[15] Obviously, the model does not fit the data satisfactorily.

Before discarding it completely, the model can be ransacked to see where it breaks down. Looking ahead, it is partitioned into two components, one pertaining to the full four-way table and the other to a three-way marginal table, $\{ACD\}$. The first component is itself further partitioned. One component involves the four-way table again, one a three-way table, $\{ABC\}$, and one a two-way table, $\{AB\}$. In other words, after making the initial partition, we split one component into three additional parts, each of which deals with a substantively interesting hypothesis.

To obtain the first partition (see Table 6.5a), let $Y_s = \{B\}$, $U_s = (B)$, and $U_s' = \{ACD\}$. Substituting the corresponding frequencies into (6.17) gives

$$\hat{\bar{F}}^Z = \frac{f_{i+kl}f_{+j++}}{n}.$$

(The n in the denominator reflects the fact that U_s^* is empty.) These estimated frequencies are used in the first likelihood-ratio chi square (6.16) to test the component $[ACD \otimes B]$. (See (6.18b).)

After B has been removed, the modified model for the variables in U_s' (that is A, C, and D) is $\{AC\}$, $\{AD\}$, and $\{CD\}$. Clearly, this is the hypothesis of no three-factor interaction in $\{ACD\}$. Estimated frequencies under this model, $\hat{F}' = \hat{F}_{i+kl}$, are obtained by iteration.

Thus, the model has initially been divided into two components, M_1: $[ACD \otimes B]$ and M_2: $[ACD = 0]$. The relevant chi squares for each part are $LRX^2(M_1) = 115.16$ with 34 degrees of freedom and $LRX^2(M_2) = 6.37$ with 4 degrees of freedom (see Table 6.5a). (The degrees of freedom are found by counting the number of parameters excluded from each submodel. In the three-way table, for instance, only μ_{ikl}^{ACD} has been excluded, giving $(I-1)(K-1)(L-1) = (2-1)(3-1)(3-1) = 4$ degrees of freedom. Alternatively, the chi squares and degrees of freedom can be obtained by finding the results for either M_1 or M_2 and subtracting from M.

---

15. Incidentally, the estimated expected frequencies under this model have to be calculated by iteration, as the reader can verify by applying the algorithm in Section 6.1.3.

TABLE 6.5.   **Partitioning of Models for Cowart's Voting Data**

a. Original Partition

Model	Component Due to:	LRX^2	df
M_1: $[ACD \otimes B]$	Interaction of B with joint variable ACD	115.16	34
M_2: $[ACD = 0]$	Three-factor interaction	6.37	4
	M Total	121.53	38

b. Further Partition of $[ACD \otimes B]$

Model	Component Due to:	LRX^2	df
$[B \otimes D \mid AC]$	Conditional association between incumbency and party	18.05	24
$[B \otimes C \mid A]$	Conditional association between incumbency and attitude	7.85	8
$[A \otimes B]$	Association between voting and incumbency	89.26	2
	M_1 Total	115.16	34

Key: A = vote for Senate, B = incumbent's party affiliation, C = partisan attitude, D = party identification.

Table 6.5a clearly points to the source of the trouble: incumbency is not unrelated to the joint variable ACD. Obviously, one or more interactions involving B must be added. But which ones? Further partitioning the submodel $[ACD \otimes B]$ yields some clues.

First note that the hypothesis $[ACD \otimes B]$ is equivalent to the model $\{ACD\}\{B\}$. This fact, ascertained from an inspection of the μ terms, means that further partitioning is possible because it is a direct model.

To begin, let $U_s = (D)$, $Y_s = \{ACD\}$, $U'_s = (ABC)$, and $U^*_s = (AC)$. Using (6.16) and (6.17), the estimated frequencies for the first part of the partition are derived from the f's corresponding to these sets:

$$\hat{\hat{F}}_{ijkl} = \frac{f_{ijk+} f_{i+kl}}{f_{i+k+}}$$

These estimates pertain to the model $[B \otimes D \mid AC]$. (See (6.18a).) The likelihood-ratio chi square for this component turns out to be 18.05 with 24 degrees of freedom, a good fit.

Estimated frequencies for the second half of (6.16) are found by *starting over*. That is, having removed D, we now have an $\{ABC\}$ marginal table and the new model is $\{AC\}\{B\}$. Using (6.16) and (6.17) again, we can divide this model into two parts. for the first, let U_s be (C), $Y_s = \{AC\}$, $U'_s = (AB)$, and $U^*_s = (A)$. The estimated frequencies for this component (see (6.17)).

$$\hat{F}_{ijk+} = \frac{f_{ij++}f_{i+k+}}{f_{i+++}},$$

correspond to the model $[B \otimes C \mid A]$. (See expression (6.18a).) Here the $LRX^2 = 7.85$ with 8 degrees of freedom, another good fit.

Only one part remains, the second half of (6.16) applied to $\{AB\}$. With C eliminated, the remaining model—$\{A\}\{B\}$—asserts the independence of voting and incumbency. The expected values under this model, the ones that go in the second half of (6.16), are obviously

$$\hat{F}_{ij++} = \frac{f_{i+++}f_{+j++}}{n}.$$

The LRX^2 for this model, $[B \otimes A]$, is 89.26 with 2 degrees of freedom. At last the source of difficulty is clear: incumbency is strongly related to voting. We ought at the least to add μ_{ij}^{AB} to the original model. Under the model with this term added—namely, $\{AB\}\{AC\}\{AD\}\{CD\}$—the LRX^2 is 32.28 with 36 degrees of freedom. Not only does this model fit the data, but it also agrees with other research on voting.

Table 6.5 summarizes the partitions. The original model was partitioned into two components, the first of which was further subdivided into three submodels each with an interpretation of its own. The example thus shows how partitioning improves the selection and understanding of log-linear models.

6.6.4 Partitioning Two Common Models. The successive application of Goodman's procedure leads to the partition of two frequently encountered models, joing independence and mutual independent.

Suppose that an m-dimensional cross-classification consists of variables $A_1, A_2, \ldots, A_m$. The model, M, of independence of the joint variable $A_1, A_2, \ldots, A_{m-2}$, from A_{m-1} given A_m, is denoted by

$$[A_1 A_2, \ldots, A_{m-2} \otimes A_{m-1} \mid A_m].$$

Successive application of Goodman's method shows that this model can be partitioned as follows:

$$LRX^2(M) = LRX^2(A_1 \otimes A_{m-1} \mid A_m) + LRX^2(A_2 \otimes A_{m-1} \mid A_m A_1) + \cdots$$
$$+ LRX^2(A_{m-2} \otimes A_{m-1} \mid A_m A_1 A_2, \ldots, A_{m-3}). \quad (6.20)$$

The model can be divided, in other words, into components involving fewer and fewer variables. The likelihood-ratio statistics (and their degrees of freedom) sum to the likelihood-ratio test for M (and its degrees of freedom). Table 6.5 provides a numerical example where $[ACD \otimes B]$ is divided into three submodels. (Note that there is no conditioning variable in this particular case.)

The model of mutual independence—$[A_1 \otimes A_2 \otimes \cdots \otimes A_{m-1} \mid A_m]$—is partitioned as

$$LRX^2(M) = LRX^2(A_1 \otimes A_2 \mid A_m) + LRX^2(A_1A_2 \otimes A_3 \mid A_m) + \cdots$$
$$+ LRX^2(A_1A_2 \cdots A_{m-2} \otimes A_{m-1} \mid A_m). \quad (6.21)$$

Again, the separate chi square tests and their degrees of freedom sum to the overall chi square and its degrees of freedom. Further, some of the separate components can also be partitioned to refine the analysis even further.

Orum and McCranie's data on gubernatorial voting (Table 6.2) demonstrate the partitioning of mutual independence. Mutual independence between (A) voting, (B) place of birth, and (C) education does not fit the data very well: $LRX^2 = 34.08$ with 4 degrees of freedom. To locate the model's weakness, partition it using (6.21) as follows:

Model	Component Due to:	LRX^2	df
$[C \otimes B]$	Marginal association between B and C	4.23	1
$[CB \otimes A]$	Joint association of CB with A	<u>29.85</u>	<u>3</u>
$[C \otimes B \otimes A]$	Associations among A, B, and C	34.08	4

These statistics are computed from appropriate tables by using the formulas for estimated expected frequencies given earlier (Sections 6.2 and 6.3). In the threeway table, for example, the model $[CB \otimes A]$ has minimal marginal configurations $\{CB\}$, $\{A\}$. Therefore, letting $U_s = (A)$, $U'_s = (BC)$, and U_s^* be empty, the expected frequencies according to (6.5) are

$$\hat{F}_{ijk} = \frac{\hat{F}_{+jk}f_{i++}}{n} = \frac{f_{+jk}f_{i++}}{n}.$$

This model, incidentally, can itself be partitioned with expression (6.20):

Model	Component Due to:	LRX^2	df
$[B \otimes A]$	Marginal association between A and B	5.31	1
$[C \otimes A \mid B]$	Association between A and C	<u>24.54</u>	<u>2</u>
$[CB \otimes A]$	Association of joint variable CB with A	29.85	3

Further partitions are possible but are not explored here.

6.7 CRITERIA FOR ACCEPTING MODELS

An investigator obviously has a wide choice of models. Even with a few variables, the number to analyze is quite large. In a three-way table, there are eight distinct models; in a four-way table there are twenty-seven. Furthermore, many of these types have several versions, depending on the particular arrangement of the variables.

Out of all of the possibilities, how can an investigator find the one that best suits his data? He could, of course, test every conceivable model. But a mindless technique like this involves both practical and theoretical difficulties. Certainly the computational task would be awesome for even moderate-sized tables. Computing one significance test after another clouds the interpretation of the significance level, and the resulting "best-fitting model" may have little or no relevance for substantive theory.

Clearly, more systematic methods for choosing among the alternatives are required. Goodman (1970, 1971a, 1973b, 1973c) and Bishop, Fienberg, and Holland (1975), among others, describe objective ways to narrow the range. The best procedures appear to be the following:

Standardized μ terms. Compute μ terms in a saturated model; divide them by their estimated variances to obtain standardized values; and look for terms having the largest standardized values.

Stepwise techniques. Analogous to stepwise regression, this model selection technique involves successively entering (or deleting) interactions into (or from) a base model, keeping those terms that significantly affect the chi square.

Instead of describing these methods in detail—they are completely described in the literature cited above—it seems preferable to discuss general criteria for accepting log-linear models.

6.7.1 Problems in Defining Acceptance Criteria.
To be acceptable, a model should obviously agree with the observed data. The simplest and most direct measures of agreement are the two chi square statistics, LRX^2 and GFX^2. They seem to provide objective standards for assessing a model's adequacy.

Yet an analyst should not be a slave to a single summary statistic. There are instances when he might accept a model on grounds other than its chi square value. Suppose that M_1 and M_2, two log-linear models, both fit a set of data in the sense that the LRX^2's are not significant at some level, but that $LRX^2 (M_1)$ is less than $LRX^2(M_2)$. On this basis one might be tempted to prefer M_1. But is the decision always wise? Probably not, because there may be more compelling reasons for accepting M_2. M_2 may contain fewer parameters, for example, and might therefore have a clearer interpretation. After all, one can *always* find a good fit by (if nothing else) computing a saturated model.

Furthermore, as in all test statistics, the sample size affects the LRX^2 and GFX^2. Anyone working with two-way cross-classification knows that very large samples lead to significant chi squares, even if the variables are for all practical purposes unrelated. A similar phenomenon occurs in log-linear analysis. If a cross-classification contains a large number of cases, it frequently turns out that comparatively trivial interactions are significant. In these situations, where the n is large, only complex models seem to fit. Determining which interactions are artifacts of the sample size and which have substantive importance rests on other criteria. In other words, the omission of complex interactions may or may not create biases in parameter estimates but their importance often has to be judged on other grounds.

6.7.2 Congruence with Substantive Theory.

To be useful, a model should bear some relationship to one's knowledge of the problem at hand. Social scientists have accumulated a vast literature showing the interrelationship between partisanship and voting. It would be fruitless to build models of electoral behavior asserting independence among these variables.

Other things being equal, theory and common sense should guide one's choices. A model that is compatible with theory is usually preferred to one that is not. Naturally, existing theory can be wrong and may have to be amended. The investigator, needless to say, ought to keep an open mind.

Nevertheless, experience with log-linear analysis shows that model searching can rapidly get out of hand. With the help of an efficient computer program it is possible to test dozens of models in a matter of moments. It is indeed tempting to examine as many alternatives as possible. But without guidance, the investigator may find more acceptable models than he can interpret. In the absence of a substantive theory or other working hypothesis, the choice turns on arbitrary or happenstance circumstances, and the researcher ends up with a model in search of an explanation.

6.7.3 Simplicity.

Simplicity, a long-established principle in scientific investigation, is another criterion of acceptance. Confronted with two models that fit the data, and that conform to theoretical expectations, a social scientist will normally pick the simplest one. Very often simple models fit almost as well as ones with higher-order interactions, and they are certainly easier to account for theoretically.

Complex models cannot always be avoided. One has to live with them. The point is merely that several models are often compatible with one's theory and data. In these circumstances, the best strategy is to select the simplest among them.

6.7.4 Alternative Measures of Fit.

Statisticians distinguish between the presence of association (that is, the lack of statistical independence) and the *strength* or *magnitude* of a relationship (see Chapter 2). A chi square test in an $I \times J$ table may be statistically significant while the variables are only weakly associated. A large chi square in and of itself indicates only the need to explore the relationship further. An index or measure of association is invaluable for this purpose.

A similar problem arises in log-linear analysis. Here, unfortunately, there is no completely adequate solution. Either chi square statistic, LRX^2 or GFX^2, measures the goodness of fit of a model to set of observations. But goodness of fit in this context has a different meaning than it does in, regression analysis. Regression analysis attempts to explain variation in a dependent variable. One measure of the fit of the regression model is R^2, the multiple correlation coefficient. Although it can be misleading in its own way, this index tells how much of the variation in the dependent variable is attributable to the independent variables. As the technique is normally applied, only two-factor and, very rarely, three-factor interactions are included in the regression equation. The number of independent variables of all types is usually small compared to the sample size. Finally, variation in the dependent variable has a clear meaning.

Consequently, if R^2 is numerically small, one infers that the independent variables have little explanatory power, even though the relationships may be statistically significant. The interpretation of goodness of fit in this sense is unambiguous.

In log-linear analysis, by contrast, a good fit can *always* be found, just by adding parameters. Goodness of fit, however, has to be interpreted cautiously. Suppose that a political scientist wants to know why people vote for Democrats or Republicans. He obviously has to decide ahead of time what variables to include in the study. Having made the decision, he then looks for models that fit the data as determined by his choice of variables. If the variables are in fact mutually independent, no difficulties arise because very simple models (mutual independence, for example) are acceptable. Yet, if there are weak interdependencies, a model containing several two-factor interactions might be required. The problem is that although this model provides a good fit as measured by chi square, the political scientist still does not know how well voting behavior has been explained.

A small chi square value for a given number of degrees of freedom might be interpreted as a full explanation of the dependent variable when in fact all the model accomplishes is to account for a particular distribution of cell frequencies. In the absence of yardstick-like variation, it is hard to determine how well it *actually* explains voting. The R^2 of regression analysis signals possible weaknesses in the regression equation. A significant chi square, on the other hand, means that the expected frequencies do not conform to the observed data. It does not say whether or not the particular cross-classification (that is, choice of variables) is meaningful.

All of this implies the need for an alternative measure, one comparable to R^2 or similar statistics. In this regard, however, there does not seem to be a convincing analogue. The magnitudes of parameter estimates are perhaps the best measures of relationships, but with polychotomous variables, these are difficult to interpret for the reasons noted previously.

Goodman (1971a, 1972a) has also proposed a general analogue to the familiar multiple and partial correlation coefficients:

$$R'^2 = \frac{LRX^2(M_a) - LRX^2(M_i)}{LRX^2(M_a)}. \tag{6.22}$$

where the parameters in M_a constitute a subset of the parameters in M_i.[16] In Goodman's (1972a, pp. 43–44) words, this expression is "somewhat analogous to the expression of the coefficients of multiple and partial [correlation], in the usual multiple regression analysis, as a ratio of the 'explained variation' (when model $[M_i]$ is used to 'explain' the variation that was not explained by $[M_a]$ to the 'unexplained variation' (when model $[M_a]$ is used)." Since M_a has fewer parameters than M_i, its associated chi square is larger. Thus, R'^2 varies between 0 and 1.0.

Seen from another perspective, R'^2 measures the proportional improvement in fit of M_i over M_a. Following this logic, R'^2 is somewhat similar to a "proportional-reduction-in-error" measure. If $LRX^2(M_a)$ represents the "error" in fitting the data from model M_a, then R'^2 gives the reduction in error obtained by moving to a more complicated model, M_i.

Whatever its interpretation, R'^2 is potentially misleading. To see why, consider Cowart's voting data. The LRX^2 for M_a, the mutual independence model in which only main effects are present, is 2283.45, with 46 degrees of freedom—clearly an unsatisfactory fit. Thinking of this model as a very crude analogy to the unexplained variation in, say, A, the dependent variable, one wonders how much understanding is gained by introducing two-factor interactions between A and the remaining variables.

$LRX^2(M_a)$ corresponds roughly to the total variation in A, and the difference, $LRX^2(M_a) - LRX^2(M_i)$, corresponds roughly to the unexplained variation after the variables in M_i have been introduced. Table 6.6 illustrates the calculation of R'^2 for various models. Models M_1, M_2, and

---

16. We could just as well define this measure by using GFX^2 instead of LRX^2.

M_3 contain only a single interaction with the dependent variable, voting, and the associated R'^2's are thus analogous to simple r^2. The remaining R'^2's pertain to models having more than one interaction and are analogous to multiple R's. For example, when M_i includes all possible interactions between A and the remaining variable, the proportional reduction in error gained by adding these terms is .84. Introducing the three interactions considerably reduces the error.

TABLE 6.6. **Examples of R'^2 Applied to Cowart Voting Data**

Model	LRX^2	R'^2
M_a: {A}{B}{C}{D}	2283.45	*
M_1: {AB}{C}{D}	2258.82	.011
M_2: {AC}{B}{D}	1652.23	.276
M_3: {AD}{B}{C}	1085.85	.524
M_4: {AD}{AC}{B}	454.64	.801
M_5: {AD}{AC}{AB}	365.38	.840

But, of course, 84 percent of the variance in voting has not been explained in either substantive or statistical terms. In fact, the model {AD}{AC}{AB} does not even provide a satisfactory fit. By itself, R'^2 does not say whether or not a model adequately explains the data. It only compares one model's fit with another.

The problem in analyzing cross-classifications is that we do not have an accurate measure of the variation in the dependent variable. In usual regression analysis, small values of R^2 alert us to possible weaknesses in the regression model. In log-linear analysis, on the other hand, a model's fit applies to a particular arrangement of cell probabilities. Although a model may account for *this* pattern, the question still remains: is this choice of variables and the resultant layout of observations worth studying in the first place? Once partisanship, attitudes, and incumbency have been selected, one can always develop a model showing their connection to voting, but neither the test statistics (LRX^2 and GFX^2) nor R'^2, by themselves, measure the true explanatory power of the model. For this purpose other devices are needed, not the least of which are theoretical knowledge, intuition, and common sense.[17]

---

17. Actually, Goodman only considers models in which a variable (for example, A) is considered dependent. These models, described in more detail in Section 5.5, assume that the marginal totals pertaining to the independent variables are fixed. For Example, the model

$$\Phi_{jkl}^A = \beta^A$$

is equivalent to the model {BCD}{A}. He uses this kind of model as M_a in expression (6.22). Nevertheless, the previous remarks about R'^2 apply to these types of models as well.

7 REGRESSION ANALYSIS OF CROSS-CLASSIFICATIONS

7.1 INTRODUCTION

Although the maximum likelihood method described previously is quite popular, it is certainly not the only way to study multivariate categorical data. In fact, statisticians and social scientists have developed a bewildering array of techniques.[1] Fortunately, many of these approaches involve the same ideas and occasionally give identical results. For hierarchical models, the choice often depends more on personal taste and convenience than on substantive differences.

Explaining all of these methods, however, would require several volumes. Instead, it seems advisable to concentrate on a single but quite broad orientation: regression analysis.

The regression perspective has several advantages. For one, it brings together two well-known statistical tools, analysis of variance and regular correlation and regression. Researchers familiar with the general linear model appreciate the convenience of having a common framework for analyzing continuous and categorical data.

More important, however, the regression point of view also permits exploration of a wide variety of models and hypotheses, a much wider variety than considered heretofore. Advocates of regression methods believe that its breadth and flexibility are the main benefits. In contrast to the more restrictive log-linear analysis, the spectrum of admissible models

---

1. Among the best-known approaches are those based on information theory—Ku and Kullback (1968), Ku, Varner, and Kullback (1971), Kullback (1973, 1974); those based on graph theory—Davis (1975); those based on Bayesian analysis—Lindley (1964); those based on likelihood inference—Lindsey (1973); as well as miscellaneous approaches (e.g., Coleman, 1964).

seems limitless. Statisticians have found, for instance, that many disparate statistical tests and measures of association from numerous disciplines are easily subsumed under regression analysis. Indeed, one is restricted only by the limits of his imagination and insight in applying regression concepts to categorical data.

These advantages are not without cost, however. Compared to log-linear analysis, a few approaches based on regression analysis have less desirable statistical properties. Although these deficiencies appear to have little practical significance, particularly for large samples, the shortcomings trouble many statisticians. More serious from the beginner's viewpoint, perhaps, is the difficulty in comprehending the computations. One cannot understand even the basic ideas without the rudiments of matrix algebra.[2] Furthermore, it is impossible to tackle any meaningful cross-tabulation without a computer, since the computations are long and tedious. But the wide availability of necessary programs has mitigated—if not eliminated—the problem.

7.2 MULTIPLE REGRESSION WITH CATEGORICAL VARIABLES

In the usual multiple regression model, scores on the dependent variable, Y, are predicted from scores on the independent variables, denoted by X's.[3] For two independent variables, a typical regression model is

$$Y_i = \beta_0 + \beta_1 X_{1i} + \beta_2 X_{2i} + \varepsilon_i, \qquad (7.1)$$

where i runs from 1 to n, the number of observations, β's are regression coefficients, and ε_i is an error term. The least-squares estimate of the model is

$$\hat{Y}_i = \hat{\beta}_0 + \hat{\beta}_1 X_{1i} + \hat{\beta}_2 X_{2i}, \qquad (7.2)$$

where $\hat{Y}_i$ is the estimated or predicted value of Y_i.

In order to make valid estimates and tests of significance, one assumes among other things that the error term in (7.1) is independent of the X's, that its expected value is nil (that is, $E(\varepsilon_i) = 0$), and that it has a constant variance (that is, $\text{var}(\varepsilon_i) = \sigma^2$, a constant). The last assumption, referred to as *homoscedasticity*, means that magnitude of the error is not related to the level of the independent variables.

Regression analysis of nominal variables raises three problems. First,

---

2. Fortunately, the basics (some of which are covered in Appendix A) are not hard to grasp, especially if one is willing to take results on faith.

3. A switch to a new notation, with Y's and X's denoting variables, is necessary to maintain consistency with other treatments of the topic.

the nominal variables have to be entered into the regression equation in some manner. After all, one cannot put category labels into a formula requiring numeric data. Second, if the dependent variable is a dichotomy or a proportion, the least-squares estimates, β_i, may produce misleading or inadmissible estimates of Y. Third, when the dependent variable is a dichotomy or a proportion, homoscedasticity does not hold. Even though the least-squares estimates of β_i are unbiased, their variances are larger than they should be.

Each of these difficulties is surmounted by modifying regular regression procedures.

7.2.1 Coding Categorical Independent Variables.   First consider an interval-scale dependent variable and one or more nominal or qualitative independent variables. Model (7.1) still applies, but it is necessary to represent the categorical independent variables in the equation. Dummy variables accomplish this task.

The basic idea is that each category of each variable is treated as a separate variable. The new variables, not the original ones, are put in the equation. How are the categories transformed? Although there are several methods, the two most common are dummy and effect coding (Suits, 1957; Kerlinger and Pedhazur, 1973; Miller and Erikson, 1974).

Dummy Coding. Given a nominal variable with K categories, one creates a series of K dichotomous variables, each scored 1 if an individual belongs in the corresponding category and 0 otherwise. Suppose that a variable, party identification, has $K = 3$ categories: Democrat, Independent, and Republican. Then there are three dichotomous variables:

$$X_1 = \begin{cases} 1 & \text{if an individual is a Democrat,} \\ 0 & \text{otherwise.} \end{cases}$$

$$X_2 = \begin{cases} 1 & \text{if an individual is an Independent,} \\ 0 & \text{otherwise.} \end{cases}$$

$$X_3 = \begin{cases} 1 & \text{if an individual is a Republican,} \\ 0 & \text{otherwise.} \end{cases}$$

The individual's score on these three dummy variables represents his party affiliation. The X's for two Democrats, a Republican, and an Independent would be

Party	X_1	X_2	X_3
D	1	0	0
D	1	0	0
I	0	1	0
R	0	0	1

Notice that one dummy variable is superfluous because if one knows a person's score on two of the X's, he can exactly predict the person's score on the remaining X. In this sense, one X is redundant and in fact is always excluded from the equation. It is mathematically immaterial which variable is eliminated, the decision turning solely on how one wants to interpret the remaining coefficients.

Hence a categorical variable with K categories is transformed into $K-1$ dichotomous variables, each scored 0 and 1 and which constitute the independent variables in the regression model. The regression of Y on party identification, model (7.1), is thus

$$\hat{Y}_i = \hat{\beta}_0 + \hat{\beta}_1 X_{1i} + \hat{\beta}_2 X_{2i} \qquad i = 1, \ldots, n, \qquad (7.3a)$$

where X_1 is the dummy variable pertaining to the category "Democrat" and X_2 is the dummy variable pertaining to the category "Independent."

Actually, any two real numbers, not just 0 and 1, can represent the values of X_1 and X_2. But using 0 and 1 has distinct advantages. Notice, for example, that with $K-1$ dummy variables, one category, a reference category, is always coded 0. This fact simplifies the interpretation of the parameters. Suppose that the ith individual happens to be a Republican. Equation (7.3a) then reduces to

$$\hat{Y}_i = \hat{\beta}_0$$

since $X_{1i} = X_{21} = 0$. From this result it is easy to show that the estimate of β_0 equals the mean of the Republicans (the reference group) on Y. If Y measured political ideology, for example, $\hat{\beta}_0$ would equal the average observed liberalism-conservatism score among Republicans. The remaining parameters have related meanings, but they will be discussed in Section 7.3.4.

Of course, one can code any number of categorical variables in this manner, provided that the number of included dummy variables does not exceed n, the sample size.

There are several methods of coding interaction effects, the easiest being the multiplication of all appropriate pairs of dummy variables. If an investigator believed that the impact of party identification on Y depended on sex, he would want to include a term measuring the party by sex interaction. Suppose that the dummy variable for sex is

$$W_1 = \begin{cases} 1 & \text{if male} \\ 0 & \text{if female} \end{cases}$$

whereas the dummy variables for party identification are defined above. The interaction terms are

$$Z_1 = X_1 W_1 \qquad \text{and} \qquad Z_2 = X_2 W_1.$$

For the following individuals, the dummy variables are

Party	Sex	X_1	X_2	W_1	Z_1	Z_2
D	M	1	0	1	1	0
D	F	1	0	0	0	0
I	M	0	1	1	0	1

The equation for predicting Y is now

$$\hat{Y}_i = \hat{\beta}_0 + \hat{\beta}_1 X_{1i} + \hat{\beta}_2 X_{2i} + \hat{\beta}_3 W_{1i} + \hat{\beta}_4 Z_{1i} + \hat{\beta}_5 Z_{2i}. \tag{7.3b}$$

More generally, the interaction between two variables with I and J classes requires $(I-1)(J-1)$ dummy variables. Similarly, higher-order interactions between three or more variables are coded by multiplying the appropriate dummy variables.

Effect Coding. Another mathematically equivalent way of recoding categorical variables is effect coding. This method is useful because it leads to alternative interpretations of the regression coefficients. Assuming that there are no significant interactions, the two methods are equivalent in the sense that they produce the same R^2, the measure of the model's fit, and the same significance tests.

Instead of 1 or 0, one scores category memberships with 1, 0, and -1 or, if the variable is dichotomous, 1 and -1. Continuing with the party identification example, $K - 1 = 2$ variables are created as follows:

$$X_1 = \begin{cases} 1 & \text{if an individual is a Democrat,} \\ 0 & \text{if an individual is an Independent,} \\ -1 & \text{if an individual is a Republican.} \end{cases}$$

$$X_2 = \begin{cases} 0 & \text{if an individual is a Democrat,} \\ 1 & \text{if an individual is an Independent,} \\ -1 & \text{if an individual is a Republican.} \end{cases}$$

As with dummy coding, a third variable, X_3, would be redundant, since from knowledge of X_1 and X_2 one could predict scores on X_3.

Notice, too, that here the category "Republican" serves as a reference group: Republicans are scored -1 on both X_1 and X_2. It is not hard to show that $\hat{\beta}_0$, the intercept, equals the grand mean of the predicted Y's, whereas $\hat{\beta}_1$ and $\hat{\beta}_2$ equal "treatment effects," that is, deviations of category means from the grand mean. For instance, $\hat{\beta}_1$ reflects the effects on Y of being a Democrat. If its numerical value is small, then Democrats do not differ much from the average person with respect to the dependent variable.

Interaction effects, like those in dummy coding, are obtained by multiplying relevant variables. For example:

Party	Sex	X_1	X_2	W_1	Z_1	Z_2
D	M	1	0	1	1	0
D	F	1	0	−1	−1	0
I	M	0	1	1	0	1
R	M	−1	−1	1	−1	−1
R	F	−1	−1	−1	1	1

Of course, all of these coefficients—those obtained either from dummy or effect coding—can be given conventional regression interpretations: they represent the change in Y expected from a unit change in a given X with other variables held constant.[4]

7.2.2 Dichotomous Dependent Variables.   As long as the dependent variable is continuous, there is no difficulty in developing regression models for categorical variables: they are simply transformed to dummy variables which are included along with any interval-level independent variables. When Y is a dichotomy or a proportion, however, ordinary least squares breaks down.

One problem is that the regression model may produce misleading or meaningless predicted values (Nerlove and Press, 1973; Goodman, 1975b). Suppose that Y is coded 0 (for example, vote for Democratic) and 1 (for example, vote for Republican). A regression equation might lead to estimates of Y lying outside the range 0 to 1. How does one interpret $Y = 1.1$, for example?

Conditional Probabilities. The same remarks hold when the dependent variable is a proportion or conditional probability. It is common to investigate the proportion of respondents who are in a given category of a dependent variable, conditional on their having certain combinations of attributes on the independent variables. One may be interested, for instance, in the proportion of Democratic voters among Democrats, Republicans, and Independents. Expressing the proportions as P_j ($j = 1, 2, 3$), a model similar to (7.1) is

$$P_j = \beta_0 + \beta_1 X_1 + \beta_2 X_2 + \varepsilon_j, \tag{7.4}$$

where X_1 and X_2 are dummy variables for the categories of party identification. (Note that the subscript j refers to the jth level of the

---

4. Regression with dummy variables, it might be noted, is equivalent to a widely used technique, *multiple classification analysis* (MCA) (Andrews, Morgan, and Sonquist, 1967). MCA is based on an extensive computer program and is appealing because of its convenience in terms of the input of data and the provision of summary statistics.

independent variable.[5] The quantity P_j stands for the proportion of Democratic voters among individuals who belong in the jth category of party identification.) It can thus be viewed as a conditional probability: given that a person is in the jth category of the independent variable, P_j is the probability that he will vote Democratic.[6]

Since model (7.4) is equivalent to scoring the dependent variable 0 and 1, ordinary least squares breaks down for the same reason: estimates of P_j may lie outside the interval 0 to 1.

The Log Odds (Logit) Transformation. One solution to this problem is to transform the proportion into a log odds or logit:

$$\Phi_j = \log\left(\frac{P_j}{1 - P_j}\right) \qquad j = 1, \ldots, J, \qquad (7.5)$$

where log refers to the natural logarithm. Whereas $0 \le P \le 1$, the log odds Φ_j takes any value from minus to plus infinity. One therefore avoids the possibility of obtaining meaningless estimates.

It should be emphasized, however, that the model for Φ_j is not equivalent nor even necessarily an approximation to a model for P_j. The regression parameters and the fit to the data can be quite different. The differences between the two types may or may not be substantial, depending on the values of P_j (Goodman, 1972a, 1975b; Knoke, 1975). Consequently the choice of dependent variable P_j or Φ_j depends on one's substantive interests as well as statistical considerations.

Many statisticians, especially those emphasizing the practical aspects of analysis, do not regard the possibility of obtaining inadmissible estimates as a serious problem. As n increases, the likelihood of accepting a model with estimates outside the range of 0 to 1 diminishes, especially if the true proportions are not too close to 0 or 1. If one has a relatively large sample size, they argue, he should not sacrifice the analysis of P_j's (assuming that they are theoretically interesting) for the sake of statistical niceties.

7.2.3 Heteroscedasticity. In spite of the fact that Φ_j takes on any values whereas P_j does not, even models for the log odds cannot be analyzed by ordinary least-squares methods because the assumption of homoscedasticity is violated. Homoscedasticity means that the error terms, ε_i, are unrelated to the independent variables. In other words, the variance of the errors, $\sigma^2_{\varepsilon_i}$, is constant.

---

5. When there are several independent variables, j refers to the jth class of the combined independent variable. In the previous example with party identification and sex, j runs from 1 to 6; $j = 1$ for Democratic–male; $j = 2$ for Independent–male, and so forth. The independent variables constitute a *joint* predictor with $J = 6$ classes.

6. This probability differs from P_{ij}, the probability of being in the ijth cell of an $I \times J$ table.

The variances of observed proportions, p_j, and log odds Φ_j, on the other hand, depends on the number of cases in each level of the (joint) independent variable, meaning that the variances of disturbances for these models are not constant across levels of the independent variables. Under heteroscedasticity, estimates of the regression parameters are unbiased but their standard errors are too large. This in turn compromises the efficiency of the parameter estimates and tests of significance. The problem's seriousness depends on how much the error variances differ from one another.

Some investigators working with large n's ignore the problem. It is common, however, to turn to an alternative procedure, weighted least squares. Weighted least squares, it turns out, is the basis of a very general framework for analyzing cross-classifications.

7.3 WEIGHTED LEAST SQUARES: THE GSK APPROACH

Grizzle, Starmer, and Koch (1969) recognized that many problems in categorical data analysis could be solved by weighted least squares. For some of the models considered in Chapter 5, their method (hereafter abbreviated GSK) gives identical results to the maximum likelihood techniques. GSK is considerably more general, however, and handles a vast array of hypotheses.[7]

7.3.1 An Overview of GSK.   Like log-linear analysis, the GSK approach consists of a series of steps.

Definition of the Dependent Variable. Most regression models predict scores for individual cases. By contrast, the dependent variable in GSK analysis does not refer to individuals *per se* rather to probabilities or functions of probabilities. The dependent variable, for example, might be the conditional probability of voting Democratic. Or it might be a log odds. Whatever the case, the analyst's first task is to define an appropriate dependent variable, often called a *response function*. The choice of a response function, which turns mostly on substantive interests, must be made carefully because a model's interpretation depends on its definition.

Definition of a Model. Since the response function is treated as a dependent variable, one can construct models to account for its "variance." Having the same appearance as ordinary regression equations, the models explicitly introduce independent variables, including main and interaction effects. As will be apparent shortly, the range of permissible models is quite broad.

7. For a general description and various applications, see, among others, Grizzle, Starmer, and Koch (1969), Grizzle and Williams (1972), Johnson and Koch (1970, 1971), Koch and Reinfurt (1970, 1971), Koch, Imrey, and Reinfurt (1972), Koch, Freeman, and Lehnen (1975), Lehnen and Koch (1974a, 1974b). Also see Theil (1970).

Estimation and Testing. After proposing a model, one estimates its parameters and, assuming that it is unsaturated, tests its fit to the data. If the model proves adequate, one can estimate values of the dependent variable, obtain residuals, and test the significance of individual parameters. In these respects, the GSK method resembles regular regression analysis.

7.3.2 **The Arrangement of the Data in GSK Analysis.** The basic table is usually arranged according to *responses* and *subpopulations.* Responses are values of the dependent variable (which may be multivariate), whereas subpopulations consist of combinations of categories of the independent variables, frequently called *factors.*

Table 7.1 illustrates one possible arrangement of the data. The entries in the table refer to population probabilities. Unlike those in the previous chapters, the P's are conditional probabilities: P_{sr} represents the probability that an observation makes response r, given that he belongs in the sth subpopulation ($s = 1, \ldots, S$, where S is the number of subpopulations; $r = 1, \ldots, R$, where R is the number of response categories). Since the P's are probabilities, we have for each subpopulation

$$\sum_r P_{sr} = 1.0, \tag{7.6}$$

where, in accordance with previous notation, the summation is over all R responses.

TABLE 7.1. **Typical Layout in GSK Analysis**

Subpopulation	Response Category		Total
	1	$2 \cdots r \cdots R$	
1	P_{11}	$P_{12} \cdots P_{1r} \cdots P_{1R}$	1.0
2	P_{21}	$P_{22} \cdots P_{2r} \cdots P_{2R}$	1.0
.	.	. . . .	.
.	.	. . . .	.
s	P_{s1}	$P_{s2} \cdots P_{sr} \cdots P_{sR}$	1.0
.	.	. . . .	.
.	.	. . . .	.
S	P_{S1}	$P_{S2} \cdots P_{Sr} \cdots P_{SR}$	1.0

Estimates of the conditional probabilities are found from the table of observed frequencies, which is usually viewed as a set of S independent samples from the subpopulations with the marginal totals fixed. The observed conditional probabilities or proportions are

$$p_{sr} = \frac{f_{sr}}{f_{s+}},$$ (7.7)

where f_{sr} is the number of observations in the rth response category of the sth subpopulation $(s = 1, \ldots, S; \; r = 1, \ldots, R)$ and where

$$f_{s+} = \sum_r f_{sr}.$$

GSK technique also permits the analysis of single subpopulation data. The table can be thought of as having a single row or as a regular contingency table (see Section 7.4.7 for an example).

Since specific examples may clarify these points, consider Tables 7.2 and 7.3 (The two data sets demonstrate different aspects of GSK analysis.) The first table pertains to senatorial voting. Although these data have been used in log-linear analysis, they shall be reanalyzed in order to compare the two approaches. Here "vote," the response variable, has two categories, whereas the nine combinations of party identification and partisan attitude define the subpopulations. Each of the row totals is now considered fixed.

Table 7.2 also presents the observed conditional proportions obtained from expression (7.7). The conditional probability of voting Democratic among Democrats with pro-Democratic attitudes is

$$p_{11} = 620/700 = .886.$$

It is often helpful to display the probabilities in a *vector*—that is, an array of numbers. For the general case, all of the SR population probabilities can be represented by an $SR \times 1$ vector denoted **P**:

$$\mathbf{P} = \begin{bmatrix} P_{11} \\ P_{12} \\ \cdot \\ \cdot \\ \cdot \\ P_{SR} \end{bmatrix}.$$

The vector **P** has SR rows and one column, with the probabilities strung out one after another, those in the first row coming first, those in the second row coming next, and so forth.

TABLE 7.2. **Voting for Senate by Party Identification and Partisan Attitude**

Subpopulation	Party	Attitude	Frequency				Conditional Probability		Log Odds
			D	R	Total		D	R	
1	D	D	620	80	700		.886	.114	2.051
2	D	N	367	64	431		.852	.148	1.750
3	D	R	116	63	179		.648	.352	.610
4	I	D	89	40	129		.690	.310	.800
5	I	N	151	150	301		.502	.498	.008
6	I	R	69	153	222		.311	.689	-.795
7	R	D	13	55	68		.191	.809	-1.444
8	R	N	52	200	252		.206	.793	-1.348
9	R	R	50	511	561		.089	.911	-2.326

Key: D = Democrat, I = Independent, R = Republican, N = Neutral.
Source: See Table 4.1.

Observed *p*'s are displayed in a similar fashion. For the voting data [where $SR = (9)(2) = 18$], the vector **p** is an 18×1 vector:

$$\mathbf{p} = \begin{bmatrix} 620/700 \\ 80/700 \\ 367/431 \\ \cdot \\ \cdot \\ \cdot \\ 50/561 \\ 511/561 \end{bmatrix} = \begin{bmatrix} .886 \\ .114 \\ .852 \\ \cdot \\ \cdot \\ \cdot \\ .089 \\ .911 \end{bmatrix}$$

Table 7.3, drawn from a study of the 1972 presidential election, shows the relationship between political activity (the response variable) and education and occupation. The proportions or probabilities are calculated according to (7.7) and may be arranged in a 36×1 vector, **p**, just as in the previous case. For clarity the rows of Table 7.3 are treated as 12 independent samples with fixed marginal totals from subpopulations defined by the combinations of education and occupation. Since there are three responses for each subpopulation, the vector **p** has 36 rows.

Weighted least-squares analysis, the heart of the GSK approach, requires estimates of the variances and covariances of the *p*'s. These quantities are estimated by

$$\text{var}\,[p_{sr}] = \frac{p_{sr}(1 - p_{sr})}{f_{s+}} \tag{7.8a}$$

$$\text{cov}\,[p_{sr}p_{sr'}] = \frac{-p_{sr}p_{sr'}}{f_{s+}} \qquad r \neq r', \tag{7.8b}$$

where p_{sr} is defined by (7.7). Because the samples from different sub-populations are assumed to be independent, the covariation across rows should be zero:

$$\text{cov}\,[p_{sr}p_{s'r}] = 0 \qquad s \neq s'. \tag{7.8c}$$

Matrix notation simplifies the representation and manipulation of these quantities. Let $\hat{\mathbf{V}}$ be an $SR \times SR$ matrix, that is, a matrix with SR rows and SR columns:

$$\underset{(SR \times SR)}{\hat{\mathbf{V}}} = \begin{bmatrix} \hat{\mathbf{V}}_1 & \mathbf{0} & \cdots & \mathbf{0} \\ \mathbf{0} & \hat{\mathbf{V}}_2 & \cdots & \mathbf{0} \\ \cdot & \cdot & & \cdot \\ \cdot & \cdot & & \cdot \\ \cdot & \cdot & & \cdot \\ \mathbf{0} & \mathbf{0} & \cdots & \hat{\mathbf{V}}_S \end{bmatrix}. \tag{7.9}$$

$\hat{\mathbf{V}}$ is really a huge matrix comprised of several smaller matrices, **0** and $\hat{\mathbf{V}}_s$.

TABLE 7.3. **Political Activity by Education and Occupation**

Subpopulation	Education	Occupation	Number of Political Activities				Probability			Average Score
			0	1	2+	Total	0	1	2+	
1	G	P	32	7	2	41	.780	.171	.049	.317
2	G	Cl	15	3	1	19	.789	.158	.053	.316
3	G	S	158	15	6	179	.883	.084	.034	.184
4	G	U	58	4	2	64	.906	.062	.031	.156
5	H	P	166	42	15	223	.744	.188	.067	.390
6	H	Cl	115	18	9	142	.810	.127	.063	.317
7	H	S	373	72	29	474	.787	.152	.061	.335
8	H	U	105	14	5	124	.847	.113	.040	.234
9	C	P	199	84	76	359	.554	.234	.212	.869
10	C	Cl	69	11	15	95	.726	.116	.158	.589
11	C	S	72	23	11	106	.679	.217	.104	.528
12	C	U	26	6	6	38	.684	.158	.158	.632

Key: *Education:* G = grade school, H = high school, C = at least some college; *occupation:* P = professional, Cl = clerical and sales, S = skilled laborer, U = unskilled laborer.

Source: 1972 National Election Study (see Appendix C).

The $R \times R$ **0** matrices contain only zeroes, whereas the $\hat{\mathbf{V}}_s$ give the variances and covariances among the probabilities in the sth row or subpopulation:

$$
\hat{\mathbf{V}}_s = \frac{1}{f_{s+}}
\begin{bmatrix}
p_{s1}(1-p_{s1}) & -p_{s1}p_{s2} & \cdots & -p_{s1}p_{sR} \\
-p_{s2}p_{s1} & p_{s2}(1-p_{s2}) & \cdots & -p_{s2}p_{sR} \\
\cdot & \cdot & & \cdot \\
\cdot & \cdot & & \cdot \\
\cdot & \cdot & & \cdot \\
-p_{sR}p_{s1} & -p_{sR}p_{s2} & \cdots & p_{sR}(1-p_{sR})
\end{bmatrix}. \tag{7.10}
$$

As an example, the estimate of the variance-covariances of the probabilities in the *second* row of Table 7.3 is

$$
\hat{\mathbf{V}}_2 = \frac{1}{19}
\begin{bmatrix}
(.789)(1-.789) & -(.789)(.158) & -(.789)(.053) \\
-(.158)(.789) & (.158)(1-.158) & -(.158)(.053) \\
-(.053)(.789) & -(.053)(.158) & (.053)(1-.053)
\end{bmatrix},
$$

$$
=
\begin{bmatrix}
.00876 & -.00656 & -.00220 \\
-.00656 & .00700 & -.00044 \\
-.00220 & -.00044 & .00264
\end{bmatrix}.
$$

This submatrix is only one of twelve on the main diagonal of the supermatrix of $\hat{\mathbf{V}}$. (At this point, one can appreciate the computational difficulties of GSK analysis.)

These estimates are valid if the data have been obtained from independent random samples of the subpopulations and one assumes a product multinomial distribution. (A multinomial distribution is assumed for single population data.) (See Section 1.1.) When the tables have been generated by more complex designs, the results hold (if at all) only approximately. Nevertheless, many investigators apply GSK techniques to complex sample surveys, apparently without serious difficulty. And as long as the observed proportions are based on at least ten cases per row, the estimates should provide reasonable approximations for many practical purposes. (For justification of GSK applications to sample surveys, see, among others, Koch and Reinfurt, 1970, and Johnson and Koch, 1970.) In any event, the data in Tables 7.2 and 7.3 are only illustrative.

7.3.3 Defining the Dependendent Variable: Response Functions.
Having arranged the data in this manner, an analyst must next decide which aspect of them should be investigated. He might, for example, treat some subset of the conditional probabilities (such as the probability of voting Democratic) as the dependent variable. Or he might combine the probabilities into a more complicated relationship. Since there are innumerable possibilities, the definition of the dependent

variable, called a response function, must be guided by substantive considerations. Fortunately, many response functions usually fall into two groups, linear and logarithmic.

Linear relationships arise when the investigator wants to analyze the probabilities themselves or some additive function of them. Suppose that interest centers on the conditional probability of voting Democratic, p_{s1}. These probabilities are derived or selected from the basic set, $\mathbf{p}$, by a series of matrix operations. Let $\mathbf{f}$ be a vector containing the responses functions to be analyzed. In the example, $\mathbf{f}$ contains the observed conditional probabilities of voting Democratic:

$$\mathbf{f}_{(9\times1)} = \begin{bmatrix} p_{11} \\ p_{21} \\ \cdot \\ \cdot \\ \cdot \\ p_{91} \end{bmatrix} = \begin{bmatrix} .886 \\ .852 \\ \cdot \\ \cdot \\ \cdot \\ .089 \end{bmatrix}.$$

(See Table 7.2.)

This vector is effectively obtained by premultiplying $\mathbf{p}$ by a matrix $\mathbf{A}$,

$$\mathbf{f} = \mathbf{Ap}, \tag{7.11}$$

where $\mathbf{A}$ is a 9×18 matrix of the form

$$\mathbf{A} = \begin{bmatrix} \mathbf{A}^* & \mathbf{0}' & \cdots & \mathbf{0}' \\ \mathbf{0} & \mathbf{A}^* & \cdots & \mathbf{0}' \\ \cdot & & & \cdot \\ \cdot & & & \cdot \\ \cdot & & & \cdot \\ \mathbf{0}' & \mathbf{0}' & \cdots & \mathbf{A}^* \end{bmatrix}. \tag{7.12}$$

$\mathbf{A}$ consists of vectors $\mathbf{0}'$ and $\mathbf{A}^*$, which are

$$\mathbf{0}' = [0\ 0], \tag{7.13a}$$

$$\mathbf{A}^* = [1\ 0]. \tag{7.13b}$$

Written out in its full form, $\mathbf{A}$ is

$$\mathbf{A} = \begin{bmatrix} 1 & 0 & 0 & 0 & 0 & 0 & 0 & 0 & 0 & 0 & 0 & 0 & 0 & 0 & 0 & 0 & 0 & 0 \\ 0 & 0 & 1 & 0 & 0 & 0 & 0 & 0 & 0 & 0 & 0 & 0 & 0 & 0 & 0 & 0 & 0 & 0 \\ 0 & 0 & 0 & 0 & 1 & 0 & 0 & 0 & 0 & 0 & 0 & 0 & 0 & 0 & 0 & 0 & 0 & 0 \\ 0 & 0 & 0 & 0 & 0 & 0 & 1 & 0 & 0 & 0 & 0 & 0 & 0 & 0 & 0 & 0 & 0 & 0 \\ 0 & 0 & 0 & 0 & 0 & 0 & 0 & 0 & 1 & 0 & 0 & 0 & 0 & 0 & 0 & 0 & 0 & 0 \\ 0 & 0 & 0 & 0 & 0 & 0 & 0 & 0 & 0 & 0 & 1 & 0 & 0 & 0 & 0 & 0 & 0 & 0 \\ 0 & 0 & 0 & 0 & 0 & 0 & 0 & 0 & 0 & 0 & 0 & 0 & 1 & 0 & 0 & 0 & 0 & 0 \\ 0 & 0 & 0 & 0 & 0 & 0 & 0 & 0 & 0 & 0 & 0 & 0 & 0 & 0 & 1 & 0 & 0 & 0 \\ 0 & 0 & 0 & 0 & 0 & 0 & 0 & 0 & 0 & 0 & 0 & 0 & 0 & 0 & 0 & 0 & 1 & 0 \end{bmatrix}.$$

$$\tag{7.14}$$

It is easy to see the advantage of writing **A** in its abbreviated form, as in (7.12).

The reader can verify that when **p** is premultiplied by **A**, the result is **f**, the vector of the conditional probabilities of voting Democratic. Thus, matrix equation (7.11) defines a response function that serves as the dependent variable in subsequent analyses.

For a different example, consider the data in Table 7.3. One might also be interested in probabilities such as the conditional probability of zero activities. These probabilities could be obtained from **p** by using a 12×36 matrix **A** consisting of vectors **0**′ and **A***, where

$$\mathbf{0}' = [0 \quad 0 \quad 0] \quad \text{and} \quad \mathbf{A}^* = [1 \quad 0 \quad 0].$$

On the other hand, a response function of greater interest might be the mean number of activities within each subpopulation. These means, calculated by, say, $0p_{s1} + 1p_{s2} + 3p_{s3}$, can be constructed by choosing[8]

$$\mathbf{A}_{(12 \times 36)} = \begin{bmatrix} 013 & 000 & \cdots & 000 \\ 000 & 013 & \cdots & 000 \\ & \cdot & & \cdot \\ & \cdot & & \cdot \\ & \cdot & & \cdot \\ 000 & 000 & \cdots & 013 \end{bmatrix}. \tag{7.15}$$

(**A** could, of course, be written in the form of (7.12) with $\mathbf{0}' = [0 \quad 0 \quad 0]$ and $\mathbf{A}^* = [0 \quad 1 \quad 3]$.)

In general, U linear response functions can be derived from the basic set of observed proportions by

$$\underset{(U \times 1)}{\mathbf{f}} = \underset{(U \times SR)}{\mathbf{A}} \underset{(SR \times 1)}{\mathbf{p}}, \tag{7.16}$$

where

$$\mathbf{A} = \begin{bmatrix} a_{111} & \cdots & a_{11R} & a_{121} & \cdots & a_{12R} & \cdots & a_{1S1} & \cdots & a_{1SR} \\ a_{211} & \cdots & a_{21R} & a_{221} & \cdots & a_{22R} & \cdots & a_{2S1} & \cdots & a_{2SR} \\ \cdot & & \cdot & \cdot & & \cdot & & \cdot & & \cdot \\ \cdot & & \cdot & \cdot & & \cdot & & \cdot & & \cdot \\ \cdot & & \cdot & \cdot & & \cdot & & \cdot & & \cdot \\ a_{U11} & \cdots & a_{U1R} & a_{U21} & \cdots & a_{U2R} & \cdots & a_{US1} & \cdots & a_{USR} \end{bmatrix}. \tag{7.17}$$

The first subscript of the a entries refers to the response function (usually there is one response function for each subpopulation; that is, $U = S$); the second refers to the subpopulation, and the third refers to the level of the response variable. The **A** matrices (7.14) and (7.15) are specific instances

---

8. Of course, this response function would be appropriate only for ordinal variables. The particular values depend on the spacing of the categories.

of (7.17). By appropriately defining **A**, one can construct an extremely wide variety of response functions. Only two rather simple examples have been presented.

Naturally, the **A** matrix cannot be constructed blindly; doing so would violate important principles of matrix algebra. For details on the limitations in the construction of **A**, see Grizzle, Starmer, and Koch (1969).

As an alternative to linear relationships, one might analyze logarithmic functions of the probabilities, the most common being the log odds. Returning to Table 7.2, suppose that an investigator wished to treat the log odds of voting Democratic as the dependent variable. For the sth population, the observed log odds is

$$\phi_s = \log\left(\frac{p_{s1}}{p_{s2}}\right) = \log(p_{s1}) - \log(p_{s2}). \tag{7.18}$$

A vector of these functions is produced from **p** by a series of matrix operations. In this example let **f** be

$$\underset{(9\times1)}{\mathbf{f}} = \begin{bmatrix} \log(p_{11}/p_{12}) \\ \log(p_{21}/p_{22}) \\ \cdot \\ \cdot \\ \cdot \\ \log(p_{91}/p_{92}) \end{bmatrix} = \begin{bmatrix} \log(p_{11}) - \log(p_{12}) \\ \log(p_{21}) - \log(p_{22}) \\ \cdot \\ \cdot \\ \cdot \\ \log(p_{91}) - \log(p_{92}) \end{bmatrix}. \tag{7.19}$$

The vector **f** can be obtained by a two-step matrix operation:

$$\mathbf{f} = \mathbf{K}[\log(\mathbf{Ap})], \tag{7.20}$$

where **A** is an 18×18 identity matrix (that is, a matrix with 1's in the main diagonal and 0's elsewhere) and **K** is a 9×18 matrix:

$$\mathbf{K} = \begin{bmatrix} 1 & -1 & 0 & 0 & 0 & 0 & 0 & 0 & 0 & 0 & 0 & 0 & 0 & 0 & 0 & 0 & 0 & 0 \\ 0 & 0 & 1 & -1 & 0 & 0 & 0 & 0 & 0 & 0 & 0 & 0 & 0 & 0 & 0 & 0 & 0 & 0 \\ 0 & 0 & 0 & 0 & 1 & -1 & 0 & 0 & 0 & 0 & 0 & 0 & 0 & 0 & 0 & 0 & 0 & 0 \\ 0 & 0 & 0 & 0 & 0 & 0 & 1 & -1 & 0 & 0 & 0 & 0 & 0 & 0 & 0 & 0 & 0 & 0 \\ 0 & 0 & 0 & 0 & 0 & 0 & 0 & 1 & -1 & 0 & 0 & 0 & 0 & 0 & 0 & 0 & 0 & 0 \\ 0 & 0 & 0 & 0 & 0 & 0 & 0 & 0 & 0 & 1 & -1 & 0 & 0 & 0 & 0 & 0 & 0 & 0 \\ 0 & 0 & 0 & 0 & 0 & 0 & 0 & 0 & 0 & 0 & 0 & 1 & -1 & 0 & 0 & 0 & 0 & 0 \\ 0 & 0 & 0 & 0 & 0 & 0 & 0 & 0 & 0 & 0 & 0 & 0 & 0 & 1 & -1 & 0 & 0 & 0 \\ 0 & 0 & 0 & 0 & 0 & 0 & 0 & 0 & 0 & 0 & 0 & 0 & 0 & 0 & 0 & 1 & -1 \end{bmatrix}. \tag{7.21}$$

The effect of premultiplying **p** by **A**, the identity matrix in this case, is to reproduce **p**. At the second step after taking the log of each member, we premultiply (**Ap**) by **K**. This multiplication carries out the subtraction indicated in expression (7.18). The reader can easily verify that this operation leads to the desired $\mathbf{f}$ vector. For example, multiplying $\log(\mathbf{Ap})$ by the first row of $\mathbf{K}$ gives

$$(1) \log(p_{11}) + (-1) \log(p_{12}) + (0) \log(p_{21}) + \cdots + (0) \log(p_{92})$$
$$= \log(p_{11}) - \log(p_{12}).$$

Suppose that T logarithmic functions are desired. They can be derived from $\mathbf{p}$ by similar matrix algebra:

$$\underset{(T \times 1)}{\mathbf{f}} = \underset{(T \times U)}{\mathbf{K}} [\log(\underset{(U \times SR)}{\mathbf{A}} \underset{(SR \times 1)}{\mathbf{p}})], \qquad (7.22)$$

where $\mathbf{K}$ and $\mathbf{A}$ are matrices of appropriate constants. In sum, we first construct U functions out of the probabilities in $\mathbf{p}$, take their logarithims, and finally derive T response functions by applying $\mathbf{K}$. Note that in the previous example $T = U = 9$, but this is not always the case.

Since $\mathbf{f}$, whether linear or logarithmic, constitutes a dependent variable, it is only natural and reasonable to estimate its variance. The variance of $\mathbf{f}$, actually a variance-covariance matrix because $\mathbf{f}$ contains several elements, is used in the calculation of parameter estimates and test statistics. In the linear case, the covariance matrix, $\mathbf{S}$, is

$$\underset{(U \times U)}{\mathbf{S}} = \underset{(U \times SR)}{\mathbf{A}} \underset{(SR \times SR)}{\hat{\mathbf{V}}} \underset{(SR \times U)}{\mathbf{A}'}, \qquad (7.23)$$

where $\hat{\mathbf{V}}$ is given by (7.9) and $\mathbf{A}$ is the matrix defining the linear response functions. (Note that $\mathbf{A}'$ denotes the transpose of $\mathbf{A}$; see Appendix A.)

The variance-covariance matrix of logarithmic functions, a $T \times T$ matrix, is given by

$$\underset{(T \times T)}{\mathbf{S}} = \underset{(T \times U)}{\mathbf{K}} \underset{(U \times U)}{\mathbf{D}^{-1}} \underset{(U \times SR)}{\mathbf{A}} \underset{(SR \times SR)}{\hat{\mathbf{V}}} \underset{(SR \times U)}{\mathbf{A}'} \underset{(U \times U)}{\mathbf{D}^{-1}} \underset{(U \times T)}{\mathbf{K}'} \qquad (7.24)$$

where $\hat{\mathbf{V}}$ was defined in (7.9), $\mathbf{A}$ and $\mathbf{K}$ are the matrices used in constructing the response functions, and $\mathbf{D}^{-1}$ is the inverse (see Appendix A) of

$$\underset{(U \times U)}{\mathbf{D}} = \begin{bmatrix} \mathbf{a}_1'\mathbf{p} & 0 & \cdots & 0 \\ 0 & \mathbf{a}_2'\mathbf{p} & \cdots & 0 \\ \cdot & \cdot & & \cdot \\ \cdot & \cdot & & \cdot \\ \cdot & \cdot & & \cdot \\ 0 & 0 & \cdots & \mathbf{a}_U'\mathbf{p} \end{bmatrix}. \qquad (7.25)$$

Here $\mathbf{a}_i'$ represents the entries from the ith row of $\mathbf{A}$.

These expressions for the covariance matrix of $\mathbf{f}$ seem rather forbidding. Although hand calculations are nearly impossible, they can be obtained rather easily with appropriate computer programs. These matrices, however, are normally of less substantive concern than are estimates of the parameters and tests of significance. From the point of view of the average social scientist, then, the formulas are necessary evils which are presented without further detail or discussion.

7.3.4 Defining Models.   The elements of $\mathbf{f}$, the response function, are the individual values of the dependent variable. GSK analysis tries to find a model that accounts for their variance. The models closely resemble ordinary multiple regression since they contain a constant plus regression coefficients. But occasionally they are also interpretable from a log-linear point of view. Before discussing the meaning of these parameters, however, it is important to see how the models are actually constructed.

Again, consider a specific example. Suppose that an investigator, interested in the conditional probability of voting Democratic, believes that two variables, party identification and partisan attitude, explain the variation in these probabilities. Therefore, he wants a model that treats the values of $\mathbf{f}$, as defined by (7.11), as an additive function of partisanship and attitude. He also believes that the interaction effects between party and attitude are nil. A convenient way of expressing the model is

$$\underset{(9\times 1)}{\hat{\mathbf{f}}} = \underset{(9\times 5)}{\mathbf{X}} \; \underset{(5\times 1)}{\hat{\boldsymbol{\beta}}} \tag{7.26}$$

where $\hat{\mathbf{f}}$ is a vector of the predicted values of $\mathbf{f}$; $\mathbf{X}$, called a *design matrix*, contains dummy variables representing the categories of the independent variables, party identification, and attitude; and $\hat{\boldsymbol{\beta}}$ is a vector of estimated coefficients. The model may be clearer if written out in full form:

$$\begin{bmatrix} \hat{p}_{11} \\ \hat{p}_{21} \\ \hat{p}_{31} \\ \hat{p}_{41} \\ \hat{p}_{51} \\ \hat{p}_{61} \\ \hat{p}_{71} \\ \hat{p}_{81} \\ \hat{p}_{91} \end{bmatrix} = \begin{bmatrix} 1 & 1 & 0 & 1 & 0 \\ 1 & 1 & 0 & 0 & 1 \\ 1 & 1 & 0 & 0 & 0 \\ 1 & 0 & 1 & 1 & 0 \\ 1 & 0 & 1 & 0 & 1 \\ 1 & 0 & 1 & 0 & 0 \\ 1 & 0 & 0 & 1 & 0 \\ 1 & 0 & 0 & 0 & 1 \\ 1 & 0 & 0 & 0 & 0 \end{bmatrix} \begin{bmatrix} \hat{\beta}_0 \\ \hat{\beta}_1 \\ \hat{\beta}_2 \\ \hat{\beta}_3 \\ \hat{\beta}_4 \end{bmatrix}, \tag{7.27}$$

where the $\hat{p}$'s are estimates based on the model.

There is, in effect, a different equation for each $\hat{p}_{s1}$. Multiplying $\hat{\boldsymbol{\beta}}$ by the first row of $\mathbf{X}$ yields:

$$\hat{p}_{11} = \hat{\beta}_0 + \hat{\beta}_1 + \hat{\beta}_3, \tag{7.28a}$$

whereas multiplying $\hat{\boldsymbol{\beta}}$ by the second row gives

$$\hat{p}_{21} = \hat{\beta}_0 + \hat{\beta}_1 + \hat{\beta}_4. \tag{7.28b}$$

$\hat{\beta}$ multiplied by the last row of $\mathbf{X}$ is simply

$$p_{91} = \hat{\beta}_0. \tag{7.28c}$$

Equation (7.28a), for instance, asserts that the probability of someone in the first subpopulation (namely, a Democrat with pro-Democratic attitudes) voting for a Democratic candidate depends on or is a function of three parameters, $\hat{\beta}_0$, $\hat{\beta}_1$, and $\hat{\beta}_3$. Thus, $\mathbf{X}$ controls the parameters in $\boldsymbol{\beta}$ that will appear in a given equation. By defining $\mathbf{X}$ in a suitable manner, a researcher can construct almost any kind of model.

Seen from another perspective, the columns of $\mathbf{X}$ contain dummy variables, coded either with dummy or effect codes (see Section 7.2.1). (Here dummy codes have been used.) The second and third columns of $\mathbf{X}$ represent party identification: a Democrat is scored 1 on X_1 and 0 on X_2; an independent receives a 0 on X_1 and a 1 on X_2; whereas Republicans, serving as the reference category, have zeroes on both variables. Variables for partisan attitude, scored in the same way, appear in the fourth and fifth columns. The first column, corresponding to X_0, contains only 1's because it is used to represent the constant $\hat{\beta}_0$ appearing in every equation. By examining Table 7.2, one should be able to see the construction of the design matrix; still other examples are given shortly.

Since (7.26) is only a model, the predicted values in $\hat{\mathbf{f}}$ usually do not equal those in $\mathbf{f}$. Residuals are defined by

$$\underset{(9\times1)}{\mathbf{R}} = \underset{(9\times1)}{\mathbf{f}} - \underset{(9\times1)}{\hat{\mathbf{f}}} \tag{7.29}$$

where $\mathbf{R}$ is a vector containing the differences $p_{s1} - \hat{p}_{s1}$, for $s = 1, \ldots, S$. As in regular regression analysis, the residuals should be calculated and carefully studied, because they often reveal patterns of association or interaction worth exploring in greater detail (see Draper and Smith, 1966).

So far only a specific model has been considered. But the general case is really the same. For a vector of, say, U response functions, a model is defined by

$$\underset{(U\times1)}{\hat{\mathbf{f}}} = \underset{(U\times G)}{\mathbf{X}} \underset{(G\times1)}{\hat{\boldsymbol{\beta}}}, \tag{7.30}$$

where $\mathbf{X}$ is an appropriate design matrix—appropriate in the sense that it generates the desired equations for the response functions—and $\hat{\boldsymbol{\beta}}$ is a vector of G estimated parameters. When the number of parameters equals the number of response functions ($G = U$), the model is *saturated*. Having the same meaning as in log-linear analysis, the term "saturated" implies that the predicted values in $\hat{\mathbf{f}}$ equal the observed values. For $G < U$, the models are "unsaturated" and the fit is usually not exact. In this case it is necessary to measure a model's adequacy with a chi square statistic, as is explained shortly.

Weighted least-squares estimates of the model's parameters, $\hat{\boldsymbol{\beta}}$, are obtained from the formula

$$\hat{\boldsymbol{\beta}} = (\mathbf{X}'\mathbf{S}^{-1}\mathbf{X})^{-1}\mathbf{X}'\mathbf{S}^{-1}\mathbf{f}, \qquad (7.31)$$

where $\mathbf{X}$ is the design matrix, $\mathbf{f}$ is the response function vector, and $\mathbf{S}$ is the covariance matrix of $\mathbf{f}$. The mechanics of these calculations, which normally have to be done on a computer, are not particularly instructive and are not discussed further.

7.3.5 Interpretation of Model Parameters. A model's definition and interpretation depend on the construction of the design matrix. Each function is expressed as the sum of a set of coefficients. The meanings of these parameters is determined by, among other things, the coding of the variables.

Dummy Coding. A saturated model for p_j, the conditional probability in Table 7.2, is given by the following design matrix containing both main and interaction effects:

$$\mathbf{X}_s = \begin{bmatrix} 1 & 1 & 0 & 1 & 0 & 1 & 0 & 0 & 0 \\ 1 & 1 & 0 & 0 & 1 & 0 & 1 & 0 & 0 \\ 1 & 1 & 0 & 0 & 0 & 0 & 0 & 0 & 0 \\ 1 & 0 & 1 & 1 & 0 & 0 & 0 & 1 & 0 \\ 1 & 0 & 1 & 0 & 1 & 0 & 0 & 0 & 1 \\ 1 & 0 & 1 & 0 & 0 & 0 & 0 & 0 & 0 \\ 1 & 0 & 0 & 1 & 0 & 0 & 0 & 0 & 0 \\ 1 & 0 & 0 & 0 & 1 & 0 & 0 & 0 & 0 \\ 1 & 0 & 0 & 0 & 0 & 0 & 0 & 0 & 0 \end{bmatrix},$$

where $\mathbf{X}_s$ denotes the design matrix for a saturated model. Columns 2 through 5 represent dummy codes for the main effects of party identification and partisan attitudes, whereas columns 6 through 9 stand for the interaction terms. When $\hat{\boldsymbol{\beta}}$ is premultiplied by $\mathbf{X}$, a set of equations results. The equations, shown in abbreviated form in Figure 7.1, illustrate the parameter's interpretation.

First note that the coefficients in a typical equation such as

$$p_{11} = X_0\hat{\beta}_0 + X_1\hat{\beta}_1 + X_3\hat{\beta}_3 + X_5\hat{\beta}_5$$
$$= \hat{\beta}_0 + \hat{\beta}_1 + \hat{\beta}_3 + \hat{\beta}_5$$

may be interpreted in the same way as in regular regression analysis. A $\hat{\beta}_k(k = 1, \ldots, 8)$ measures the increase in p_{s1} per unit change in X_k; more

Figure 7.1. **The Interpretation of GSK Parameters**

		Democrat	Party Independent	Republican
	Pro-Democratic	$\hat{\beta}_0 + \hat{\beta}_1 + \hat{\beta}_3 + \hat{\beta}_5$	$\hat{\beta}_0 + \hat{\beta}_2 + \hat{\beta}_3 + \hat{\beta}_7$	$\hat{\beta}_0 + \hat{\beta}_3$
Attitude	Neutral	$\hat{\beta}_0 + \hat{\beta}_1 + \hat{\beta}_4 + \hat{\beta}_6$	$\hat{\beta}_0 + \hat{\beta}_2 + \hat{\beta}_4 + \hat{\beta}_8$	$\hat{\beta}_0 + \hat{\beta}_4$
	Pro-Republican	$\hat{\beta}_0 + \hat{\beta}_1$	$\hat{\beta}_0 + \hat{\beta}_2$	$\hat{\beta}_0$

precisely, as X_k increases from 0 to 1, p_{s1} changes by $\hat{\beta}_k$ units, assuming that the other variables are held constant.

As a further aid in their interpretation, note that the parameters in this model roughly correspond to parameters in a saturated log-linear model for log (F_{ijk}). Both models contain main and interaction effects. In a GSK model, however, the main effects correspond to two-factor interactions in log-linear analysis since they measure the impact of a given category of an independent variable on the dependent variable. The interaction terms—$\hat{\beta}_5$ through $\hat{\beta}_8$ in the above model—correspond to three-factor interactions in log-linear analysis. β_0 is a grand mean somewhat like μ in log-linear models.

In general, when the dependent variable is a conditional probability, the parameters will have roughly the same meaning as in log-linear models. (Neither the models nor the parameters will be numerically equivalent, however.) If the dependent variable is a log odds, then both GSK and log-linear analysis lead to identical goodness-of-fit tests and conclusions. In other words, a model for the log odds can be constructed either with GSK or maximum likelihood methods. That this relationship is true should come as no surprise. The general form of the log odds model given in Section 5.5 resembles a weighted least-squares equation. Although the β's are not numerically equal, there are simple relationships between them and chi square tests for the models will be equivalent.

Although this correspondence does not extend to models not included in the log-linear framework, it is clear that one understands either type of model in roughly the same terms.

Figure 7.1 provides a different and more specific view of the coefficients. Consider the lower right corner. The predicted value of the dependent variable, p_{91}, is simply $\hat{\beta}_0$. Whenever dummy coding is used, the constant term, $\hat{\beta}_0$, equals the value of the response function for the combination of variables (i.e., for the subpopulation) coded zero throughout. Here Republicans with pro-Republican attitudes are given 0's on X_1 through X_8; thus, $\hat{\beta}_0$ equals the conditional probability of a Republican with pro-Republican attitudes voting Democratic.

Assuming that one is willing to think in causal terms, $\hat{\beta}_2$ is interpreted as the effect on the probability of voting Democratic of a change in party identification from Republican to Independent. Suppose, in other words, that a person changes his party affiliation by switching from Republican to Independent but does not change his political attitudes. Then the probability of his voting Democratic will change by an amount equal to $\hat{\beta}_2$. Should this quantity be numerically large, one would conclude that party identification has a large impact on voting; if it is small, on the other hand, party has little or no relationship to voting. (As in log-linear analysis, it is somewhat difficult to find an intuitively clear definition of large and small changes, although one can certainly test the parameters for significance.) By the same token, $\hat{\beta}_1$ is the effect of a two-level jump from Republican to Democrat, providing that attitude does not change.

The coefficients pertaining to attitude, $\hat{\beta}_3$ and $\hat{\beta}_4$, have similar interpretations: they give the change in probability of voting Democratic resulting from changes in partisan attitude, assuming that party identification remains constant. It might be useful to remind the reader that these interpretations are meant to apply to the dependent variable, however defined. With the log odds, for instance, the text would read, "they give the change in log odds of voting Democratic resulting from . . . ."

One should note, incidentally, that the interpretation of these parameters has assumed a saturated model. But their meaning in unsaturated models is the same except that one is dealing with *estimates* of the response functions. The constant term, $\hat{\beta}_0$, in an unsaturated model, for example, equals the average *estimated* response function among the members of the subpopulation coded zero on all dummy variables. In the present context, $\hat{\beta}_0 = \hat{p}_{91}$, where $\hat{p}_{91}$ is the estimated conditional probability of a Republican with pro-Republican attitudes voting Democratic.

Now suppose that someone changes not only his party affiliation (from Republican to Independent), but also his partisan attitude (from pro-Republican to neutral). What happens to the probability of his voting Democratic? Not only is the probability affected by $\hat{\beta}_2$ and $\hat{\beta}_4$, but it is also influenced by an additional parameter, $\hat{\beta}_8$, representing the interaction effect. (Refer to Figure 7.1.) In this model, party and attitude do not act in a simple additive fashion, but instead the effect of one depends on the level of the other.

Figure 7.2a provides another way of looking at interaction terms. The three graphs, one for each level of partisan attitude, show the relationship between party identification and the dependent variable, the conditional probability of voting Democratic. Notice that the lines are not parallel, indicating that the form of the relationship depends on the level of partisan attitudes. Naturally, the statistical significance of the terms cannot be determined from graphs alone. From the shape of the curves, however, it is likely that at least some of them are important.

Figure 7.2b shows what the lines would look like if there were no interactions between party and attitude. For these hypothetical data, the graphs parallel one another, suggesting that the relationship between

FIGURE 7.2.   **Examples of Interaction and No Interaction in a Model for Conditional Probabilities**

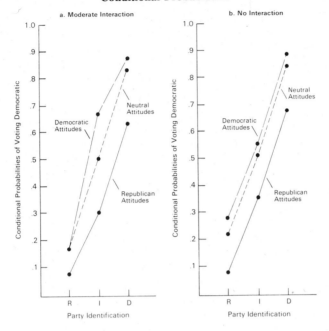

partisanship and voting does not depend on the level of partisan attitude. Remember too that interaction is "symmetric": were one to graph the association between partisan attitudes and voting, he would discover that, if interaction is not operative, the relationship would be the same for all categories of party identification.

The parameters in unsaturated models have identical interpretations. An advantage of the GSK approach, however, is that a researcher is not bound to hierarchical models. By appropriately constructing the design matrix **X**, he can include higher-order interactions without including their lower-order relatives. Or he can eliminate some but not all categories of an independent variable or an interaction term by leaving out the appropriate dummy variables. This flexibility in designing models is very useful because a nonhierarchical model may fit the data quite well, whereas a hierarchical one does not.

It is worth noting that since a GSK model for the log odds is equivalent in various ways to a corresponding log-linear model (see Section 5.5), the numerical estimates of the parameters found in each type of model are simple functions of each other. When all variables are dichotomous, the relationships can be simply expressed, as in, for instance,

$$\hat{\beta}_1 = 2\hat{\beta}_1^A,$$

where $\hat{\beta}_1$ is the GSK parameter and $\hat{\beta}_1^A$ is a corresponding term from log-linear analysis.[9] If the variables are not dichotomous, the relationships are more complicated but can be worked out rather easily. (See Goodman, 1975b, for additional details.)

Effect Coding. Using effect codes for the independent variables changes the numerical values of the parameters but does not affect either the significance test of the model as a whole or the substantive inferences drawn from it. This conclusion holds for any response function. When effect coding is used, however, the individual parameters have slightly different interpretations.

For the voting data with p_{s1}, the response function of interest, the design matrix is now

$$\mathbf{X}_s = \begin{bmatrix} 1 & 1 & 0 & 1 & 0 & 1 & 0 & 0 & 0 \\ 1 & 1 & 0 & 0 & 1 & 0 & 1 & 0 & 0 \\ 1 & 1 & 0 & -1 & -1 & -1 & -1 & 0 & 0 \\ 1 & 0 & 1 & 1 & 0 & 0 & 0 & 1 & 0 \\ 1 & 0 & 1 & 0 & 1 & 0 & 0 & 0 & 1 \\ 1 & 0 & 1 & -1 & -1 & 0 & 0 & -1 & -1 \\ 1 & -1 & -1 & 1 & 0 & -1 & 0 & -1 & 0 \\ 1 & -1 & -1 & 0 & 1 & 0 & -1 & 0 & -1 \\ 1 & -1 & -1 & -1 & -1 & 1 & 1 & 1 & 1 \end{bmatrix}.$$

As with dummy coding, the first column pertains to the constant, $\hat{\beta}_0^*$, columns 2 through 5 to the main effects, and columns 6 through 9 to the interaction effects. The interaction terms are obtained by multiplying the appropriate pairs of independent variables. The star notation (*) distinguishes the parameters from the coefficients obtained from dummy coding.

Premultiplying $\hat{\boldsymbol{\beta}}$ by $\mathbf{X}$ leads to a series of equations. For example,

$$\hat{p}_{11} = X_0\hat{\beta}_0^* + X_1\hat{\beta}_1^* + X_2\hat{\beta}_3^* + X_5\hat{\beta}_5^*$$
$$= \hat{\beta}_0^* + \hat{\beta}_1^* + \hat{\beta}_3^* + \hat{\beta}_5^*.$$

Like the other set of parameters, these have the usual regression interpretations. Or they can be described in analysis-of-variance terminology. The constant term, $\hat{\beta}_0^*$, for example, equals the grand mean of the dependent variable:

$$\hat{\beta}_0^* = \frac{\sum\limits_s \hat{f}_s}{S}, \tag{7.32}$$

---

9. When interactions are present they have to be coded slightly differently than described in Section 7.2.1 for the equality to hold. Goodman (1975b) gives the details.

where $\hat{f}_s$ is an estimate of the response function, however defined, in the sth subpopulation. For the voting data where $\hat{f}_s = \hat{p}_{s1}$, $\hat{\beta}_0^*$ is .486 when the response functions are the conditional probabilities and $-.078$ when the response functions are log odds. These values are reached by simply averaging the appropriate functions across all nine subpopulations. (Note that since the model is saturated, estimates of the response functions equal their observed values.)

As in analysis of variance, main effects give the difference between category means and the grand mean. Let $\bar{\hat{f}}_i$ designate the mean of the response functions of those people in the ith category of a particular variable. (The subscript i runs from 1 to $I-1$, the number of categories of the variable that are actually included in the model.) Then the main effect pertaining to that category is

$$\hat{\beta}_i^* = \bar{\hat{f}}_i - \hat{\beta}_0^*. \tag{7.33}$$

For instance, the mean $\hat{p}_{s1}$ among Democrats is .795. Therefore the estimated main effect of being a Democrat is

$$\hat{\beta}_1^* = .795 - .486 = .309.$$

If an effect is numerically large, it suggests that the average score on the dependent variable in a particular category differs substantially from the average scores in other categories. If, on the other hand, the effect is small, the category mean lies close to the grand mean, implying that the category does not explain much variation in the dependent variable.

Interaction effects are interpreted in the usual way as indications that the form or magnitude of a relationship between one independent variable and the response function depends on categories of another independent variable. Graphs similar to those introduced in Figure 7.2 could be presented here to show the effects of interaction terms. Alternatively, these parameters may be interpreted as deviations of the response functions around the main effects. In any event, their presence in a model indicates that the independent variables do not work together in a simple additive way, but have a more complex relationship to the dependent variable.

7.3.6 Significance Tests. Having decided upon a model, one tests its fit to the data by calculating a goodness-of-fit chi square

$$W^2 = \mathbf{f}'\mathbf{S}^{-1}\mathbf{f} - (\mathbf{X}\hat{\boldsymbol{\beta}})'\mathbf{S}^{-1}(\mathbf{X}\hat{\boldsymbol{\beta}}), \tag{7.34}$$

where $\mathbf{f}$, $\mathbf{S}$, and $\hat{\boldsymbol{\beta}}$ are the vectors and matrices defined previously and where $\mathbf{X}$ is the design matrix for the particular model under investigation. If this model fits, the statistic has an approximately chi square distribution with $(U-G)$ degrees of freedom, U being the number of response functions and G the number of parameters estimated. Small values for a given number of degrees of freedom of W^2 suggest that the model fits the data.

As with the estimates of the parameters, the actual calculation of W^2 is not especially instructive and usually has to be done by computer.

After finding an acceptable model, one can test various hypotheses about its parameters. Perhaps the most common step is to test the coefficients separately. Or, an investigator may want to test the hypothesis that one β equals another. Besides these tests, there are literally dozens of other hypotheses to explore.

In each instance, however, the hypothesis about the parameters in $\hat{\boldsymbol{\beta}}$ has a general form

$$H: \mathbf{C}\hat{\boldsymbol{\beta}} = \mathbf{0} \tag{7.35}$$

where $\mathbf{C}$ is a $Q \times G$ vector or matrix which specifies the hypothesis to be tested and $\mathbf{0}$ is a vector of zeroes. To test the hypothesis that the parameter pertaining to Democratic partisans, β_1, in the saturated model is nil (that is, $H_0: \beta_1 = 0$), one chooses

$$
\begin{bmatrix} 0 & 1 & 0 & 0 & 0 & 0 & 0 & 0 & 0 \end{bmatrix}
\begin{bmatrix} \beta_0 \\ \beta_1 \\ \beta_2 \\ \beta_3 \\ \beta_4 \\ \beta_5 \\ \beta_6 \\ \beta_7 \\ \beta_8 \end{bmatrix} = 0.
$$

The hypothesis that both β_1 and β_2 equal zero—that is, $H_0: \beta_1 = \beta_2 = 0$—is tested by

$$
\begin{bmatrix} 0 & 1 & 0 & 0 & 0 & 0 & 0 & 0 & 0 \\ 0 & 0 & 1 & 0 & 0 & 0 & 0 & 0 & 0 \end{bmatrix}
\begin{bmatrix} \beta_0 \\ \beta_1 \\ \beta_2 \\ \beta_3 \\ \beta_4 \\ \beta_5 \\ \beta_6 \\ \beta_7 \\ \beta_8 \end{bmatrix} = \begin{bmatrix} 0 \\ 0 \end{bmatrix}.
$$

The equality of two parameters—$\beta_1 = \beta_2$, for example—can be tested by

$$[0 \quad 1 \quad -1 \quad 0 \quad 0 \quad 0 \quad 0 \quad 0 \quad 0] \begin{bmatrix} \beta_0 \\ \beta_1 \\ \beta_2 \\ \beta_3 \\ \beta_4 \\ \beta_5 \\ \beta_6 \\ \beta_7 \\ \beta_8 \end{bmatrix} = 0$$

since the hypothesis is equivalent to H_0: $\beta_1 - \beta_2 = 0$. Finally, a test of all of the main effects together is based on

$$\mathbf{C} = \begin{bmatrix} 0 & 1 & 0 & 0 & 0 & 0 & 0 & 0 & 0 \\ 0 & 0 & 1 & 0 & 0 & 0 & 0 & 0 & 0 \\ 0 & 0 & 0 & 1 & 0 & 0 & 0 & 0 & 0 \\ 0 & 0 & 0 & 0 & 1 & 0 & 0 & 0 & 0 \end{bmatrix}$$

Whatever the case, by appropriately defining $\mathbf{C}$, one can test a wide variety of hypotheses. The general test statistic is

$$W^2 = \hat{\boldsymbol{\beta}}' \mathbf{C}' [\mathbf{C}(\mathbf{X}'\mathbf{S}^{-1}\mathbf{X})^{-1}\mathbf{C}']^{-1} \mathbf{C}\hat{\boldsymbol{\beta}}, \tag{7.36}$$

where W^2 is also approximately distributed as chi square with degrees of freedom equal to the number of rows, Q, in C. Here too the computation of W^2 is not very revealing, so we do not describe the mechanics. It is a matter best left to a computer: one simply enters the required matrices and pushes a button.

7.3.7 Examples. First, consider models for both the conditional probability and log odds of voting Democratic. Table 7.4 contains estimates of the parameters for saturated models together with their significances. (Note that only dummy coding has been used in this section.) These values could, of course, be substituted into an appropriate equation to get the estimated response function. (In a saturated model the estimate equals the observed value.) The equation for Republicans with pro-Republican attitudes is

$$\hat{p}_{91} = \hat{\beta}_0 = .089.$$

This value equals the observed conditional probability. For log odds the equation is

$$\hat{\phi}_9 = \hat{\beta}_0 = -2.324,$$

which agrees with the observed log odds in Table 7.2, except for a small rounding error.

Since the models are saturated, no overall goodness-of-fit test is possible—the predicted and observed values equal—but as in log-linear analysis, the estimates guide the selection of simpler models.

Note in particular the nonsignificance of most interaction terms. This pattern suggests testing models having only main effects. It is likely, however, that the final model for the conditional probabilities may differ from the one for the log odds.

Using the designed matrix given in (7.27), a main effects model, we obtain the estimates shown in Table 7.5. Clearly, the goodness-of-fit tests indicate that although main effects satisfactorily explain the log odds, they do not explain the conditional probabilities. This result could have been anticipated from the previous table where one interaction, $\hat{\beta}_7$ (Independent × pro-Democrat) was highly significant in the conditional probability model, but not in the log odds model. Consequently, we accept the main effects model for the log odds. Notice, incidentally, that this model is equivalent to a log-linear model with fitted marginals $\{AB\}\{AC\}\{BC\}$, where A stands for vote, B is party identification, and C is partisan attitudes. The goodness-of-fit test calculated by the methods described in Chapter 6 is 6.11 with 4 degrees of freedom, the same result as in Table 7.5 except for rounding error. As noted before, GSK models for log odds are equivalent to hierarchical log-linear models in the sense

TABLE 7.4. **Saturated Models for Conditional Probabilities and Log Odds for Table 7.2**

Parameter	Interpretation	Conditional Probability Estimate	Log Odds Estimate
$\hat{\beta}_0$	Mean	.089*	−2.324*
	Main Effects of Party		
$\hat{\beta}_1$	Democrat	.559*	2.935*
$\hat{\beta}_2$	Independent	.222*	1.528*
	Main Effects of Attitude		
$\hat{\beta}_3$	Pro-Democrat	.102†	.882‡
$\hat{\beta}_4$	Neutral	.117*	.997*
	Interactions		
$\hat{\beta}_5$	Democrat × pro-Democrat	.113†	.555
$\hat{\beta}_6$	Democrat × pro-Democrat	.086	.159
$\hat{\beta}_7$	Independent × pro-Democrat	.277*	.714
$\hat{\beta}_8$	Independent × Neutral	.074	−.174

*Significant at .001 level.   † Significant at .05 level.   ‡ Significant at .01 level.

TABLE 7.5. **Main Effects Models for Conditional Probabilities and Log Odds for Table 7.2**

Parameter	Interpretation	Conditional Probability Estimate	Log Odds Estimate
$\hat{\beta}_0$	Mean	.078*	−2.366*
	Main Effects of Party		
$\hat{\beta}_1$	Democrat	.604*	3.062*
$\hat{\beta}_2$	Independent	.285*	1.536*
	Main Effects of Attitude		
$\hat{\beta}_3$	Pro-Democrat	.209*	1.381*
$\hat{\beta}_4$	Neutral	.154*	.949*
		$W^2 = 19.300$, 4 *df*	$W^2 = 6.11$, 4 *df*

* Significant at .001 level.

that the overall tests are the same. Furthermore, the parameters of one model will be simple functions of the parameters of the other.

Observe, too, that the log-linear model contains an explicit interaction term between party and attitude, but that this term "cancels out" in rewriting the equation as a model for the log odds (see Section 5.5). The fact that it drops out does not mean that its effects have not been included in the goodness-of-fit test. Finally, in the log-linear analysis of these data, the three-factor interaction term, $\{ABC\}$, is not significant. Correspondingly, no interaction term between party and attitude is needed in the GSK model. (Remember, two-factor interactions in GSK analysis correspond to three-factor terms in log-linear analysis.)

A slightly expanded model is required for the conditional probabilities model. The following design matrix gives the estimates shown in Table 7.6:

$$\mathbf{X} = \begin{bmatrix} 1 & 1 & 0 & 1 & 0 & 0 \\ 1 & 1 & 0 & 0 & 1 & 0 \\ 1 & 1 & 0 & 0 & 0 & 0 \\ 1 & 0 & 1 & 1 & 0 & 1 \\ 1 & 0 & 1 & 0 & 1 & 0 \\ 1 & 0 & 1 & 0 & 0 & 0 \\ 1 & 0 & 0 & 1 & 0 & 0 \\ 1 & 0 & 0 & 0 & 1 & 0 \\ 1 & 0 & 0 & 0 & 0 & 0 \end{bmatrix}.$$

The last column, giving the interaction between Independents and pro-Democrats, is obtained by multiplying the entries in columns 3 and 4.

TABLE 7.6. **Model for Conditional Probabilities for Table 7.2**

Parameter	Interpretation	Estimate
$\hat{\beta}_0$	Mean	$-.080^*$
	Main Effects of Party	
$\hat{\beta}_1$	Democrat	$.620^*$
$\hat{\beta}_2$	Independent	$.254^*$
	Main Effects of Attitude	
$\hat{\beta}_3$	Pro-Democrat	$.181^*$
$\hat{\beta}_4$	Neutral	$.148^*$
	Interaction	
$\hat{\beta}_5$	Independent $\times$ pro-Democrat	$.175^*$

* Significant at .001 level.

Having found an adequate model for the conditional probabilities, an investigator might test the various parameters and summarize the results in an analysis-of-variance table. Using equations (7.35) and (7.36) with

$$\mathbf{C} = \begin{bmatrix} 0 & 1 & 0 & 0 & 0 & 0 \\ 0 & 0 & 1 & 0 & 0 & 0 \end{bmatrix},$$

he can test the hypothesis that $\beta_1 = \beta_2 = 0$. Similar analysis are carried out for the remaining main and interaction terms. The findings for the conditional probability model are as follows:

Component	W^2	df
Main Effects of Party	900.434	2
Main Effects of Attitude	73.575	2
Single Interaction (Ind. × pro-Dem.)	12.526	1
Error (residual)	6.776	3

Clearly, the effects of party and attitude are highly significant. The component due to the residual is nonsignificant, suggesting that the model adequately fits the data.[10] In addition, the test for the difference between β_1 and β_2, which is carried out by letting $\mathbf{C} = \begin{bmatrix} 0 & 1 & -1 & 0 & 0 & 0 \end{bmatrix}$, is significant ($W^2 = 192.596$ with 1 degree of freedom) whereas the difference between β_3 and β_4 is not ($W^2 = 2.984$ with 1 degree of freedom).

We can see how well the model fits by calculating estimated values for the response functions p_{s1}. For Democrats with pro-Republican attitudes, the equation is

$$\hat{p}_{31} = \hat{\beta}_0 + \hat{\beta}_1 = -.080 + .620 = .540.$$

Since the observed value is $p_{31} = .648$ and the residual is thus $R_{31} = p_{31} - \hat{p}_{31} = .108$, the agreement seems reasonable.

---

10. It is entirely possible that other models also fit these data. In a thorough analysis, one would investigate these possibilities more completely.

Finally, let us return briefly to the political activity data where the dependent variable or response function is the average number of activities. A preliminary analysis of the saturated model, not shown here, indicates that only main effects are needed. The left side of Table 7.7 shows the results. Although the model has a satisfactory fit, two parameters, $\hat{\beta}_4$ and $\hat{\beta}_5$, are not significant. It seems possible, then, to fit an even simpler model using

$$\mathbf{X} = \begin{bmatrix} 1 & 1 & 0 & 1 \\ 1 & 1 & 0 & 0 \\ 1 & 1 & 0 & 0 \\ 1 & 1 & 0 & 0 \\ 1 & 0 & 1 & 1 \\ 1 & 0 & 1 & 0 \\ 1 & 0 & 1 & 0 \\ 1 & 0 & 1 & 0 \\ 1 & 0 & 0 & 1 \\ 1 & 0 & 0 & 0 \\ 1 & 0 & 0 & 0 \\ 1 & 0 & 0 & 0 \end{bmatrix}.$$

The results appear on the right side of Table 7.7. Education, for example, accounts for most of the variation in the average activity scores.

In all of these models, one could use the parameter estimates to obtain predicted or estimated values for the dependent variables. By examining how these predictions deviate from the observed scores, further insights into the strengths and weaknesses of a particular model are obtained.

7.3.8 Conclusion: A Test for Marginal Symmetry.

The advocates of GSK analysis argue that one of its main benefits is flexibility. The procedure can be adapted to an astonishingly wide variety of problems. To illustrate this versatility, we conclude with a test for marginal symmetry (see Chapter 1).

The hypothesis of marginal symmetry asserts that in an $I \times I$ table (that is, a square table) corresponding row and column proportions equal each other:[11]

$$P_{i+} = P_{+i} \qquad \text{for all } i. \tag{7.37}$$

---

11. Note that the P's now refer to proportions or probabilities based on the table as a whole.

TABLE 7.7. **Two Models for Political Activity Index**

Parameter	Interpretation	Main Effects Model Estimate	Reduced Model Estimate
$\hat{\beta}_0$	Mean	.598*	.647*
	Main Effects of Education		
$\hat{\beta}_1$	Grade school	−.459*	−.465*
$\hat{\beta}_2$	High school	−.348*	−.351*
	Main Effects of Occupation		
$\hat{\beta}_3$	Professional	194*	.147*
$\hat{\beta}_4$	Clerical sales	.063	—
$\hat{\beta}_5$	Skilled	.058	—
		$W^2 = 6.285$, 6 df	$W^2 = 8.696$, 8 df

*Significant at .001 level.

As noted in Chapter 1, testing this hypothesis can present mathematical difficulties. Fortunately, the test is rather easily performed within the GSK framework.

Referring to the data in Table 1.6 showing the relationship between spouses' votes in the 1968 presidential election, the problem is formulated as follows: we want to know if the table comes from a population in which the row proportions equal the corresponding column proportions. Consequently, observed marginal proportions constitute the response function of interest. These proportions can be obtained from Table 1.6 by multiplying $\mathbf{p}$, the vector of observed probabilities, by $\mathbf{A}$, which is

$$\mathbf{A} = \begin{bmatrix} 1 & 1 & 1 & 0 & 0 & 0 & 0 & 0 & 0 \\ 0 & 0 & 0 & 1 & 1 & 1 & 0 & 0 & 0 \\ 1 & 0 & 0 & 1 & 0 & 0 & 1 & 0 & 0 \\ 0 & 1 & 0 & 0 & 1 & 0 & 0 & 1 & 0 \end{bmatrix}.$$

The first two rows of $\mathbf{A}$ give the first two row marginal proportions (p_{1+}, p_{2+}), whereas the last two rows of $\mathbf{A}$ give the column marginal proportions (p_{+1}, p_{+2}). For mathematical reasons it is not possible to include p_{3+} and p_{+3}. But if the hypothesis (7.37) holds for $(I-1)$ rows and columns, it will also hold for the remaining proportions as well.

Note that the hypothesis can be thought of as asserting that

$$P_{i+} = P_{+i} = \hat{\beta}_i \quad \text{for} \quad i = 1,2.$$

In other words, both P_{i+} and P_{+i} equal the same number. Thus, an alternative statement of the hypothesis using GSK concepts is

$$\hat{\mathbf{f}} = \mathbf{X}\hat{\boldsymbol{\beta}}, \tag{7.38}$$

where

$$X = \begin{bmatrix} 1 & 0 \\ 0 & 1 \\ 1 & 0 \\ 0 & 1 \end{bmatrix}$$

and $\hat{\beta}' = [\hat{\beta}_1 \hat{\beta}_2]$ and $\hat{f}$ is a vector of estimated marginal proportions. The reader can verify that by premultiplying $\hat{\beta}$ by X leads to, for example,

$$\hat{f}_1 = \hat{p}_{1+} = \hat{\beta}_1 \quad \text{and} \quad \hat{f}_{+1} = \hat{p}_{+1} = \hat{\beta}_1.$$

If (7.38) fits the data, the hypothesis holds. The test statistic is given by expression (7.34) with $v = U - G$ degrees of freedom. (In the example, there are four response functions and two estimated parameters, so the degrees of freedom is 2.)

For the data at hand, $W^2 = 10.508$ with 2 degrees of freedom. Although it is statistically significant, the value is not particularly large and the significance seems partly a function of the huge sample size.

In any event, the example illustrates the wide applicability of GSK. In order to appreciate fully its advantages, the reader is advised to consult the literature cited earlier. This approach to the analysis of categorical data, although not without pitfalls, will no doubt become an increasingly important tool in survey research.

Appendix A
VECTORS AND MATRICES

Although it is impossible to explain matrix and vector operations in a short space, these notes may clarify the ideas presented in Chapter 7. For more rigorous and thorough presentations, consult, among others, Hadley (1961) and Horst (1963).

A.1.1 Matrices and Vectors. A matrix is a rectangular array of numbers with r rows and c columns. It can be denoted by $\underset{r \times c}{\mathbf{X}}$ or more simply $\mathbf{X}$ when the dimensions are clear from the context. For example,

$$\underset{3 \times 2}{\mathbf{X}} = \begin{pmatrix} 3 & 5 \\ 1 & 2 \\ 8 & 0 \end{pmatrix}.$$

A diagonal matrix is a square matrix (that is $r = c$) with entries in the main diagonal and zeroes elsewhere. For example,

$$\underset{3 \times 3}{\mathbf{X}} = \begin{pmatrix} 5 & 0 & 0 \\ 0 & 1 & 0 \\ 0 & 0 & 3 \end{pmatrix}.$$

A diagonal matrix with only 1's in the main diagonal, called an identity matrix and denoted $\mathbf{I}$, is frequently used in matrix operations. For example,

$$\mathbf{I} = \begin{pmatrix} 1 & 0 & 0 \\ 0 & 1 & 0 \\ 0 & 0 & 1 \end{pmatrix}.$$

Vectors are matrices with one row or column, such as

$$\underset{3 \times 1}{\mathbf{Z}} = \begin{pmatrix} 2 \\ 4 \\ 5 \end{pmatrix}.$$

One has to distinguish between column vectors (for example, **Z** above) and row vectors, which are denoted with primes ('). (See the next section.)

A.1.2 Transpose of a Matrix.   The transpose of a matrix, denoted by a prime ('), is a matrix having as its rows the columns of the original matrix.

For example, the transpose of $\underset{3\times2}{\mathbf{X}}$ above is a matrix with two rows and three columns:

$$\underset{2\times3}{\mathbf{X'}} = \begin{pmatrix} 3 & 1 & 8 \\ 5 & 2 & 0 \end{pmatrix}.$$

Another way of expressing the idea of matrix transposition is thus: if x_{ij} is an element in the ith row and jth column of **X**, x_{ji} is the element in the jth row and ith column of **X'**. The transpose of the vector **Z** above is

$$\mathbf{Z'} = (2 \quad 4 \quad 5).$$

A.1.3 Equality of Matrices.   Two matrices, **X** and **W**, having the same dimensions, are equal if they have the same elements in corresponding positions: that is, $x_{ij} = w_{ij}$ for all i and j.

A.1.4 Addition and Subtraction of Matrices.   If two matrices have the same dimensions, their sum is a matrix containing the sums of corresponding elements. The sum of **X** and **W**, assuming that they have the same dimensions, is a matrix **T** with the same dimensions as **X** or **W** and elements $t_{ij} = x_{ij} + w_{ij}$ for all i and j. For example, let

$$\underset{3\times2}{\mathbf{X}} = \begin{pmatrix} 3 & 5 \\ 1 & 2 \\ 8 & 0 \end{pmatrix} \quad \text{and} \quad \underset{3\times2}{\mathbf{W}} = \begin{pmatrix} 7 & 4 \\ 2 & 3 \\ 0 & 1 \end{pmatrix}.$$

Then

$$\underset{3\times2}{\mathbf{T}} = \underset{3\times2}{\mathbf{X}} + \underset{3\times2}{\mathbf{W}} = \begin{pmatrix} 3+7 & 5+4 \\ 1+2 & 2+3 \\ 8+0 & 0+1 \end{pmatrix} = \begin{pmatrix} 10 & 9 \\ 3 & 5 \\ 8 & 1 \end{pmatrix}.$$

The addition of matrices with unequal dimensions is undefined. The subtraction of matrices follows the same principles.

A.1.5 Multiplication by a Scalar.   The multiplication of a matrix by a scalar yields a new matrix of the same dimension, but in which each element is the scalar times the corresponding original element. Let **X** be defined as in the previous examples. Then, for example,

$$2\mathbf{X} = \begin{pmatrix} 6 & 10 \\ 2 & 4 \\ 16 & 0 \end{pmatrix}.$$

The same idea applies to multiplication of a vector by a scalar.
For $\mathbf{Z}' = (2 \quad 4 \quad 5)$:

$$3\mathbf{Z}' = (6 \quad 12 \quad 15).$$

A.1.6 Matrix Multiplication.   Two matrices can be multiplied only if
the columns of the premultiplier equals the rows of the postmultiplier. If
$\mathbf{X}$ is an $r \times c$ matrix and $\mathbf{W}$ is a $c \times s$ matrix, the product $\mathbf{T} = \mathbf{XW}$ is an $r \times s$
matrix with elements

$$t_{ij} = \sum_{k=1}^{c} x_{ik} w_{kj}.$$

In effect, one finds the ijth element of $\mathbf{T}$ by multiplying the elements
in the ith row of $\mathbf{X}$ by the corresponding elements in the jth column of $\mathbf{W}$
and adding the product. For example, if

$$\underset{3\times2}{\mathbf{X}} = \begin{pmatrix} 3 & 5 \\ 1 & 2 \\ 8 & 0 \end{pmatrix} \quad \text{and} \quad \underset{2\times3}{\mathbf{W}} = \begin{pmatrix} 3 & 5 & 1 \\ 0 & 6 & 2 \end{pmatrix},$$

then

$$\underset{3\times3}{\mathbf{T}} = \underset{3\times2}{\mathbf{X}} \, \underset{2\times3}{\mathbf{W}} = \begin{bmatrix} (3)(3)+(5)(0) & (3)(5)+(5)(6) & (3)(1)+(5)(2) \\ (1)(3)+(2)(0) & (1)(5)+(2)(6) & (1)(1)+(2)(2) \\ (8)(3)+(0)(0) & (8)(5)+(0)(6) & (8)(1)+(0)(2) \end{bmatrix}$$

$$= \begin{pmatrix} 9 & 45 & 13 \\ 3 & 17 & 5 \\ 24 & 40 & 8 \end{pmatrix}.$$

Multiplication of matrices by vectors is handled in the same way.
For example, if

$$\mathbf{Z}' = (4 \quad 2) \quad \text{and} \quad \mathbf{Y} = \begin{pmatrix} 3 & 9 \\ 6 & 1 \end{pmatrix},$$

then

$$\underset{1\times2}{\mathbf{U}} = \underset{1\times2}{\mathbf{Z}'} \, \underset{2\times2}{\mathbf{Y}} = [(4)(3)+(2)(6) \quad (4)(9)+(2)(1)] = [24 \quad 38].$$

Note that the dimensions of the matrices must conform. Also note
that $\mathbf{XW}$ usually does not equal $\mathbf{WX}$ and in fact may not be defined. For
example, if

$$\mathbf{W} = \begin{pmatrix} 8 & 4 & 7 & 1 \\ 5 & 5 & 3 & 2 \end{pmatrix},$$

then the product $\mathbf{XW}$ (where $\mathbf{X}$ is defined above) is defined but $\mathbf{WX}$ is
not. Thus, it is important to keep in mind the size of matrices and the
order of their multiplication.

A.1.7 The Inverse of a Matrix. Consider the following relationship between two *square* matrices:

$$\mathbf{X}\mathbf{X}^{-1} = \mathbf{I},$$

where $\mathbf{I}$ is an identity matrix. The matrix, $\mathbf{X}^{-1}$, is called the *inverse* of $\mathbf{X}$. It has the property that its premultiplication by $\mathbf{X}$ produces the identity matrix.

Not every square matrix has an inverse, and it is not easy to find inverses. To appreciate the complexity, consider a simple example. Let

$$\underset{2\times 2}{\mathbf{X}} = \begin{pmatrix} 2 & 3 \\ 1 & 4 \end{pmatrix} \quad \text{and} \quad \underset{2\times 2}{\mathbf{X}^{-1}} = \begin{pmatrix} a & b \\ c & d \end{pmatrix}.$$

Since $\mathbf{X}\mathbf{X}^{-1} = \mathbf{I}$, we have

$$\begin{pmatrix} 2 & 3 \\ 1 & 4 \end{pmatrix}\begin{pmatrix} a & b \\ c & d \end{pmatrix} = \begin{pmatrix} 1 & 0 \\ 0 & 1 \end{pmatrix},$$

which amounts to

$$2a + 3c = 1 \qquad 2b + 3b = 0$$
$$a + 4c = 0 \qquad b + 4d = 1$$

Hence, to find the elements of $\mathbf{X}^{-1}$ one must solve several simultaneous equations. In this instance, the task might not be too difficult, but with large matrices it is not an easy matter.

Although GSK (Chapter 7) makes extensive use of matrix inversion, one usually does not have to perform the actual computations because nearly every computer and many desk calculators as well have preprogrammed routines for doing the work.[1] Thus for a practical comprehension of weighted least squares, a general familiarity with inverses should suffice.

---

1. One should note, however, that the inversion of large matrices can be time consuming even on large computers.

Appendix B   DISTRIBUTION OF CHI SQUARE

Probability

v	.99	.98	.95	.90	.80	.70	.50	.30	.20	.10	.05	.02	.01	.001
1	$.0^3157$	$.0^3628$	.00393	.0158	.0642	.148	.455	1.074	1.642	2.706	3.841	5.412	6.635	10.827
2	.0201	.0404	.103	.211	.446	.713	1.386	2.408	3.219	4.605	5.991	7.824	9.210	13.815
3	.115	.185	.352	.584	1.005	1.424	2.366	3.665	4.642	6.251	7.815	9.837	11.345	16.266
4	.297	.429	.711	1.064	1.649	2.195	3.357	4.878	5.989	7.779	9.488	11.668	13.277	18.467
5	.554	.752	1.145	1.610	2.343	3.000	4.351	6.064	7.289	9.236	11.070	13.388	15.086	20.515
6	.872	1.134	1.635	2.204	3.070	3.828	5.348	7.231	8.558	10.645	12.592	15.033	16.812	22.457
7	1.239	1.564	2.167	2.833	3.822	4.671	6.346	8.383	9.803	12.017	14.067	16.622	18.475	24.322
8	1.646	2.032	2.733	3.490	4.594	5.527	7.344	9.524	11.030	13.362	15.507	18.168	20.090	26.125
9	2.088	2.532	3.325	4.168	5.380	6.393	8.343	10.656	12.242	14.684	16.919	19.679	21.666	27.877
10	2.558	3.059	3.940	4.865	6.179	7.267	9.342	11.781	13.442	15.987	18.307	21.161	23.209	29.588
11	3.053	3.609	4.575	5.578	6.989	8.148	10.341	12.899	14.631	17.275	19.675	22.618	24.725	31.264
12	3.571	4.178	5.226	6.304	7.807	9.034	11.340	14.011	15.812	18.549	21.026	24.054	26.217	32.909
13	4.107	4.765	5.892	7.042	8.634	9.926	12.340	15.119	16.985	19.812	22.362	25.472	27.688	34.528
14	4.660	5.368	6.571	7.790	9.467	10.821	13.339	16.222	18.151	21.064	23.685	26.873	29.141	36.123
15	5.229	5.985	7.261	8.547	10.307	11.721	14.339	17.322	19.311	22.307	24.996	28.259	30.578	37.697
16	5.812	6.614	7.962	9.312	11.152	12.624	15.338	18.418	20.465	23.542	26.296	29.633	32.000	39.252
17	6.408	7.255	8.672	10.085	12.002	13.531	16.338	19.511	21.615	24.769	27.587	30.995	33.409	40.790
18	7.015	7.906	9.390	10.865	12.857	14.440	17.338	20.601	22.760	25.989	28.869	32.346	34.805	42.312
19	7.633	8.567	10.117	11.651	13.716	15.352	18.338	21.689	23.900	27.204	30.144	33.687	36.191	43.820
20	8.260	9.237	10.851	12.443	14.578	16.266	19.337	22.775	25.038	28.412	31.410	35.020	37.566	45.315
21	8.897	9.915	11.591	13.240	15.445	17.182	20.337	23.858	26.171	29.615	32.671	36.343	38.932	46.797
22	9.542	10.600	12.338	14.041	16.314	18.101	21.337	24.939	27.301	30.813	33.924	37.659	40.289	48.268
23	10.196	11.293	13.091	14.848	17.187	19.021	22.337	26.018	28.429	32.007	35.172	38.968	41.638	49.728
24	10.856	11.992	13.848	15.659	18.062	19.943	23.337	27.096	29.553	33.196	36.415	40.270	42.980	51.179
25	11.524	12.697	14.611	16.473	18.940	20.867	24.337	28.172	30.675	34.382	37.652	41.566	44.314	52.620

v														
26	12.198	13.409	15.379	17.292	19.820	21.792	25.336	29.246	31.795	35.563	38.885	42.856	45.642	54.052
27	12.879	14.125	16.151	18.114	20.703	22.719	26.336	30.319	32.912	36.741	40.113	44.140	46.963	55.476
28	13.565	14.847	16.928	18.939	21.588	23.647	27.336	31.391	34.027	37.916	41.337	45.419	48.278	56.893
29	14.256	15.574	17.708	19.768	22.475	24.577	28.336	32.461	35.139	39.087	42.557	46.693	49.588	58.302
30	14.953	16.306	18.493	20.599	23.364	25.508	29.336	33.530	36.250	40.256	43.773	47.962	50.892	59.703
32	16.362	17.783	20.072	22.271	25.148	27.373	31.336	35.665	38.466	42.585	46.194	50.487	53.486	62.487
34	17.789	19.275	21.664	23.952	26.938	29.242	33.336	37.795	40.676	44.903	48.602	52.995	56.061	65.247
36	19.233	20.783	23.269	25.643	28.735	31.115	35.336	39.922	42.879	47.212	50.999	55.489	58.619	67.985
38	20.691	22.304	24.884	27.343	30.537	32.992	37.335	42.045	45.076	49.513	53.384	57.969	61.162	70.703
40	22.164	23.838	26.509	29.051	32.345	34.872	39.335	44.165	47.269	51.805	55.759	60.436	63.691	73.402
42	23.650	25.383	28.144	30.765	34.157	36.755	41.335	46.282	49.456	54.090	58.124	62.892	66.206	76.084
44	25.148	26.939	29.787	32.487	35.974	38.641	43.335	48.396	51.639	56.369	60.481	65.337	68.710	78.750
46	26.657	28.504	31.439	34.215	37.795	40.529	45.335	50.507	53.818	58.641	62.830	67.771	71.201	81.400
48	28.177	30.080	33.098	35.949	39.621	42.420	47.335	52.616	55.993	60.907	65.171	70.197	73.683	84.037
50	29.707	31.664	34.764	37.689	41.449	44.313	49.335	54.723	58.164	63.167	67.505	72.613	76.154	86.661
52	31.246	33.256	36.437	39.433	43.281	46.209	51.335	56.827	60.332	65.422	69.832	75.021	78.616	89.272
54	32.793	34.856	38.116	41.183	45.117	48.106	53.335	58.930	62.496	67.673	72.153	77.422	81.069	91.872
56	34.350	36.464	39.801	42.937	46.955	50.005	55.335	61.031	64.658	69.919	74.468	79.815	83.513	94.461
58	35.913	38.078	41.492	44.696	48.797	51.906	57.335	63.129	66.816	72.160	76.778	82.201	85.950	97.039
60	37.485	39.699	43.188	46.459	50.641	53.809	59.335	65.227	68.972	74.397	79.082	84.580	88.379	99.607
62	39.063	41.327	44.889	48.226	52.487	55.714	61.335	67.322	71.125	76.630	81.381	86.953	90.802	102.166
64	40.649	42.960	46.595	49.996	54.336	57.620	63.335	69.416	73.276	78.860	83.675	89.320	93.217	104.716
66	42.240	44.599	48.305	51.770	56.188	59.527	65.335	71.508	75.424	81.085	85.965	91.681	95.626	107.258
68	43.838	46.244	50.020	53.548	58.042	61.436	67.335	73.600	77.571	83.308	88.250	94.037	98.028	109.791
70	45.442	47.893	51.739	55.329	59.898	63.346	69.334	75.689	79.715	85.527	90.531	96.388	100.425	112.317

For odd values of v between 30 and 70, the mean of the tabular values for $v-1$ and $v+1$ may be taken. For larger values of v, the expression $\sqrt{2X}, -\sqrt{2v-1}$ may be used as a normal deviate with unit variance, remembering that the probability for X^2 corresponds with that of a single tail of the normal curve.

Source: This table is reprinted from Table IV of R. A. Fisher and F. Yates, *Statistical Tables for Biological, Agricultural and Medical Research,* published by Longman Group Ltd., London (previously published by Oliver and Boyd, Edinburgh), by permission of the authors and publishers.

Appendix C
DATA SOURCES

Data used in this book were supplied in part by the Inter-University Consortium for Political Research (University of Michigan) and by the Lou Harris Political Data Center (University of North Carolina). The studies are as follows:

CPS 1974 American Election Study (ICPR)
CPS 1972 American National Election Study (ICPR)
The 1956 Election Study (ICPR)
M. Kent Jennings, The Student-Parent Socialization Study (ICPR)
D. Kovenock et al., Comparative State Election Project (LHPDC)
J. Davis, National Data Program for the Social Sciences, Spring, 1975 General Social Survey (ICPR)

Neither the ICPR nor the Lou Harris Center is responsible for either the analysis or interpretation of these data, but their assistance in making them available is greatly appreciated.

REFERENCES

AGRESTI, ALAN. 1976. "The Effect of Category Choice on Some Ordinal Measures of Association." *Journal of the American Statistical Association* 71:49–55.

ALLAN, G. J. BORIS. 1976. "Ordinal-Scaled Variables and Multivariate Analysis: Comment on Hawkes." *American Journal of Sociology* 81:1498–1500.

ANDERSON, NORMAN H. 1961. "Scales and Statistics: Parametric and Non-parametric." *Psychological Bulletin* 58:305–15.

ANDREWS, F. M., JAMES N. MORGAN, and JOHN SONQUIST. 1967. *Multiple Classification Analysis.* Ann Arbor, Mich.: Institute for Social Research.

ARMITAGE, P. 1955. "Tests for Linear Trends in Proportions and Frequencies." *Biometrics* 11:375–86.

BAKER, BELA O., et al. 1966. "Weak Measurement vs. Strong Statistics." *Educational and Psychological Measurement* 26:291–309.

BERKSON, JOSEPH. 1968. "Application of Minimum Logit χ^2 Estimate to a Problem of Grizzle with Notation on the Problem of 'No Interaction.'" *Biometrics* 24:75–95.

BHAPKAR, V. P., and GARY KOCH. 1968a. "Hypothesis of 'No Interaction' in Multidimensional Contingency Tables." *Technometrics* 10:107–22.

———. 1968b. "On the Hypothesis of 'No Interaction' in Contingency Tables." *Biometrics* 24:567–94.

BIRCH, M. W. 1963. "Maximum Likelihood in Three-Way Contingency Tables." *Journal of the Royal Statistical Society*, Series B, 25:220–33.

———. 1964. "The Detection of Partial Association, I: The 2×2 Case." *Journal of the Royal Statistical Society*, Series B, 26:313–24.

———. 1965. "The Detection of Partial Association, II: The General Case." *Journal of the Royal Statistical Society*, Series B, 27:111–24.

BISHOP, YVONNE M. M. 1969. "Full Contingency Tables, Logits, and Split Contingency Tables." *Biometrics* 25:383–99.

———. 1971. "Effects of Collapsing Multidimensional Contingency Tables." *Biometrics* 27:545–62.

221

BISHOP, YVONNE M. M., and STEPHEN E. FIENBERG. 1969. "Incomplete Two-Dimensional Contingency Tables." *Biometrics* 25 (March): 119–28.

BISHOP, YVONNE M. M., STEPHEN E. FIENBERG, and PAUL W. HOLLAND. 1975. *Discrete Multivariate Analysis: Theory and Practice.* Cambridge, Mass.: MIT Press.

BLALOCK, HUBERT M. 1961. *Causal Inferences in Nonexperimental Research.* Chapel Hill, N.C.: University of North Carolina Press.

———. 1972. *Social Statistics.* 2d ed. New York: McGraw-Hill.

———. 1975. "Can We Find a Genuine Ordinal Slope Analogue?" In *Sociological Methodology 1976*, edited by David R. Heise, pp. 195–229. San Francisco: Jossey-Bass.

BOUDON, RAYMOND. 1973. *Mathematical Structures of Social Mobility.* San Francisco: Jossey-Bass.

BOYLE, RICHARD P. 1966. "Causal Theory and Statistical Measures of Effect: A Convergence." *American Sociological Review* 31: 843–51.

———. 1970. "Path Analysis and Ordinal Data." *American Journal of Sociology* 75: 461–80.

BRESNAHAN, JEAN L., and MARTIN M. SHAPIRO. 1966. "A General Equation and Technique for the Exact Partitioning of Chi Square Contingency Tables." *Psychological Bulletin* 66: 252–62.

BURKE, CLETUS J. 1953. "Additive Scales and Statistics." *Psychological Bulletin* 60: 73–75.

CASTELLAN, N. JOHN. 1965. "On the Partitioning of Contingency Tables." *Psychological Bulletin* 64: 330–38.

COCHRAN, WILLIAM G. 1954. "Some Methods of Strengthening the Common χ^2 Tests." *Biometrics* 10: 417–51.

COHEN, JACOB. 1960. "A Coefficient of Agreement for Nominal Scales." *Educational and Psychological Measurement* 20: 37–46.

———. 1968. "Weighted Kappa." *Psychological Bulletin* 70: 213–20.

COLEMAN, JAMES S. 1964. *Introduction to Mathematical Sociology.* New York: Free Press.

CONOVER, W. J. 1974. "Some Reasons for Not Using the Yates Continuity Correction on 2×2 Contingency Tables." *Journal of The American Statistical Association* 69: 374–76.

COSTNER, HERBERT L. 1965. "Criteria for Measures of Association." *American Sociological Review* 30: 341–53.

COWART, ANDREW T. 1973. "Electoral Choice in American States: Incumbency Effects, Partisan Forces, and Divergent Partisan Majorities." *American Political Science Review* 67: 835–53.

DALY, C. 1962. "A Simple Test for Trends in a Contingency Table." *Biometrics* 18: 114–19.

DANIELS, H. E. 1944. "The Relation between Measure of Correlation in the Universe of Sample Permutations." *Biometrika* 33: 129–35.

DARROCH, J. N. 1974. "Multiplicative and Additive Interaction in Contingency Tables." *Biometrika* 61: 207–14.

DAVIS, JAMES A. 1967. "A Partial Coefficient for Goodman and Kruskal's Gamma." *Journal of the American Statistical Association* 62:189–93.

―――. 1974. "Hierarchical Models for Significance Tests in Multivariate Contingency Tables." In *Sociological Methodology 1973–1974*, edited by Herbert L. Costner, pp. 189–231. San Francisco: Jossey-Bass.

―――. 1975. "Analyzing Contingency Tables with Linear Flow Graphs: D Systems." In *Sociological Methodology 1976*, edited by David R. Heise, pp. 111–45. San Francisco: Jossey-Bass.

DRAPER, N. H., and H. SMITH. 1966. *Applied Regression Analysis*. New York: Wiley.

DUNCAN, OTIS DUDLEY. 1974. "Measuring Social Change Via Replication of Surveys." In *Social Indicator Models*, edited by Kenneth C. Land and Seymour Spilerman, pp. 105–27. New York: Russell Sage.

―――. 1976. "Partitioning Polytomous Variables in Multiway Contingency Tables." *Social Science Research* 4:167–82.

EDWARDS, A. W. F. 1963. "The Measure of Association in a 2×2 Table." *Journal of the Royal Statistical Society*, Series A, 126:109–14.

EVERS, MARK, and N. KRISHNAN NAMBOODIRI. 1976. "Weighted Least-Squares versus Maximum Likelihood Estimates of Non-Hierarchical Models." Paper presented at American Statistical Association, Boston.

FIENBERG, STEPHEN E. 1969. "Preliminary Graphical Analysis and Quasi-independence for Two-Way Contingency Tables." *Applied Statistics* 18:153–68.

―――. 1970a. "The Analysis of Multidimensional Contingency Tables." *Ecology* 51:419–33.

―――. 1970b. "Quasi-Independence and Maximum Likelihood Estimation in Incomplete Contingency Tables." *Journal of the American Statistical Association* 65:1610–16.

―――. 1971. "A Statistical Technique for Historians: Standardizing Tables of Counts." *Journal of Interdisciplinary History* 1:305–15.

―――. 1972. "The Analysis of Incomplete Multi-way Contingency Tables." *Biometrics* 28:177–202.

FIENBERG, STEPHEN E., and PAUL W. HOLLAND. 1973. "Simultaneous Estimation of Multinomial Cell Probabilities." *Journal of the American Statistical Association* 68:683–91.

FLEISS, JOSEPH L. 1971. "Measuring Nominal Scale Agreement among Many Raters." *Psychological Bulletin* 76:378–82.

―――. 1973. *Statistical Methods for Rates and Proportions*. New York: Wiley.

―――. 1975. "Measuring Agreement between Two Judges on the Presence or Absence of a Trait." *Biometrics* 31:651–59.

FLEISS, JOSEPH L., JACOB COHEN, and B. S. EVERITT. 1969. "Large Sample Standard Errors of Kappa and Weighted Kappa." *Psychological Bulletin* 72:323–27.

FORTHOFER, RONALD N., and GARY G. KOCH. 1973. "An Analysis for Compounded Functions of Categorical Data." *Biometrics* 29:143–57.

FREUND, JOHN. 1962. *Mathematical Statistics.* Englewood Cliffs, N.J.: Prentice-Hall.

GAIL, M. H. 1972. "Mixed Quasi-Independent Models for Categorical Data." *Biometrics* 28:703–12.

GART, JOHN J. 1972. "Interaction Tests for $2 \times s \times t$ Contingency Tables." *Biometrika* 59:309–16.

GOODMAN, LEO A. 1963. "On Methods for Comparing Contingency Tables." *Journal of the Royal Statistical Society*, Series A, 126:94–108.

———. 1964a. "Simultaneous Confidence Limits for Cross-Product Ratios in Contingency Tables." *Journal of the Royal Statistical Society*, Series B, 26:86–102.

———. 1964b. "Simple Methods for Analyzing Three-Factor Interaction in Contigency Tables." *Journal of the American Statistical Association* 59:319–52.

———. 1964c. "Interactions in Multidimensional Contingency Tables." *Annals of Mathematical Statistics* 35:632–46.

———. 1964d. "Simultaneous Confidence Intervals for Contrasts among Multinomial Populations." *Annals of Mathematical Statistics* 35:716–25.

———. 1965a. "On Simultaneous Confidence Intervals for Multinomial Proportions." *Technometrics* 7:247–54.

———. 1965b. "On the Statistical Analysis of Mobility Data." *American Journal of Sociology* 70:564–85.

———. 1965c. "On the Multivariate Analysis of Three Dichotomous Variables." *American Journal of Sociology* 71:290–301.

———. 1968. "The Analysis of Cross-Classified Data: Independence, Quasi-Independence, and Interactions in Contingency Tables with or without Missing Entries." *Journal of the American Statistical Association* 63:1091–1131.

———. 1969a. "How to Ransack Social Mobility Tables and Other Kinds of Cross-Classification Tables." *American Journal of Sociology* 75:1–40.

———. 1969b. "On Partitioning X^2 and Detecting Partial Association In Three-Way Contingency Tables." *Journal of the Royal Statistical Society*, Series B, 31:486–98.

———. 1970. "The Multivariate Analysis of Qualitative Data." *Journal of the American Statistical Association* 65:226–56.

———. 1971a. "The Analysis of Multidimensional Contingency Tables: Stepwise Procedures and Direct Estimation Methods for Building Models for Multiple Classifications." *Technometrics* 13:33–61.

———. 1971b. "Partitioning of Chi Square, Analysis of Marginal Contingency Tables, and Estimation of Expected Frequencies in Multidimensional Contingency Tables." *Journal of the American Statistical Association* 66:339–44.

———. 1972a. "A Modified Multiple Regression Approach to the Analysis of Dichotomous Variables." *American Sociological Review* 37:28–46.

———. 1972b. "A General Model for the Analysis of Surveys." *American Journal of Sociology* 77:1035–86.

———. 1972c. "Some Multiplicative Models for the Analysis of Cross-Classified

Data." *Proceedings of the Sixth Berkeley Symposium on Mathematical Statistics and Probability* 1:649–96.

———. 1973a. "Casual Analysis of Data from Panel Studies and Other Kinds of Surveys." *American Journal of Sociology* 78:1135–91.

———. 1973b. "The Analysis of Multidimensional Contingency Tables When Some Variables Are Posterior to Others: A Modified Path Analysis Approach." *Biometrika* 59:579–96.

———. 1973c. "Guided and Unguided Methods for the Selection of Models for a Set of *T* Multidimensional Contingency Tables." *Journal of the American Statistical Association* 68:165–75.

———. 1974a. "The Analysis of Systems of Qualitative Variables When Some of the Variables Are Unobservable. Part I—A Modified Latent Structure Approach." *American Journal of Sociology* 79:1179–1259.

———. 1974b. "Exploratory Latent Structure Analysis Using both Identifiable and Unidentifiable Models." *Biometrika* 61:215–31.

———. 1975a. "A New Model for Scaling Response Patterns: An Application of the Quasi-Independence Concept." *Journal of the American Statistical Association* 70:755–68.

———. 1975b. "The Relationship between Modified and Usual Multiple-Regression Approaches to the Analysis of Dichotomus Variables." In *Sociological Methodology 1976*, edited by David R. Heise, pp. 83–110. San Francisco: Jossey-Bass.

GOODMAN, LEO A., and WILLIAM H. KRUSKAL. 1954. "Measures of Association for Cross-Classifications." *Journal of the American Statistical Association* 49:732–64.

———. 1959. "Measures of Association for Cross-Classifications. II: Further Discussion and References." *Journal of the American Statistical Association* 54:123–63.

———. 1963. "Measure of Association for Cross-Classifications. III: Approximate Sampling Theory." *Journal of the American Statistical Association* 58:310–64.

———. 1972. "Measures of Association for Cross-Classifications. IV: Simplification of Asymptotic Variances." *Journal of the American Statistical Association* 67:415–21.

———. 1974. "Empirical Evaluation of Formal Theory." *Journal of Mathematical Sociology* 3:187–96.

GRIZZLE, JAMES E., C. FRANK STARMER, and GARY G. KOCH. 1969. "Analysis of Categorical Data by Linear Models." *Biometrics* 25:489–504.

GRIZZLE, JAMES E., and O. DALE WILLIAMS. 1972. "Log Linear Models and Tests of Independence for Contingency Tables." *Biometrics* 28:137–56.

HABERMAN, SHELBY J. 1973. "The Analysis of Residuals in Cross-Classified Tables." *Biometrics* 29:205–20.

———. 1974. *The Analysis of Frequency Data.* Chicago: University of Chicago Press.

HADLEY, GEORGE. 1961. *Linear Algebra.* Reading, Mass.: Addison-Wesley.

HALLINAN, MAUREEN T., and MAURICE J. MOORE. 1975. "Some Multiplicative

Models for Interpreting Psychological Mobility." Working Paper 75-7. Madison, Wisc.: Center for Demography and Ecology.

HAWKES, ROLAND K. 1971. "The Multivariate Analysis of Ordinal Measures." *American Journal of Sociology* 76:908–26.

———. 1973. "Reply to Reynolds." *American Journal of Sociology* 78:1516–21.

———. 1975. "Effects of Grouping on Measures of Ordinal Association." In *Sociological Methodology 1976*, edited by David R. Heise, pp. 176–94. San Francisco: Jossey-Bass.

HAYS, WILLIAM L. 1963. *Statistics for Psychologists.* New York: Holt, Rinehart & Winston.

HILDEBRAND, DAVID K., JAMES D. LAING, and HOWARD L. ROSENTHAL. 1974a. "Prediction Logic: A Method for Empirical Evaluation of Formal Theory." *Journal of Mathematical Sociology* 3:1963–85.

———. 1974b. "Prediction Logic and Quasi-Independence in Empirical Evaluation of Formal Theory." *Journal of Mathematical Sociology* 3:197–209.

———. 1975. "A Prediction-Logic Approach to Causal Models of Qualitative Variates." In *Sociological Methodology 1976*, edited by David R. Heise, pp. 146–75. San Francisco: Jossey-Bass.

———. 1976. "Prediction Analysis in Political Research." *American Political Science Review* 70:509–35.

HOEL, PAUL G. 1962. *Introduction to Mathematical Statistics.* 3d ed. New York: Wiley.

HORST, PAUL. 1963. *Matrix Algebra for Social Scientists.* New York: Holt, Rinehart & Winston.

HYMAN, HERBERT H. 1955. *Survey Design and Analysis.* New York: Free Press.

JOHNSON, WILLIAM D., and GARY G. KOCH. 1970. "Analysis of Qualitative Data: Linear Functions." *Health Services Research* 5:358–69.

———. 1971. "A Note on the Weighted Least Squares Analysis of the Ries-Smith Contingency Table Data." *Technometrics* 13:438–47.

KALTON, G. 1968. "Standardization: A Technique to Control for Extraneous Variables." *Applied Statistics* 17:118–36.

KASTENBAUM, MARVIN A. 1960. "A Note on the Additive Partitioning of Chi Square in Contingency Tables." *Biometrics* 16:416–22.

KASTENBAUM, MARVIN A., and D. E. LAMPHIEAR. 1959. "Calculation of Chi-Square to Test the No Three-Factor Interaction Hypothesis." *Biometrics* 15:107–22.

KENDALL, MAURICE G. 1970. *Rank Correlation Methods.* 4th ed. New York: Hafner.

KENDALL, MAURICE G., and ALAN STUART. 1966. *The Advanced Theory of Statistics.* 3 vols. London: Griffin.

KERLINGER, FRED N., and ELAZAR J. PEDHAZUR. 1973. *Multiple Regression in Behavioral Research.* New York: Holt, Rinehart & Winston.

KIM, JAE-ON. 1971. "Predictive Measures of Ordinal Association." *American Journal of Sociology* 76:391–907.

———. 1975. "Multivariate Analysis of Ordinal Variables." *American Journal of Sociology* 81:261–98.

KIMBALL, A. W. 1954. "Short-Cut Formulas for the Exact Partition of X^2 in Contingency Tables." *Biometrics* 10:452–459.

KNOKE, DAVID. 1975. "A Comparison of Log-Linear and Regression Models for Systems of Dichotomous Variables." *Sociological Methods and Research* 3:416–34.

KOCH, GARY G., JEAN L. FREEMAN, and ROBERT G. LEHNEN. 1975. "A General Methodology for the Analysis of Ranked Policy Preference Data." Mimeo No. 1005. Chapel Hill, N.C.: Institute of Statistics.

KOCH, GARY G., PETER B. IMREY, and DONALD W. REINFURT. 1972. "Linear Model Analysis of Categorical Data with Incomplete Response Vectors." *Biometrics* 28:663–92.

KOCH, GARY G., and DONALD W. REINFURT. 1970. "The Analysis of Complex Contingency Table Data from General Experimental Designs and Sample Surveys." Mimeo No. 716. Chapel Hill, N.C.: Institute of Statistics.

———. 1971. "The Analysis of Categorical Data from Mixed Models." *Biometrics* 27:157–73.

KRUSKAL, WILLIAM H. 1958. "Ordinal Measures of Association." *Journal of the American Statistical Association* 53:814–61.

KU, H. H., and SOLOMON KULLBACK. 1968. "Interaction in Multidimensional Contingency Tables: An Information Theoretic Approach." *Journal of Research of the National Bureau of Standards* 72B:159–99.

KU, H. H., R. N. VARNER, and S. KULLBACK. 1971. "On the Analysis of Multidimensional Contingency Tables." *Journal of the American Statistical Association* 66:155–64.

KULLBACK, SOLOMON. 1973. "Estimating and Testing Linear Hypotheses on Parameters in the Log-Linear Model." *Biometrische Zeltschrift* 15:371–88.

———. 1974. *Information in Contingency Tables—Final Technical Report.* Washington, D.C.: George Washington University, Department of Statistics.

LABOVITZ, SANFORD. 1967. "Some Observations on Measurement and Statistics." *Social Forces* 46:151–60.

———. 1970. "The Assignment of Numbers to Rank Order Categories." *American Sociological Review* 35:515–24.

LANCASTER, H. O. 1949. "The Derivation and Partition of χ^2 in Certain Discrete Distribution." *Biometrika* 36:117–29.

LAZARSFELD, PAUL F. 1955. "Interpretation of Statistical Relations as a Research Operation." In *The Language of Social Research*, edited by Paul F. Lazarsfeld and Morris Rosenberg, pp. 115–40. New York: Free Press.

LEHNEN, ROBERT G., and GARY G. KOCH. 1974a. "Analyzing Panel Data with Uncontrolled Attrition." *Public Opinion Quarterly* 38:40–56.

———. 1974b. "A General Linear Approach to the Analysis of Non-Metric Data: Applications for Political Science." *American Journal of Political Science* 18:283–313.

LEIK, ROBERT K., and WALTER R. GOVE. 1969. "The Conception and Measurement of Asymmetric Monotonic Relationships in Sociology." *American Journal of Sociology* 74:696–709.

————. 1971. "Integrated Approach to Measuring Association." In *Sociological Methodology 1971*, edited by Herbert L. Costner, pp. 279–301. San Francisco: Jossey-Bass.

LEWIS, B. N. 1962. "On the Analysis of Interaction in Multi-Dimensional Contingency Tables." *Journal of the Royal Statistical Society*, Series A, 125:88–117.

LIGHT, RICHARD. 1971. "Measures of Response Agreement for Qualitative Data: Some Generalizations and Alternatives." *Psychological Bulletin* 76:365–77.

LIGHT, RICHARD J., and BARRY H. MARGOLIN. 1971. "An Analysis of Variance for Categorical Data." *Journal of the American Statistical Association* 66:534–44.

LINDLEY, DENNIS V. 1964. "The Bayesian Analysis of Contingency Tables." *Annals of Mathematical Statistics* 35:1622–43.

LINDSEY, J. K. 1973. *Inferences from Sociological Survey Data: A Unified Approach.* San Francisco: Jossey-Bass.

MCNEMAR, QUINN, 1969. *Psychological Statistics.* 4th ed. New York: Wiley.

MANTEL, NATHAN. 1963. "Chi Square Tests with One Degree of Freedom: Extensions of the Mantel-Haenszel Procedure." *Journal of the American Statistical Association* 58:690–700.

————. 1970. "Incomplete Contingency Tables." *Biometrics* 26:291–304.

MANTEL, NATHAN, and W. HAENSZEL. 1959. "Statistical Aspects of the Analysis of Data from Retrospective Studies of Disease." *Journal of the National Cancer Institute* 22:719–48.

MARGOLIN, BARRY H., and RICHARD J. LIGHT. 1974. "An Analysis of Variance for Categorical Data, II: Small Sample Comparisons with Chi Square and Other Competitors." *Journal of the American Statistical Association* 69:755–64.

MAXWELL, A. E. 1961. *Analyzing Qualitative Data.* London: Methuen.

MAYER, LAWRENCE S., and I. J. GOOD. 1974. "On Ordinal Prediction Problems." *Social Forces* 52:543–49.

MILLER, J., and M. ERICKSON. 1974. "On Dummy Variable Regression Analysis: A Description and Illustration of the Method." *Sociological Methods and Research* 2:409–30.

MOSTELLER, FREDERICK. 1968. "Association and Estimation in Contingency Tables." *Journal of the American Statistical Association* 63:1–28.

NAMBOODIRI, N. KRISHNAN, LEWIS F. CARTER, and HUBERT M. BLALOCK, JR. 1975. *Applied Multivariate Analysis and Experimental Designs.* New York: McGraw-Hill.

NERLOVE, MARC, and S. JAMES PRESS. 1973. "Univariate and Multivariate Log-Linear and Logistic Models." Report No. R-1306-EDA/NIH. Santa Monica: Rand Corporation.

ORUM, ANTHONY, and EDWARD W. MCCRANIE. 1970. "Class, Tradition and Partisan Alignments in a Southern Urban Electorate." *Journal of Politics* 32:156–76.

PIRIE, W. R., and M. A. HAMDAN. 1972. "Some Revised Continuity Corrections for Discrete Distributions." *Biometrics* 28:693–701.

PLACKETT, R. L. 1974. *The Analysis of Categorical Data.* New York: Hafner.

PLOCH, DONALD R. 1974. "Ordinal Measures of Association and the General Linear Model." In *Measurement in the Social Sciences,* edited by Hubert M. Blalock, Jr., pp. 343–68. Chicago: Aldine-Atherton.

PULLUM, THOMAS W. 1970. "What Can Mathematical Models Tell Us about Occupational Mobility?" *Sociological Inquiry* 40 : 258–80.

QUADE, DANA. 1971. "Nonparametric Partial Correlation." Report SW 13/71. Amsterdam: Mathematisch Centrum.

———. 1974. "Nonparametric Partial Correlation." In *Measurement in the Social Sciences,* edited by Hubert M. Blalock, Jr., pp. 369–98. Chicago: Aldine-Atherton.

RAE, DOUGLAS W., and MICHAEL TAYLOR. 1970. *The Analysis of Political Cleavages.* New Haven, Conn.: Yale University Press.

REYNOLDS, H. T. 1971. "Making Causal Inferences with Ordinal Data." Working Paper No. 5. Chapel Hill, N.C.: Institute for Research in Social Science.

———. 1973. "On 'The Multivariate Analysis of Ordinal Measures.'" *American Journal of Sociology* 78:1513–16.

———. 1974a. "Nonparametric Partial Correlation and Causal Analysis." *Sociological Methods and Research* 2:376–92.

———. 1974b. "Ordinal Partial Correlation and Causal Inferences." In *Measurement in the Social Sciences,* edited by Hubert M. Blalock, Jr., pp. 399–423. Chicago: Aldine.

———. 1976. "Some Comments on the Causal Analysis of Surveys with Log Linear Models." University of Delaware, unpublished manuscript.

ROSENBERG, MORRIS. 1962. "Test Factor Standardization as a Method of Interpretation." *Social Forces.* 41:53–61.

———. 1968. *The Logic of Survey Analysis.* New York: Basic Books.

SENDERS, VIRGINIA L. 1953. "A Comment on Burke's Additive Scales and Statistics." *Psychological Bulletin* 60:423–24.

SHAFFER, JULIET POPPER. 1973. "Defining and Testing Hypotheses in Multidimensional Contingency Tables." *Psychological Bulletin* 79:127–41.

SIMON, GARY. 1974. "Alternative Analysis for the Singly-Ordered Contingency Table." *Journal of the American Statistical Association* 69:971–76.

SIMPSON, C. H. 1951. "The Interpretation of Interaction in Contingency Tables." *Journal of the Royal Statistical Society,* Series B, 13:238–41.

SMITH, J. E. KEITH. 1976. "The Analysis of Qualitative Data." *Annual Review of Psychology* 27:487–99.

SMITH, KENT W. 1976. "Marginal Standardization and Table Shrinking." *Social Forces* 54:669–93.

SMITH, ROBERT B. 1972. "Neighborhood Context and College Plans: An Ordinal Path Analysis." *Social Forces* 51:199–217.

————. 1974. "Continuities in Ordinal Path Analysis." *Social Forces* 53:200–29.

SOMERS, ROBERT H. 1962. "A New Asymmetric Measure for Ordinal Variables." *American Sociological Review* 27:799–811.

————. 1968. "On the Measurement of Association." *American Sociological Review* 33:291–92.

————. 1970. "A Partitioning of Ordinal Information in a Three-Way Cross-Classification." *Multivariate Behavioral Research* 5:217–39.

————. 1974. "Analysis of Partial Rank Correlation Measures Based on the Product-Moment Model: Part One." *Social Forces* 53:229–46.

STUART, ALAN. 1953. "The Estimation and Comparison of Strengths of Association in Contingency Tables." *Biometrika* 42:412–16.

SUITS, DANIEL. 1957. "The Use of Dummy Variables in Regression Equations." *Journal of the American Statistical Association* 52:548–51.

THEIL, HENRI. 1970. "On the Estimation of Relationships Involving Qualitative Variables." *American Journal of Sociology* 76:103–54.

WEISBERG, HERBERT. 1974. "Models of Statistical Relationships." *American Political Science Review* 68:1638–55.

WILSON, THOMAS P. 1969. "A Proportional-Reduction-in-Error Interpretation for Kendall's Tau-b." *Social Forces* 47:340–42.

————. 1971. "Critique of Ordinal Variables." *Social Forces* 49:432–44.

————. 1974a. "On Interpreting Ordinal Analogues to Multiple Regression and Path Analysis." *Social Forces* 53:196–99.

————. 1974b. "Reply to Somers and Smith." *Social Forces* 53:247–51.

————. 1974c. "Measures of Association for Bivariate Ordinal Hypotheses." In *Measurement in the Social Sciences*, edited by Hubert M. Blalock, Jr., pp. 327–42. Chicago: Aldine-Atherton.

INDEX